SWISS BANKING

Also by Warren J. Blackman

THE CANADIAN FINANCIAL SYSTEM

SWISS BANKING IN AN INTERNATIONAL CONTEXT

Swiss Banking

An Analytical History

Hans Bauer
sometime Director of Economic Research
Swiss Bank Corporation

and

Warren J. Blackman
Professor of Economics (Emeritus)
The University of Calgary
Canada

palgrave

Published by
PALGRAVE
Houndmills, Basingstoke, Hampshire RG21 6XS and
175 Fifth Avenue, New York, N. Y. 10010
Companies and representatives throughout the world

PALGRAVE is the new global academic imprint of
St. Martin's Press LLC Scholarly and Reference Division and
Palgrave Publishers Ltd (formerly Macmillan Press Ltd).

ISBN 0–333–72091–1

This book is printed on paper suitable for recycling and
made from fully managed and sustained forest sources.

A catalogue record for this book is available
from the British Library.

Transferred to digital printing 2001

Printed and bound in Great Britain by
Antony Rowe Ltd, Chippenham, Wiltshire

Contents

Frontispiece: Hans Bauer-Anderson 10.7.1901–5.1.1995

In Memoriam

Hans Bauer-Anderson
10/7/1901–5/1/1995

Acknowledgements

We, Dr Bauer and myself, wish to express our sincerest appreciation to all who have graciously contributed their time and efforts in creating this book. To Dr Hans Halbheer and his staff at Credit Suisse we are particularly indebted. Ms Silvia Matile-Steiner, Assistant Vice President of the Swiss Bankers Association, has been most kind in contributing not only original material but also the press releases of the SBA which have enabled us to remain in permanent contact with Swiss banks.

Finally, and by far the most important of all, we are indebted to my wife, Elizabeth Blackman, who patiently and carefully translated the documents referred to in the book from their original German and French. Without these translations, preparing and writing this book would have been impossible.

Introduction

This book strives to be more than an historical account; it is an attempt to answer the question 'why?', until either explanations are exhausted or the question can no longer be asked. While everyone must be aware of both the existence and prominence of Swiss banks in the world of this century, few can offer an explanation as to how a nation, characterised in the mid-nineteenth century by multiple cantons with scarcely more than some light industry such as textiles, watches and the like, can pull itself up by its own bootstraps to the highest per capita income level in the world in the twentieth century. This must be one of the great success stories of history.

Uncovering this story with the 'why?' question inevitably leads one into far more than just this hundred and fifty year period. Indeed, we find that the roots of success lie, firstly, in the Swiss ability to develop its banks, and secondly, the roots *themselves* of these banks, which did not begin simply with the great constitutional reform of 1848. Quite the contrary, there was a centuries-old tradition not only of money changing but all the other necessary conditions for modern banks– capital, savings, and investment practices both foreign and domestic. Therein lies the real set of answers to our 'why?' question.

Exploring these areas has proven to be a fascinating experience which we hope the reader may share with us. While we cannot measure or quantify the various influences, we can lay stress on what are obviously the most important and let readers judge for themselves. The first chapter begins the task with a discussion of mediaeval banking as practiced by the Italians, the founders of banking in all countries including Switzerland. We suggest that a basic understanding of banking in those early times will lead not only to an appreciation of early banking processes but also an appraisal of the events which were responsible for the migration of Italian banking to Switzerland and Germany – the great Basle Synod.

The second chapter discusses the early development of banking in Basle, which, though not part of the Swiss Confederation at the time, can be considered as the place of origin of Swiss banking itself. Nevertheless, circumstances of both history and economics conspired to result in the development of the Bank in Basle. Mercantilism on in England and elsewhere the Continent actually retarded the growth of banks and banking, but not in Switzerland.

Chapter 3 concentrates on the philosophical roots of Swiss banking as opposed to the historical circumstances. These roots are obviously important, for as the circumstances of history change, the banks do not disappear but simply adapt themselves to the different conditions. It is the permanency of these philosophical roots which enable the banks to continue in a different economic environment. Chapter 4 continues the analysis of these roots, including the tradition and influence of the Saint-Simonian school, which had a very practical impact upon the thinking of bankers of Basle and Zürich such that the first and most successful of the Swiss banks were Saint-Simonian.

Chapter 5 discusses the contribution, and significance, of deposit banking to economic development. In particular it considers the advantages of a deposit fund to be made available by bankers for investment purposes. These advantages are contrasted with a purely cash economy prevalent in Europe at mid-nineteenth century. The chapter includes a discussion of the difficulties of establishing banks in the old Confederation and the necessity for change in Switzerland. The sixth chapter continues this topic with the formation of new note-issuing banks in the beginnings of the new Confederation.

Chapter 7 begins with the more generalised concept of the gold standard in Victorian times and analyses its importance in restricting the supply of banknotes in circulation. This was the world in which the 'new' (post-1848) Swiss banks were to operate. Most significant, how-ever, was the development of joint-stock banking as a means by which the capital of banks could be both increased and extended throughout Europe, again a model for the Swiss. Fortunately the Swiss were able to avoid the pitfalls of Victorian banking, the 'boom-bust' credit cycles, by adhering closely to their Saint-Simonian tradition.

In Chapter 8, we attempt a broad survey of Swiss banking and its development during the nineteenth century. The importance of this survey lies in the fact that it stresses those peculiar characteristics of Switzerland which were to form the unique structure of the Swiss banking industry. Chapter 9 continues this analysis of growth and development but in the context of the environment of central Europe.

Chapter 10 explores the period preceding World War I. The nine-teenth century was generally a prosperous one for Swiss banking, characterised by a growth of both the deposit system and foreign investment. The large banks were, quite simply, outgrowing their domestic banking opportunities. All this was brought to a tragic end with the outbreak of war. Most foreign investments were irretrievably lost, with disastrous consequences for many Swiss banks.

In Chapter 11, we examine the interesting inter-war period during which the gold-exchange standard replaced the pre-1914 gold standard. By this time the affairs of Swiss banks were completely interrelated with events in other countries, particularly France, Germany and Great Britain. At the same time the emergence of the United States as a financial superpower meant that whatever occurred in that country (such as the Great Depression) was instantly reflected in Europe and, of course, Switzerland.

Chapter 12 considers the important period of the second World War and Swiss neutrality during that tragic episode. Yet, out of the ashes of Europe were to grow a new and even more dynamic banking structure than the world had yet seen.

We hope, after perusing these chapters, that readers will gain an appreciation not only of Swiss banking itself but the banking industry as a whole; even more importantly, we hope also that an understanding of banking processes will be gained and thereby add to our fund of knowledge. We regret that space limitations do not make possible an examination of the very interesting matters of the Swiss National Bank and its implementations of monetary policy. Such topics, along with the almost imperceptible development of the Grossbanken into modern international banks (no longer 'Swiss'), we must leave to the interested reader to supply. We may only hope that we have supplied the background of information.

Part 1
The Mediaeval World of Banking and Currency

1 The Mediaeval Money Economy

Modern banking, and Swiss banking in particular, is a direct descendant of the Italian commercial banks of the fourteenth and fifteenth centuries. The exhaustive research of the late Professor Raymond de Roover, economic historian at Harvard, establishes this with scarcely any doubt. These early banks were developed at the same time that Italian city-states achieved an ascendancy in the fields of commerce and trading, when Italy had become the major industrial and commercial power of Europe.[1] This coincidence of commerce, trade, and banking is not fortuitous; indeed, there is ample historical evidence that banking thrives and develops in just such an environment. Italy, or rather the city-states of Florence, Venice, and so on, being the major commercial powers of the time, created an environment of political and economic security for banks and made possible their growth and development in response to the needs of commerce.

Such a statement appears to be a 'truism' – an obvious truth; nevertheless it forms the initial premise of the analysis which follows. Societies invent banking when the need for such services arises, not before. The need, in this case, is precisely the counterpart of the movement of goods – the flow of payments in the opposite direction. Ultimately, the requirements for investment and the transfer of savings into capital for investment give rise to a further banking service, but the historical evidence is clear: commercial banking services preceded other banking activities. But even the services which we ordinarily think of as commercial banking had their predecessor in the form of money changing, and it was the money changers who were the true ancestors of modern banking.

Since gold was the acceptable form of currency in the mediaeval period, each coin had to be weighed and assayed as to its gold content. An Italian money changer, skilled in the art of determining the gold content of coins, would exchange the local currency for a foreign coin. Depending upon the ordinances within his jurisdiction, he would either cut the foreign coin in two, thereby converting it into bullion, or exchange it directly for the local coin at some pre-established price. In the event that it was cut into halves, the bullion price would be compared to the corresponding bullion price of the local coin and the exchange rate determined therefrom.

3

THE MEDIAEVAL FAIRS OF GENEVA

The business of the money changers meant that a stock of foreign coins was kept for the purpose of exchanging local currencies into foreign currencies. Whenever local businessmen embarked upon journeys to distant regions in which foreign currencies were required, a price (exchange rate) between the two currencies would have to be determined. This price did not necessarily mean a purely bullion price relationship; in fact, most of the time it did not. An inquiry into such prices, or exchange rates, ordered by Duke Louis of Savoy for the money changers of Geneva in 1454, revealed a remarkable fluctuation in these non-bullion rates of exchange. Commissioners were able to conduct interviews with the bankers of Geneva, including Francois Sasseti, the well-known representative of the Medici bank in Geneva. The result was a surprising variation of exchange rates over time.[2]

As economists, we can recognise what was happening at the time. Money changers, once they had progressed beyond the mere bullion level, were determining exchange rates by equating demand and supply, that is, they were fixing a market price. Thus, when foreign gold coins flowed into a monetary jurisdiction, the balance of trade was favourable to that area. The price of those foreign coins relative to the domestic coins tended to fall, despite the fact that the bullion price may have been higher. This meant that between the gold bullion 'shipping points', in this case the cost of transport of bullion into and out of the jurisdiction, coins were free to fluctuate in value.

All this suggests that during the great Geneva fair periods, a large-scale movement of coins flowed through Geneva, large enough to have a market, and the counterpart, a large scale movement of goods, took place as well. With fairs held four times per year, the market price, or exchange rate, of coins was set during the two-week fair period which would hold until the next fair.

Gold coins were the important currency of exchange, with rates set for the ducat, the florin, and the 'light weight' florin which was minted for the first time in 1384. During the next century, the latter years of the fairs of Geneva, the ducat had several values depending upon its gold content. The florin, on the other hand, became the all-important money of account and while the mint weight varied throughout the years, the account money remained constant at '12 deniers gros'.

Silver money tended to be the money in daily use, that is, it had a real velocity of circulation. A great variety of silver money was coined in Geneva. Duke Louis of Savoy added his own silver coin in 1457 and the coin of Charles I, the *teston*, came into existence in 1483. Copper money, of which a great variety was minted, was the most widely used of all.[3]

THE MEDIAEVAL MONETARY SYSTEM

A remarkable degree of sophistication in the art of money changing was developed by our banking ancestors. They were, in the first place, the conduits through which coin flowed into circulation from the mintmasters. By presenting bullion (halved foreign coins, and so on) to the mintmasters to be coined, they acquired the equivalent of the bullion in the form of new local coins. These, in turn, would be on hand for exchange for further bullion, in a continuous process of depletion/replenishing very much in the same fashion as modern banks replace worn-out banknotes with new ones.

In the second place, they were the means through which the *amount* of money in circulation was determined. As money changers, they operated within the limits of trade. For example, whenever exports from the jurisdiction exceeded imports, an excess of foreign coin (to pay for the excess of imports over exports) was presented to the money changers for local coin. This they provided by always having the mintmasters at their disposal to convert any excess of foreign coin, as bullion, into local coin.

In such cases additional purchasing power came into the hands of exporters who continued their profitable business activity: the purchase of additional wares from tradesmen who in turn hired more workers to increase the supply. In the case of agriculture, they made the attempt to purchase additional commodities for export. Since short-run supply elasticities for agriculture were generally low, the price of such commodities tended to rise. Peasants attempting to increase output (but not until the next season) could take advantage of higher prices with an increased area or more intensive cultivation.

Industrial workers, that minority of skilled journeymen, apprentices, and so on, found themselves in a particularly advantageous position. Again, supply elasticities for labour were low because mediaeval guilds had their own strict requirements for full membership. In short, wages in industry tended to rise.

The opposite, an unfavourable balance of trade which results in an outflow of gold, was roughly symmetrical. In this case, money changers (now the money changers resident in the gold-receiving country) were trading the excessive foreign coin for *their* local currency. In the gold-exporting country, money changers were finding themselves short of foreign coin relative to its demand. Bullion was the only way of alleviating the shortage, and mintmasters, desperate for additional supplies of bullion, could not resist the temptation to debase their own currency so that the scarce gold might stretch further and relieve the pressure on dwindling supplies of domestic coin.

The economic effects of coin shortages were the opposite of coin surpluses. A surplus of commodities, as imports competed with domestic production, relative to money, existed in the market. Unemployment grew with developing surpluses of labour. The ultimate result was that wages tended to be lowered, and, perhaps more important, agricultural prices fell as low supply elasticities worked in reverse to create commodity surpluses.

Under such conditions, it was to the advantage of the authorities to raise the price of gold bullion, thereby generating an inflow of foreign coin. 'Raising the price of bullion', in this case, meant a cheaper price for commodities relative to prices in the foreign jurisdiction. It would be to the advantage of a country to purchase imports from a neighbouring jurisdiction where commodities were cheaper relative to its home production, thereby establishing a fundamental principle of mercantilism.

Another factor influencing mercantilist thought must have been the tendency of mediaeval banks to use deposits as currency. De Roover observes this in mediaeval Bruges and, since the Italians were the 'universal bankers', the practice must have been common elsewhere.[4] There are sufficient records of mediaeval banks in existence to know that these money changers recorded deposits which were the counterpart of bullion as they came in from clients. Such bullion would eventually be handed over to mintmasters for recoining, but there is also sufficient historical evidence that money changers would, upon the orders of the deposit owners, actually change the ownership of deposits in the presence of both contracting parties. Such changes of deposit ownership constituted a transaction which involved no currency whatsoever.

At the same time that deposits changed ownership, the bullion remained intact awaiting its turnover to the mintmasters, or, if already coined, awaiting its withdrawal by a depositor. The money changer in this case was no longer in the business of changing money from bullion to coin, or from foreign to domestic coin, but was acting as a banker. Deposits were changing ownership without the use of metallic currency at all.

This is a matter of some considerable importance. When the balance of trade was favourable, gold flowed into the jurisdiction in greater amounts than flowed out. As gold entered the monetary jurisdiction, it was presented to the money changer for either the domestic currency equivalent or a recorded deposit. If a deposit was recorded and used for transactions purposes by changing its ownership, but with a corresponding idle metallic currency in the money changer's 'box', there was no effect on the local economy. However, if the deposit was recorded and used for transactions purposes and the currency of deposit itself was also used for payments, the effect of a favourable trade balance (ample stocks of money) was heightened. The metallic currency itself, otherwise idle and surplus to requirements, could have been used as a loan. Or, even further, additional deposits in the form of overdrafts, or other types of loans which merely changed ownership, could be made without the use of metallic currency at all.

We might imagine that mediaeval bankers could have served a most useful purpose by expanding their loan and deposit transactions just when money was tight, that is, when money was flowing out of the jurisdiction due to an unfavourable balance of trade. Such action might have saved coins from debasement. Not so. Such a level of sophistication had not yet been reached. During periods of unfavourable trade balances, the bankers suffered, along with everyone else, from a shortage of coin. There was an insufficient amount of metallic currency to honour their deposits and carry on the business of money changing at the same time. Fines, and even the gallows, awaited the hapless banker in such instances.

While it is to the Italians that we owe a great debt for the invention of modern banking, it is interesting that the early Italian banks suffered their greatest losses, to the point of bankruptcy, when they departed from the established practice of commercial lending. Since the capital requirement for industrial investment was minimal in mediaeval times, the temptation to extend credit to monarchs and princes proved to be sometimes irresistible, with unfortunate results.[5]

The implication here was obvious. The resources of these early banks proved to be greater than those required by commercial lending alone, and to keep the available capital continuously employed, additional outlets were required. Sometimes, as in the case of the Medici bank, it was expedient to finance the end purchase of commodities, and to the extent that royalty was the principal customer, as in the case of luxuries, the banks resorted to the finance of conspicuous consumption on the part of royalty. Unfortunately, the extravagant princes, dependent as they were upon taxation as their sole source of financing, proved in the end to be the greatest credit risks.

The great Medici bank of Florence was the epitome of Italian banking. Their branches were extensive throughout Europe and made possible much of the trade and commerce of the time. The evidence from the letters and correspondence of the bank, examined and made available to us through the scholarship of Raymond de Roover, suggests that even though the Medici did enjoy some monopoly control of the alum trade, the success of business throughout the century of their existence (until 1494) was due to the capacity of the company to adapt to the structure of trade and commerce of the day and adjust to the economic conditions as they changed.[6] Nevertheless, the deteriorating business environment in the Mediterranean after 1470, the result of the shift of trade away from the Levant, proved to be too much and became the underlying cause of the decline of the Medici.

The reason for this appears to be an inflexibility of the bank during periods of a deteriorating commercial environment, as is shown by the inability of its far-flung branches to remain solvent. Thus, while the Medici as well as the other banks of Italy were capitalists, *par excellence*, a rigidity of organisational structure grew through the years which made it difficult for their branches to maintain themselves as independent entities within the control mechanism exercised by the Florentine management.[7]

During the favourable times of economic expansion in Europe, the Italian banks found little difficulty in adapting to new circumstances, to expand and grow in prosperity along with the developing European economy. With less favourable periods of economic contraction, the rigidity of their organisational structure, which was efficient enough during growth periods, became a source of inefficiency. It is precisely during such contractionary periods that the all-too-human problems of branch loyalties and trust, which manifest themselves even today, become paramount.

THE MEDIAEVAL WORLD OF USURY

It is not easy for the modern scientific mind to appreciate the problems faced by our mediaeval ancestors constrained, as they were, by church dogma. In the case of usury, its definition consisted purely of 'any increment whether large or small, demanded above the principal...'[8] Thus, it was not merely a matter of excessive amounts of interest; *any* amount was forbidden.

It is simple enough to imagine the consequence. Since interest derives from a surplus acquired through investment in any form, it would be next to impossible for a nascent capitalist to acquire the funds necessary for a productive venture. Italian banks could hardly place any of their funds at risk without the compensation which was denied them by the church. The best they could do would be to participate in some industrial activity jointly with a mediaeval entrepreneur, thereby sharing both entrepreneurship and the profits.

In the case of loans for commercial ventures, which was the principal source of activity (and profit) for the Italian banks, another form of 'surplus' to replace interest *per se* was required. In this case it was by means of an 'exchange of bills', what we know today as the bill of exchange, which served this purpose.

The cambium (exchange contract) was not a loan; therefore it was not subject to the usury restrictions. Furthermore, since a bill of exchange was necessary for the implementation of the cambium, such implementation necessarily involved a credit transaction. This credit transaction, perhaps the most interesting aspect of the entire system, meant that the borrower of funds could pay absolutely nothing in terms of interest for the use of them. He could not pay interest since the church forbade such. The mediaeval banks that supplied the funds were entirely recompensed for their labours (and risk) from the exchange market itself. The degree to which they profited depended, therefore, on the fluctuations in that market alone.

The entire process will be instantly recognised by modern readers as arbitrage, pure and simple. Instead of the instantaneous communication between banks to take advantage of the smallest differentials, as we know it today, an arbitrage opportunity always existed in mediaeval banking. Why? If there were not sufficient exchange differentials amongst markets, a commercial loan involving the bill of exchange would never be made in the first place. These differentials were a substitute for interest, and therefore were essential to the entire process of commercial lending. Further, since credit was largely for the purpose of financing commercial transactions, as opposed to a more modern investment in productive enterprise, the system was not at all removed from the fundamental basis for the existence of mediaeval banking.

The opposition on the part of the church to usury stemmed from the hardships created by money lenders and usurers in their lending to hard-pressed landowners during the great famine of 1096. These lenders literally increased the hardship of the debtors by the simple expedient of doubling the debt if not paid at maturity.[9] Thus, any famine or pestilence was welcomed by money lenders as an opportunity for profit or for direct confiscation of property in the event that their loans could not be repaid. Since such loans were entirely for the purpose of consumption, serving no productive purpose whatsoever, they became the rationale for the banning of usury by the church.

But this was the early Middle Ages, and the economic potential inherent in commercial or productive lending had not yet arrived on the scene. It was the great mediaeval fairs which made commercial lending not only possible but necessary. Indeed, we might suggest the inverse relationship, that commercial lending made the mediaeval fairs possible and successful, and, since these fairs were the commercial centerpiece of economic life during the fifteenth century, it was commercial banking which made commerce possible during the period. This is the precise counterpart of the Italian banks in the Mediterranean region.

GENEVA, AN IMPERIAL CITY-STATE

It is important to realise that Geneva as a city had its beginnings long before the artificial national boundaries that carve up Europe today were conceived in the imagination of men. It was a true city-state, and, as part of the Holy Roman Empire, it was an Imperial town. It issued its own currency in the sense that the right of coinage belonged to the bishop. This right was the result of an agreement between Bishop Humbert and Count Aymon of the Genevese in 1124, later confirmed by the Emperor in 1154.[10]

A question which will likely remain unanswered for the rest of time will be to what extent, if any, did the church's opposition to interest actually *restrain* economic and commercial development? Should we use the example of Geneva, we must conclude that there was scarcely any actual restraint at all. Indeed, the citizens of Geneva seemed to have prospered mightily during the early years of the fifteenth century because of its famous fairs. Tradesmen, hoteliers, and even prostitutes enjoyed the patronage of visitors. Merchants from many parts of Europe, Germany, France, and Italy met there for the purpose of exchanging both commodities and currencies; indeed, Geneva, with its strategic location in central Europe, enjoyed the position of being both the principal banking and trading centre under the continuous protection of the Dukes of Savoy. (Geneva was, at that time, within the territories of the duchy of Savoy which was, in turn, part of the Holy Roman Empire.)[11]

Probably the most important of the merchants, from the standpoint of the subject which concerns us here, were those from Italy, because it was these which were not only most numerous (numbering in the hundreds) but also brought their Italian bankers with them. 'Nearly all', says Borel, 'of the banks used by the Duke, the Bishop, and the private citizens of the community were of Milanese or Florentine origin.'[12] The town council itself used the bank of Lionet de Medici when it borrowed some 24,000 Rhine florins in 1477. Additionally, on the occasion of the coronation of the son of the Duke of Savoy as king of Cyprus, a gift was provided by the town and the service of two Italian 'money changers' was used to provide a loan for this purpose in December, 1459.

The importance of foreign merchants in Geneva is indicated by the fact that when negotiations with Louis XI were ongoing for the purpose of persuading the king to abrogate the ordinances which had made permanent the fairs of Lyon (at the expense of Geneva), German and Italian merchants were selected as envoys. But it was the Italian merchants who were the most important in the town. Those from Savoy (the Genovese merchants themselves) and Milan were particularly numerous since the alliance between the houses of Savoy and Milan made commercial relations between them much simpler.[13] They tended to move from fair to fair, but the bankers and money changers, the *sine qua non* of the more mobile merchants, settled permanently in Geneva contributing to the welfare of the community as money lenders when the occasion arose.

The great annual Geneva fairs of the fifteenth century were just four in number, held throughout the year – Quasimodo (Easter), Saint-Pierre (St Peter in Chains), All Saints, and Apparition (Epiphany) – with a duration of fourteen days each.[14] During these periods, the local industry, particularly the hoteliers, literally thrived. The city bustled with activity. Different languages were heard in the streets, spoken by the commercial elite of Germany, Italy, and France. Considerable amounts of wealth flowed into the city for commercial purposes and for recreation: taverns and prostitutes prospered. But more important were the opportunities which the fairs held for the local artisans – tailors, shoemakers, cloakmakers, and so on – who were able to sell their accumulated inventory. The fairs themselves provided the commercial outlet which they required.

Why did the fairs locate in Geneva? It was actually a coincidence of geography and circumstance. Merchants from the towns of Germany, France, and Italy found a central location, at roughly the half-way point from each other, which by-passed the insurmountable passes of the high Alps. Furthermore, France under Charles VI was suffering from almost continuous hardships of plague, civil wars, and famine, and, with an undisciplined army closing French territory to trading, Geneva was the nearest appropriate commercial centre. Since the local Genevois were able to provide the facilities necessary for the accommodation of the fairs, and since the Italians were willing and able to provide the necessary credit facilities, the circumstances were ideal.[15]

All this changed when, in 1465, Louis XI issued the ordinances not only forbidding the subjects of France to attend the Geneva fairs but requiring them to use the newly created fairs of Lyon instead. Since the ordinances met with the support of the Duke of Savoy, there was little the Genevois could do except to appeal to Louis XI himself – to no avail, of course.

But of far greater significance to Geneva was the decline of the trade route system of which Geneva was a part. A medieval trade 'axis' had developed between Italy and Flanders. This axis had extended to the Levant, the trade of which Venice had a virtual monopoly, and to the cities of north Germany and England from which woollen goods had flowed. The Italians supplied the banking, bookkeeping, and insurance requirements as well as manufacturing and exporting silk and other fabrics. Flanders specialised in woollens, lace, and the like.[16]

In addition to this overland route, the sea routes to ports along the northern coasts of Europe were used. While the sea routes had the advantage of security from theft, they suffered from the uncertainties of weather; nevertheless, the sea route, though longer, was generally a favoured method of transport and travel.[17] Geneva was an important part of the overland route and participated both as an entrepot and as an important banking and money changing centre.

Largely as a result of the fairs, Geneva developed a remarkably sophisticated banking and credit system as well as money changing facilities. The money changers were banks as well, and some credit was provided by them. What was interesting, however, was the fact that the banks and the money changers were not native Genevois. Even the Medici bank was represented in Geneva by Francesco Sassetti, the most famous of the Medici 'factors'. The credit, largely commercial, was arranged on the basis of 'from fair-to-fair', and interest on loans (despite the church ban on usury) was charged for the interval between fairs.

The interesting question is why did the Genevois not develop their own banking skills directly from the tutelage and example of the Italians? From the historical evidence, it is clear that banking as an industry was still based upon commercial activity (money changing, commercial credit, and so on) and only rarely was it used for loan facilities other than these. The occasional loan to royalty (though poor credit risks) is recorded but this is the exception. We can suggest, therefore, that the Italians had the advantage of the technical skills (double entry accounting had already been invented), the advantages of location with branches throughout Europe wherever fairs existed, and the background experience with the bill of exchange, the trade instrument which avoided the usury prohibition. Hence, after 1463 with the re-location of the banks to Lyon, there was no further reason for the existence of commercial banking in Geneva.

Actually, the town and its citizens had other problems with which to concern themselves. The Reformation and the great upheavals which followed meant that Geneva, just as it had been the centre of trade and commerce in the fifteenth century, became the centre of religious activity in the sixteenth. John Calvin found Geneva, with its long history of the right to elect its syndics (magistrates), an ideal place for a theocratic government. All the more so because it was surrounded by powerful and not at all friendly neighbours, the Duke of Savoy and the Swiss canton of Berne. With an influx of refugees from religious strife, Geneva became populated not only with some of the best tradesmen of Europe but at the same time with potential soldiers to serve as a means of defense against invasion. What is most important, the banking industry and its development, for which Geneva became famous some two centuries later, had to wait while these more pressing problems were addressed.

THE PRICE REVOLUTION AND BANKS

At the same time that Italian banking reigned supreme throughout Europe, the great 'price revolution' (or, rather, inflation) began to assert itself with ever more intensity. Under ordinary circumstances, one might expect that rising prices would stimulate banking activity, that is, banks would find many customers wishing to borrow funds in anticipation of higher, though inflated, profits. Not so in this case. The great Medici bank was having considerable difficulty with its branch in London, due largely to unfortunate loans to Edward IV.[18] The Bruges branch, on the other hand, was having personnel difficulties, again suggestive of difficulties in maintaining solvency.[19]

The question, then, which requires answering is what was (or were) the causes of the so called 'price revolution' since, so it seemed, no one seemed to have prospered? Braudel's careful study of price movements during the 300 year period from 1450 to 1750 suggests that governments, attempting to maintain parity among three different types of money (gold coins, silver coins, and copper) failed, like incompetent jugglers, to keep all three in equilibrium.[20]

To understand and appreciate the problem, he identifies a fourth type of 'money', the money of account, which was a necessary method by which governments could record tax payments and set exchange rates. The money of account, in other words, was an administrative phenomenon which grew because of the simple necessity of record keeping. Tax payments were made in specie but in accordance with the rates set in money of account. It was by this means that governments sought to maintain an equilibrium between the various coins in circulation as well as between foreign coins as they appeared. To put it into practical terms, the mintmasters were prepared to accept coins as bullion in accordance with account money ratios.

Account money, therefore, had no real existence in concrete form. All debts had to be settled in the form of gold, silver, or other metallic currencies in accordance with the ratios of account. The money of account arose from the simple fact that records of some form had to be kept whenever debts were created. Yet, while simple enough to recognise as a means of record keeping, account money still served an important function in that it was the only form of money which was subject to the direct control of the authority. When a specific money was devalued in relation to a foreign currency, it was account money which was referred to.

But this led to considerable difficulties. Suppose silver, as bullion, decreases in price due to an oversupply of the commodity from the mines of the New World. It is a simple matter for those with mint rights (such as bishops and dukes) to purchase the silver with any of the other moneys (gold or copper) and convert the silver into coin, *just so long as the account money ratios remained intact*. Account money would, in fact, maintain its currency ratios in the short term for the simple reason that instantaneous adjustment of account ratios in the government accounts was impossible.

There is another aspect of mediaeval life and society which might appear somewhat foreign to modern readers. The artificial boundaries of modern nation-states, each with its own legal jurisdiction (and monetary system), did not exist in the case of feudal jurisdictions. Metallic currencies were free to move not only within feudal jurisdictions but amongst them. Thus the coins minted by a Duke within his own territory could be carried to the fairs of Geneva, Paris, or Bruges and freely exchanged via the highly skilled money changers in accordance with the gold or silver content.

Metallic currencies have a long life. They may be returned to the mint as bullion as they become worn, clipped, or damaged, to be replaced with a new issue. Because of this and their universality, any increase in the output of monetary metals must result in a net increase in monetary circulation in all political jurisdicions. The expansion of output of metals for metallic currency because of the new availabilities of mines in the New World, on the one hand, and newer and more efficient techniques of mining in both Europe and America on the other, meant price increases everywhere. Only if an increase in the output of commodities could outpace the rate of metallic currency expansion could a process of deflation exist, and this is not likely to have been the situation until much later, during the 160 year span from 1600–1750.[21]

But there is likely to be more than an increase in the supply of metallic currency involved. Braudel's prices of commodities in terms of silver suggest that more than a threefold increase in wheat prices (in terms of grams of silver, 20 to 70) occurred during the 100 year span from 1500 to 1600; they then showed little or no further tendency to rise except for occasional fluctuations due to harvest conditions.[22] At the same time fairly recent research into Spanish trade with the New World indicates that the silver trade showed an increase during the sixteenth century to peak in the year 1600. The trade rose from about 20,000 or 30,000 tons to a maximum of about 50,000 tons in 1600.[23] It is unlikely that approximately doubling the amount of trade, paid for in silver shipments, could cause a threefold increase in prices throughout all of Europe. What could have been the agent which caused the 'leverage effect' of silver on the price level?

It was the banking system of the day (what else) which must have been responsible for the upward leverage in prices. Since 'banks' really consisted of money changers combined with some elements of modern commercial banking, clearly what was happening was that the beginnings of deposit creation, using loans as a basis for new deposits, must have been taking place. Such deposit creation was generally for the purpose of commercial transactions, as in the bills of exchange discussed above, or in the form of overdrafts in one account to be credited to another account in settlement of a debt. Indeed, the Italian banks had already developed a remarkable degree of sophistication in this activity.[24]

With the development of such lending, a certain amount of metallic 'reserve' was required for the protection of depositors. Precisely what percentage of total deposits must consist of metallic reserve would vary from bank to bank; nevertheless, it was there, in some cases as much as 29 or 30 per cent. This would be sufficient to result in an approximately threefold increase in bank money (defined as both deposit money plus metallic currency) which came into the possession of the money changers. Furthermore, since such deposit creation was for the purpose of commercial transactions only, strict limits upon such creation would have been imposed by the very nature of the activity. Banking was not so developed that deposit creation could be used for consumer credit, for instance. Credit of this type was the prerogative of the Lombards and there is no evidence that a deposit expansion occurred in the case of Lombard loans.

The almost systematic inflation which developed through the fifteenth, sixteenth, and seventeenth centuries suggests just such a general increase in the supplies of metallic currencies as well as deposit creation by the banks. Indeed, the fact that prices rose throughout Europe during this period suggests further that there was a relative ease of transport of metallic currency from one jurisdiction to another.

CONCLUSIONS

The history of banking in the mediaeval period is, of course, Italian. It was invented by Italians to facilitate the great commercial activity for which the Italian city-states were famous. But the story of money and money changing is not necessarily Italian. In this activity, the Italians excelled because they happened to be there first.

In Europe, during this period, the nation-state was yet to be developed. Boundaries between dukedoms and bishoprics were flexible, and certainly there existed no currency restrictions which would retard the flow of metallic currencies. Values of local currencies *vis-à-vis* 'foreign' currencies were determined by the weight of their metallic content.

In such a complex system with a multiplicity of coins, the money changer became the centre of the entire monetary system. It is no exaggeration to say that he was the pivot round which all economic activity revolved. At the same time, the money changer's bullion counterpart, the mintmaster, completed this 'pivot service' by providing a sufficient quantity of coins for the mediaeval economy to thrive. The sheer complexity of the money changer/mintmaster task poses the question to the modern mind, how could the mediaeval economy have even functioned with any degree of success? But function it did and remarkably well under the circumstances.

There was, of course, a weakness which is characteristic of a metallic system. Bullion, both gold and silver, can enter into monetary circulation at any time. This was the function of the mint. Furthermore, since there was no political boundary to limit the area of circulation, any increase in bullion would spread quickly from one end of Europe, for example Novgorod, to the other, London. Gold and silver could move to wherever the purchasing power of bullion was the greatest (the price level of commodities in terms of gold or silver was lowest). The movement of these metals was expedited by the mediaeval fair system which meant that merchants moved from fair to fair almost continuously.

Any increase in the supply of gold and silver bullion must, therefore, result in 'inflation'. Prices would certainly rise as a result of greater supplies unless the output of commodities could either outpace or just keep pace with the increase in supply. This was the impact of the New World gold plundering, in the first place, and the increase in mine output in the second.

At the same time, the money changers were extending into the range of complete banking with both deposit taking and, more significant, deposit creation. We would not agree with some economic historians who argue that a 'bank multiplier', similar to the logic of a so-called bank multiplier in a modern system, existed at the time. The bank multiplier argument itself is hardly tenable even in the best of circumstances. There was, nevertheless, an element of deposit expansion as bankers transferred the ownership of deposits for the purpose of discharging debt obligations. Deposit expansion, particularly as overdrafts, certainly became common. The result was a heightening of the inflationary impact of the increase in supply of gold and silver bullion. This is apparent from the statistical series compiled by Braudel.

The geographic position of Geneva as an important centre for mediaeval trade between southern and northern Europe was unique. Italian bankers recognized the strategic importance of the city fairly early in the period and established their branches there until the ordinances of Louis XI brought an end to the fairs. Were it not for these ordinances and the theocratic period of Calvin which followed in the sixteenth century, we can speculate that Geneva's banking experience, under the tutelage of the Italian branch banks, could well have begun a steady evolutionary process not unlike that of the Basle bankers. Swiss banking, that is, might have developed much earlier than it did.

In particular, it is quite conceivable that a Swiss banking industry could have actually outpaced the Germans whose adventuresome banks literally displaced the more cautious, conservative, (and exhausted) Italian banks. There is just one difficulty. The Swiss did not have the necessary capital at this time. That was to come later.

Nevertheless, the lessons in the art of banking taught by the Italians must have left an important legacy. We know that Calvin did not discourage banking, nor did he exclude interest as a form of profit. He did, however, actively discourage excessive interest. Considering the enormously broad concerns of Calvin with all types of trades and industry during the period, it is to his credit that lending at interest should have occupied his attention at all.[25]

Notes

1. Between 1300 and 1345, the most powerful Florentine companies were those of the Bardi, the Peruzzi, and the Acciaiuoli. The Florentine chronicler, Giovanni Villani (1276–1348), who had been for a while a partner of the Peruzzi company, called them 'the pillars of Christian trade', by which he meant presumably the main supports of the western trade in the Mediterranean area. All three companies collapsed shortly before the Black Death (1348), which is believed to have wiped out one-third of the population of Europe. De Roover, Raymond, *The Rise and Decline of the Medici Bank, 1397–1494* (Cambridge: MA.: Harvard University Press, 1963) p. 2.
2. Borel, Frederic, *Les Foires de Genève au Quinzieme Siècle*, H. Georg, Libraire-Editeur, 10, Corraterie, Genève, 1892, 237.
3. Ibid., p. 238
4. De Roover, Raymond, *Money, Banking, and Credit in Medieval Bruges* (Cambridge MA: The Medieval Academy of America, 1948) p. 230.
5. De Roover, *Rise and Decline of Medici Bank*, 1397–1494, pp. 10–11.
6. De Roover, *Rise and Decline*, p. 156.
7. Ibid., p. 234
8. Ibid., p. 10
9. De Roover, *Money, Banking, and Credit*, p. 10.

10. Borel, *Les Foires de Geneve*, p. 228.
11. Thanks to Frederic Borel, a scholar who has left us a careful and exacting analysis of the original documents from the archives of the town, we have a fairly clear picture of economic activity in the city during this period.
12. Borel, *Les Foires de Genéve*, p. 106.
13. Borel, *Les Foires de Genéve*, p. 103.
14. Guerdon, Rene, *La Vie Quotidienne a Geneve au Temps de Calvin*, (Paris Librairie Hachette, 1973) p. 56.
15. Ibid pp.51 ff. Guerdon provides an interesting, amusing, and somewhat unsavoury account of the hotels of the period. They were not, as he points out, Hiltons. Nevertheless, they did provide a respectable source of income for local dignitaries who were the proprietors. Later, during the period of Calvin, they, the landlords, acted as 'secret police' to report on foreign visitors when it was felt necessary.
16. Koenigsberger, H.G. and Mosse, G.L., *Europe in the Sixteenth Century* (New York: Holt, Rinehart and Winston, 1968) p. 45.
17. Ibid., p. 46.
18. De Roover, *Rise and Decline*, pp. 330 ff.
19. De Roover, *Money, Banking and Credit in Mediaeval Bruges*, pp. 338 ff.
20. Braudel, F., 'Prices in Europe from 1450 to 1750', in *The Cambridge Economic History of Europe*, Cambridge University Press, 1967, p. 381. E. E. Rich and C. H. Wilson, eds.
21. Ibid., p. 470–1.
22. Ibid., p. 470–1.
23. Chaunu, P. and Chaunu, H. *Seville et l'Atlantique, 1504–1650*, (Paris, 1955–59), quoted in Koenigsberger and Mosse, *Europe in the Sixteenth Century*, p. 47.
24. See de Roover, *Money and Banking, and Credit in mediaeval Bruges*, Chapter 14.
25. Guerdon, Rene, *La Vie Quotidienne a Geneve au Temps de Calvin*, Librairie Hachette, 1973. Chapter 3. This is a most interesting account of the broader concern of the Geneva government in economic life. But Calvin did not stop with economics alone. All aspects, so it seemed, of human endeavour was embraced by his paternalistic government.

2 The Money Changers of Basle

The thoughtful reader must surely have been struck by a historical parallel which exists between the mediaeval economies of Europe and the modern vision of a united Europe with a single currency. Indeed, the European Monetary System, with its anticipated economic union, does bear a remarkable resemblance to the same Europe which existed prior to the emergence of nation states. There are obvious differences in detail, history does not repeat itself with exactitude, but the similarities are sufficient to remind us that there is really very little that is completely new in human endeavour.

One difference strikes one as significant: the function of the banking system in our modern world is very different from that of the mediaeval period. Modern banking is much broader in scope, serving with the greatest efficiency the vital economic purpose of channelling the savings of one sector of the world into investment in another. Technological differences apart, it is this banking function that our mediaeval ancestors could never have understood.

With all its faults, mediaeval society was highly successful in the pursuit of its own economic activity, if we use as a comparison our own minimal degree of success in coping with our modern economic problems of inflation, unemployment, and so on. While it is certainly correct (and obvious enough) that our own economic society is considerably more complex than that of our ancestors, in terms of the degree to which economic institutions have adapted to the requirements of commerce, exchange, and production, we have yet far to go to reach the efficiency level of our mediaeval ancestors.

To our ancestors, banking was a commercial proposition, a method of facilitating the flow of trade and commerce. After all the church itself, in an age when the authority of the church was not to be questioned, did not understand how money could beget additional money. To put it simply, the lending of capital for the purpose of gain was an act to be punished in the fires of Hell.

All this makes good sense when we consider that opportunities for capital investment were extremely limited in the pre-Industrial Revolution era. This raises the interesting point which has concerned historians for some time: did the church actually retard economic growth with its anti-usury doctrine? Or, to be more specific, did the Protestant Reformation make possible the Industrial Revolution which followed some two centuries later? These are questions which are more appropriately left to those of a more philosophical bent; our central focus in this chapter lies in the antecedents of Swiss banking.

BASLE

For all practical purposes, Basle's history as a centre for money and banking dates from the period of the Holy Roman Empire. Just as in other centres of trade and commerce, the banking process had its beginnings in the activity of money changing, a highly skilled and technical process involving the determination of weights of precious metals included in each coin to be changed.

Since the Emperor alone possessed the sovereignty necessary for the determination of both the supply and quality of money, the disposition of the right of coinage of the money supply was an important power. The Emperor decided the gold content of coins as well as their manufacture. He then disposed of these rights, amongst the various fiefs, bishoprics and monastaries, to the feudal lords of the territories within which the coins were permitted to circulate. These rights of coinage were perpetuated, at least since the tenth century, as part of the fiefdom. As a result, many types of currency appeared in circulation throughout the entire Empire.

We can picture the situation. With so many different coins in circulation, it is obvious that a spillover of 'foreign coins' into specific feudal regions must occur. This would be the consequence of normal trading activity, especially so near the boundaries of the fiefdom. A natural tendency, therefore, existed for the 'foreign coin' to depreciate in terms of the domestic coin. This simple psychological preference for the domestic coin made it necessary for a new class of professional money changers to come into existence in mediaeval society. These money changers were expert in the art of determining the precious metal content of each of the coins. Furthermore, the professional money changers had to have some regulations because of the simple fact that the coins themselves frequently changed their precious metal content. This necessitated an expertise and a knowledge of all the coin manufacturing of each of the fiefdoms with which they came into commercial contact.

As the money changers grew in this expertise, they also developed an understanding of monetary circulation. In particular, they learned that the manufacture and distribution of coins was a powerful and eagerly sought-after privelege, the result of political patronage or favours. By developing an order from this 'chaos', they made possible, without being consciously aware of their importance, the success of the mediaeval monetary system.

The underpinning of this system was the actual gold (or silver where appropriate) content of the coins. In carrying on their profession, they contributed to the classic Law of Gresham – that the coins of lesser gold content drove from circulation those of greater gold content. This arose because both types of coin (those of lesser and greater gold content) had the same nominal value in terms of purchasing power. The desire for profit made it possible for the money changers to exchange the 'heavier' coins for the 'lighter' coins at the local mint, where a simple process of melting the smaller number of 'heavier' coins and re-creating them in the form of more 'lighter' coins could take place. The profit in the transaction consisted of the greater nominal value of coins less the cost of mintage.

While the pursuit of profit was undoubtedly the immediate objective of the money changers, we should not lose sight of the larger picture, namely that there always existed a shortage of gold. This gold scarcity, while a necessary feature of money *per se*, was at times sufficiently great that the practice of clipping was resorted to, so as to stretch a small amount of gold further amongst a large amount of coins. Thus, 'profit' was not necessarily the result of acquisitiveness on the part of money chaners. The avoidance of losses when the price of bullion rose was equally important.

What is most important here is that the money changers themselves became an integral part of the monetary system; indeed, without them, the system itself would necessarily have been chaotic. In addition, the knowledge of the continuously fluctuating foreign exchange values, as well as their ability to anticipate *future* values of foreign exchange, was certainly as sophisticated as any modern banker who deals in foreign bills.

Basle had had a long tradition in matters of coinage. In the mediaeval period, one of the earliest of the mediaeval mints in the territory of modern Switzerland was located in Basle itself. This mint was already active during the reign of King Conrad of Burgundy in the tenth century.[1] When the town became part of the Holy Roman Empire, the right of coinage was bestowed by the Emperor on the bishop of Basle sometime during the reign of Bishop Adelbero (999–1025). This right of coinage was further 'corroborated' by Pope Eugene III in 1146 by the granting of the right of coinage to be Bishop Ortlieb. Since the silver mines of Breisgau, as well as access to other raw materials for coinage, had already been granted to the bishop by Konrad II in 1028, the monopoly was complete. Indeed, by the frequent withdrawal of old coins to be replaced by the minting of new ones, and the 'economising' of silver by the practice of issuing thinner, hence debased, coinage, thereby 'stretching' the limited amount of silver, some transfer of wealth from the public to the bishop took place. In effect, this was a substitute for taxation by means of an early form of money inflation.

The somewhat widespread use of this practise was confirmed by the Emperor Friedrich in 1154 who, in a deed, asserted that coins be improved in weight and purity and remain in that state forever. Neither the bishop nor his successors would ever dare to debase the Basle coinage again, nor could any one outside the town or within the bishopric imitate the coins by means of similar impressions on coins of lesser worth. Curiously, Bishop Ludwig, Ortlieb's successor, was actually placed in 'tutelage', that is, under the control of his worldly advisers for matters of coinage. Despite this, matters further deteriorated until he was dismissed by the Lateran Council in 1179.

But it was later, in 1225, that the Basle coinage received its greatest and most successful impulse toward becoming the most universally accepted money in the area. The Lord of the Town, Heinrich II of Thun, possessed the astonishing foresight ('astonishing' for that mediaeval era) to undertake the financing and building of the first Rhine bridge. It was financed by means of borrowing from Jewish sources with the church treasure as security. Most importantly, the bridge made possible commercial activity across the river to a much greater extent than the previous unreliable ferry crossings could ever have achieved. From that point on, the use of the Basle coinage was extended well beyond the bishopric, even to the Customs at the St Gothard Pass itself. This gave the town of Basle enormous importance which in turn enhanced the prestige of the money changers of the town.

As could have been expected, Basle became an important commercial and financial centre as a result of this prescience of Heinrich II. The numbers of money changers increased considerably during the thirteenth century, all within the 'financial world' of the bishopric. There were, thus, two underpinnings to this world. The first was the document, or deed, of Friedrich II which regulated the coinage as to the weight of silver and the second was the bridge over the Rhine which made possible the extension of the use of these high quality coins to a much larger geographic area than the bishopric. As Lord of the Town, the bishop had the legislative authority to maintain the purity of the coinage as well as the right to issue a new coinage annually, the weight and standard of purity of which never changed.

Along with the bishop, the master of the mint (mentioned for the first time in 1141 in an edict of Konrad II) had the authority to protect the Basle coinage against the dangers of counterfeiting as well as to bring the guilty to justice ('justice', of course, being of the harshest mediaeval type). The regulations designed to protect the Basle coinage from debasement were both stringent and epasting.

While the bishop and the mint-master enjoyed the privilege of the weighing of silver and the determination of its purity, others such as the goldsmiths or other private citizens in possession of foreign coin or precious metals could only have the metals weighed at the Fronwaage – the public scales at which all articles over 12 1/2 pounds were to be weighed when sold. Goldsmiths had to pay up to two marks for the right to purchase such silver for their business. Likewise, trading in silver was forbidden to the money changers unless the silver was first sold to the mint. A fine of 3 pounds of pfennigs was levied against those money changers who violated this regulation. Additionally, when the money changers received bullion in exchange for Basle coins, they were required to offer it to the mintmaster. On the rare occasions when the mintmaster refused to purchase the bullion, the money changers had to dispose of it themselves and pay the 3 pounds of pfennigs fine, hence a risk was incurred in the purchase of bullion with Basle coins.

While these regulations were stringent enough, there was still the right of the village mayor, acting as a judge, to sample the output of the mint without any previous warning. The mayor, generally accompanied by two or three witnesses, would then take the samples to the bishop for trial, should they be suspected of being fraudulent. In this case, 'fraudulent' meant an error of only four pfennigs, which was the maximum allowed to the mintmaster.

All these regulations and restrictions had the effect of enhancing the reputation of Basle coins throughout the region of the Empire. This was no small achievement; indeed, during an era when currencies were either imperfectly understood, or understood not at all, it is remarkable that the Basle coinage regulations should have been designed so as not only to preserve the original purity of the coins but to limit their production.[2] The famous law of Sir Thomas Gresham and the currency reform of the young Queen Elizabeth during the years 1558–1603 are sufficient testimony to the difficulties of both quality and quantity in the matter of coinage. Indeed, throughout all of Europe the difficulty of maintaining currencies at their correct weight and fineness (as discussed in detail in Chapter 1) was shown by the general trend of rising prices during the mediaeval period. The fact, therefore, that the Basle controls were so strict, testifies to a remarkable insight into the working of the mediaeval economy and the importance of a sound currency, an unusual circumstance for the period.

The Basle system consisted of a relatively complex relationship between mintmasters, the mayor, and the money changers. The mintmaster was directly under the control of the mayor whereas the money changers were office holders who had a special trust relationship with the coinage lord (the bishop). They had the exclusive right to change money and gold ingots and had their tables placed in the fish market beside the coin house with its Fronwaage. Their positions were hereditary, in that only their legitimate sons could carry on in their fathers' occupations. They formed a fraternity, along with the bishop's household, and as such, most important, could grant loans and advances to credit-worthy businessmen.

In a decree of 21 August 1289, Bishop Peter I of Reichenstein confirmed the fraternity of money changers with their own company statute along with their rights and duties. They could purchase gold and silver from goldsmiths who were in their turn subordinate to the mintmaster. With this decree the relationship between the office of money changer and the goldsmith's craft was defined, eventually to become a matter of custom.

But the bishops of Basle were by no means successful in the double role they had to play as both politicians in control of the state and masters of the church. The fundamental weakness of two different jurisdictions combined in the same person, with sometimes conflicting objectives, made it impossible for the system of administration to be successful over longer periods. Johann III von Vienne, reigning from 1365 onward, never resided in Basle at all. He found himself plagued by debts due to the secular ambitions of his predecessors as well as himself. A century of mismanagement, including military adventures, meant that the bishopric was heavily in debt, so much so that in 1373 he transferred to the town of Basle the right of coinage forever in return for 4000 'good and heavy florins'. This included, of course, the important mint.

This transfer of coinage rights to the town made possible the formation of the Upper Rhine Coin Alliance, the first attempt at regional cooperation within the Empire for the purpose of standardising coin values and weights. Thus, in 1387 the representatives of some 17 independent towns plus 11 lords with 74 towns and governments met in Basle for that purpose. In September of that year, the Basle Convention was signed which made possible the standardisation of the pfennig, and the fixing of the pfennig against the mark and the pound.[3]

In one year after the Convention, the Swiss and Alsatian towns agreed upon a new Coin Regulation which regulated the money changers both in their exchange and their profit margins. This was not just to protect the population from the greed of the money changers, but to protect the money changers from the competition of the counterfeiting population, that is, the 'greed' of the population. Or, to express it differently, the greater the geographical spread of the coin circulation, the greater the tendency of the coin to be debased or copied. Consider, for example, a list of punishments for infractions:

> Whoever breaks up or debases pfennigs shall have his finger cut off and he shall be hanged.
> Whoever debases and melts down pfennigs shall have life and goods forfeited.
> Whoever takes silver or minted gold out of the country shall have a hand cut off.
> Whoever sells silver to anyone who takes it out of the country shall incur the same punishment.
> Whoever strikes or mints coins without the right to do so shall have life and goods forfeited.[4]

This list of punishments, terrifying enough to a modern mind, underscores not so much the nature of mediaeval 'justice' but of the social and economic problems faced by the authorities of the time and, more specifically, the money changers themselves. Considering both that transactions were very largely made in cash and that the gradual improvement in the technique of minting made it more difficult for abuses to exist, a natural monopoly of the production of coins developed. Ultimately, a relatively simple inspection of the coins by the seller of a product was all that was required to distinguish between a counterfeit coin and the genuine article.

The real problem which the money changers faced, however, was not counterfeiting itself but the protection of their monopoly, hence the frightening list of punishments which were really meant less to deter a would-be miscreant than a potential competitor. It was in this way that the monetary system of the region was supposed to develop and extend itself beyond the immediate Basle area. 'Supposed' is the operative word, because the Basle Convention only lasted ten years and was not renewed in 1397. We can, however, immediately recognise that the focus of concern on the part of the public and governments alike was upon the quality of the coins: their weight and their precious metal content. That was the extent and the objective of 'monetary policy' in mediaeval times.

Shortly after the end of the Basle Convention in 1397, Basle concluded, in 1399, a coin alliance with Duke Leopold of Burgundy. The purpose of this alliance, contrary to the Convention, was to protect the domestic currency from the influx of foreign coins into the region. This was the mediaeval counterpart of a modern inflation being generated not by an overissue of domestic coins but by a surfeit of foreign coins which the local money changers were obliged to accept.

At the same time attempts were made to continue the spirit of the Basle Convention in a new form, the Rappen Coin Alliance. In 1403, Basle, Freiburg, Breissach, Colmar and Thann, along with the Habsburg lands, successfully concluded this alliance, which was to last until 1584. Based upon the Rhenish gold gulden (or sovereign), a pound (pfund) of pfennig were struck for each gulden. Additional coins, including the batzen, groschen, plapparte and rappen, were based upon the gold gulden which was, incidentally, the commercial currency of western Germany. These local coins were of silver mined from the Vosges and distributed amongst the participants of the Alliance according to a contractual agreement. Thus, the success of the entire Alliance rested on the availability of silver, on the one hand, and its fair and just distribution on the other. The fact that it lasted so long suggests that the monetary requirements of each of the participating communities did not differ to any significant degree.

Mediaeval monetary policy (the terms of the Alliance in this case) was successful in serving the requirements for a circulating medium within each community. The phenomenon of economic growth, with its expanding monetary requirement, with which we are all so familiar in our time, was non-existent. What *was* in existence was a society quite different from what we know and have experience of today. Europe, more specifically the Holy Roman Empire, in the fifteenth century was a society in turmoil, to be sure, but not concerning economic or social issues. Religious dogma occupied the centre of attention with the minorities, particularly the Jews, often the object of persecution. The central focus of human activity was spiritual, with the polar opposites of the Heavenly reward for the righteous contrasted with witchcraft, worship of Satan and necromancy. In a word, the Antichrist was the enemy, and, unfortunately, often tended to be Jewish.

Women also became the object of persecution as witches. Any strange or unusual phenomenon, illness, plague, or real or imagined variation in the normal agricultural cycle, was attributed to witches in a non-scientific age of myth and superstition. Women who were either old and ugly or young and pretty were particularly susceptible to the charge of witchcraft. Indeed, even those who were suspected often fantasised themselves as witches in a psychological confirmation of their own guilt.

Finally, the established church itself came under suspicion because of the enormous earthly wealth and power that it possessed. Instead of offering a vision of the spiritual world to come (in an age of extreme pessimism), the church itself became hopelessly entangled in the web of corrupt political practices totally unrelated to its spiritual function.

The awareness on the part of the populace of the need for general social reform led to the Reformatio Sigismundi (1439), a document which advocated massive changes in both church and feudal hierarchies. In terms of economics, it advocated the abolition of guilds and trading companies which were seen as agents which drove up prices. Additionally it appealed for revolutionary change, in that serfs were to be freed and prices and wages fixed for the benefit of the poor. As in many such instances in human history, the Reformatio was not in itself so significant in terms of the positive measures it advocated but in its being indicative of the conditions, both economic and social, of the time.

Most important, for our purposes, are the measures which protested the change of commodity prices, presumably favouring the interests of specific groups in society. Here we find the mediaeval doctrine of the 'just price'. It was a 'bootstrap' concept in the sense that a price is what it is because it has always been such a price, and any increase in that price must be the consequence of monopoly power.

It is at once apparent to the modern mind that the 'just price' system is really a static pricing system. Any economic system based upon such a pricing concept has little or no opportunity for economic growth, or, to invert the logic, it is only an economic system with no opportunity for growth which could tolerate such a pricing mechanism. Trading companies, that is, which saw the possibilities of additional profit through higher prices, not necessarily due to conditions of poor harvest, were in violation of the system.[5] One cannot but recognise in the just price the mediaeval counterpart of Adam Smith's 'natural price'.

This price was defined in a rather circular fashion by Smith as 'the central price to which the prices of all commodities are continually gravitating'.[6]

Central to the mechanism of the just price was a monetary system based upon precious metals. Such metals, by definition, were in short supply, and as such were particularly suited to the function of a circulating medium. It was, however, essential that the circulating coins be of a precise amount of precious metal, because only in that way could the just price system work successfully. Consider, as an example, a peasant selling a quantity of grains. With the proceeds of his sale he desires certain items produced by artisans in the town. Should he exchange his grains for coins of less than the full value of precious metals, he would discover that his grains had less value (in terms of the amount of manufactured items) than he had originally thought. The peasant would have a legitimate grievance since the just price mechanism had failed him. It would have failed him because should he wish to make a purchase of an 'imported product' (imports referring to an adjoining area in which another currency was used), he would be required to exchange his coin through a money changer who would determine the precious metal content of his coin. For this reason, it was essential that the quality of the coins be of the highest.

THE BASLE SYNOD

In a real sense, therefore, we can attribute to Basle the 'distinction' of being the first of the great Swiss monetary centres, even though Basle did not join the confederation until 1501. The word 'monetary' in this case includes both the minting of coins and the process of money changing. This occurred because the papal bull of 1424, which announced the Synod in Basle (a stroke of good fortune for Basle) was precisely the inducement for King Sigismund of Austria to encourage the establishment of an imperial mint there in 1429.[7]

The Basle Synod, as well as the Council of Constance, was the concrete result of a massive church reform movement which was sweeping Europe at the time. The roots of the movement, however, lay much deeper than the church alone. It was the entire social and economic hierarchy, particularly the institution of serfdom, which was being strained. The Rennaissance period had already begun. But for Basle to be the 'host' town for the Synod meant much more than social or religious reform. It meant a period of great prosperity – the mediaeval equivalent of an economic boom. At the same time, such a boom period necessitated the existence of a source of currency which could expand, temporarily at least, the local money supply so as to avoid an inevitable shortage of currency. In a word, economic growth within a relatively small region was proceeding at a much greater rate and monetary expansion within that area was essential. It was the recognition of the importance of a greater supply of currency which led to the establishment of the imperial mint at Basle.

The importance of the Basle mint was later endorsed by the Emperor Sigismund in 1435 (he was crowned by the pope in 1433) who confirmed that the florins produced by the Basle mint were superior in gold content to the competing mints of Frankfurt and Nordlingen. This was no small achievement and must be to the credit of the mint-masters, Peter Gatz and Heinrich von Romersheim. Considering, once more, that the entire 'science' of mediaeval economics rested upon the production of coins of good quality in a quantity necessary to maintain commercial activity, a well-run mint was the greatest asset to the town of Basle, especially during the period of the Synod. Even so, the mint had a stormy history. The Imperial Chamberlain, Konrad von Weinsberg, received the Basle mint as security for loans to the Emperor. Then Weinsberg himself, when later he became heavily in debt, attempted to sell the mint, first to the town of Basle and then to the competing Rhenish mint owners. He died in 1448 leaving his debts to his heirs to settle.

The Basle mint ceased to exist in 1509 when it was transferred to Augsburg. This was the consequence of the settlements of Weinsberg debts and the inheritance of another estate, bringing to an end the minting of gold coins in Basle. It was not until 1512, when Pope Julius II awarded to the people of Basle the right to mint gold coins, later confirmed by the Emperor Maximillian, that the process of minting in the town began again.

The period of prosperity which was ushered in by the Synod was so great that more than a new mint was required to satisfy the financial requirements of the city and its illustrious guests. The great Italian banks of Medici, Albertini, and Gianfigliazzi were invited to the city to provide their credit facilities. Thus, exchange orders drawn upon the Basle offices of these banks were used to provide a safe, secure means whereby visitors could transport their own funds. There was, therefore, a fundamental competition between the Basle money changers who required the personal transport of gold coins (at peril of the life of the visitor) and the more sophisticated banking facility of the Italian banks. Even more important, however, was the fact that the money changers of Basle were introduced to the techniques of Italian banking.

As far as economic activity was concerned, the Basle economy flourished. Along with the dignitaries that came to the town there were the tradesmen and artisans who accompanied them and brought their own productive skills in competition with the existing guilds. Not only new products but also new techniques of production were introduced into the economy. There was, as a consequence, a great pressure on the existing supply of housing, which in turn drove up prices. The prices of housing were often the subject of dispute, to be settled by a commission appointed by the city council. Ultimately price controls had to be imposed. Additionally, the town council itself, through the collection of more taxes, was able to greatly improve its own financial management.

During the period of the Synod, Basle was literally 'flooded' with coins from all regions – French, Spanish, Italian, Venetian, Hungarian and, of course, Savoy. The problem of the money changers, as a consequence, became enormous. Indeed, the money changers were at the centre of economic activity because the value of all the foreign coins *vis-à-vis* the Basle coins not only had to be established but also had to be consistent. The importance of consistency in value was shown by the treaty of Breisach in 1433 which settled the value ratios between foreign and Basle coins on the basis of objective tests of individual currencies. The results of the tests were read aloud in public.

At the same time, price controls were introduced into the town so that guests and visitors alike could have some security of purchasing power for their foreign funds. When gold became relatively scarce, silver was used as a supplement for coinage. Thus the mediaeval economy of Basle became an economy, in miniature, of Europe, adjusting to new and different situations as they arose – in this case the considerable prosperity of a boom situation, for the merchants and tradesmen of Basle also shared in the good fortune of the presence of the Synod.

The Italian bankers, particularly the Medici, who were invited to the Synod, were not subject to the strict rules of conduct of the money changers and found considerable profit in lending to the clergy as well as to merchants. Indeed, the returns of the Medici at the Synod were actually greater than in Brugge or London and they expanded their activity to include merchandising in addition to the ordinary business of banking. Silver articles, silks and woollens were among the more popular articles in demand at the banks.

Still, however, strict rules prevailed regarding the quality of gold coins, and the foreign banks were subject to these rules just as were the domestic money changers. Profits on exchange were regulated and the practice of melting down gold coins and the substitution of cheaper, or lighter, coins for possible additional profit was strictly prohibited.

The 'boom' reached its peak with the arrival of the Emperor Sigismund in 1433 after his coronation by the Pope in Rome. Curiously, he eschewed pomp and ceremony, and disembarked, barefoot, from his boat on the Rhine. He then walked up Freiestrasse to the Munster accompanied by the town council and the protector of the Synod.

It was then that the fortunes of Basle became linked to world history, for, indeed, it was in a real sense the centre of the Holy Roman Empire with the convening of the Imperial Diet in the town. Already, however, Pope Eugen IV, elected in 1431, had abolished the Synod and was no longer interested in the work of reform which the Synod had undertaken. The Synod assembly, on the other hand, determined to maintain its position, countered with the assertion that an assembly of the church would stand even before the Pope. Hence the question of primacy, the assembly of the Synod or the papacy, became the heart of the conflict.

The Emperor himself attempted to mediate between the two and finally reached a compromise which was solemnized both by the Pope in Rome and the Synod in Basle in December of 1433. With the convening of the Diet in 1434, Basle became in a true sense a world centre of both spiritual and political activity. Great pomp and ceremony accompanied the announcement of 'peace' between the Pope and the Synod.

The compromise peace was short-lived, because, as with all compromises, neither party was satisfied. The Pope continued his struggle against the Basle Synod which, in its turn, declared its own supremacy over the Pope. The Pope decreed in 1437 that a council of union (between himself and the Synod) would meet at Ferrara; however, the Synod's answer was a suspension of the Pope himself, and in 1439 the Pope was declared a heretic by the Synod.

It was in the spring of that year that the plague finally visited Basle, forcing the many dignitaries to flee the city. The epidemic, incidentally, was so intense that in only one day 300 lives were lost. Of course the Synod had to be temporarily suspended. The matter of an alternative Pope, Eugen having been suspended, had to await the return of the church dignitaries after the plague had run its course. When they did return, Basle experienced an even greater boom period than before the plague, because now the election of the counterpope, Duke Amadeus of Savoy, to be known as Felix V, was an event which foreshadowed the possibility of Basle becoming an alternative to Rome. The Munster was quite inadequate to hold the many dignitaries for the coronation and the Munster square was certainly not large enough to hold the estimated 50,000 spectators.

POLITICAL AND ECONOMIC BACKGROUNDS

Unfortunately for the city, other events were conspiring to decide the future of Swiss banking. The Hundred Years War between England and France had recently been concluded, leaving a large number of troublesome French mercenaries (known as Armagnacs) wandering about the countryside. At the same time a 'civil war' had developed between Zürich and the Confederation of Schwyz over the matter of the control of the valley of the Linth, which was of strategic importance because of its approach to Wallensee. Zürich managed to gain the assistance of the Habsburgs of Austria, who recognised that by assisting Zürich in the dispute there was a possibility of extending their influence into the territory of the Swiss Confederation itself. A combined force of Zürichers and Austrians was defeated by the Confederates, who then proceeded to lay siege to the city of Zürich.

At this point, in 1444, the Habsburgs appealed to Charles VII of France (with whom they happened to be on good terms) for assistance. He was relieved to be able to dispatch 30,000 of his troublesome Armagnacs, under the command of the Dauphin, to a Swiss campaign. Their very first contact with Swiss soldiers proved to be their last, for almost within sight of the walls of Basle, a tiny force of 1500 Swiss soldiers crossed the river Birs at St Jakob an der Birs and attacked the Armagnacs. Even though outnumbered 20 to 1 the Confederates fought with such ferocity, inflicting such heavy losses on the Armagnacs, that even though they were technically 'defeated', they so convinced the Dauphin (later to be Louis XI) of their fighting prowess that he refused to permit his French mercenaries to invade Switzerland itself. Moreover, as Louis XI, he found it to his advantage to enlist Swiss soldiers as mercenaries, and because many future French kings followed his example in their wars, Switzerland was able to acquire a source of capital which, as we shall see subsequently, was a principal source of funding for future Swiss banking.

Turning away from an invasion of the Swiss Confederation, the Armagnacs contented themselves with laying waste to Alsace, and in 1450 Zürich agreed to end its pact with Austria and rejoin the Confederacy so that the Confederacy itself became larger and stronger as a result of its civil war. In Basle the Synod was dissolved in 1448 with the obvious triumph of Pope Eugen; however, Basle never returned to its former status prior to the Synod. The influence of the highly educated dignitaries and the Synod fathers over a period of 18 years proved to be permanent.

Nevertheless the end of the Synod meant the end of the boom years for Basle. The Synod participants, of course, departed the town and all the employed artisans and builders who had found employment because of the Synod were thereafter redundant. Tax returns fell sharply and the Italian bankers returned to their respective homes taking with them the high profits they had earned during the Synod period. The money changers were back to a more normal activity, exploiting the advantageous position of Basle as a transport and commercial route, the importance of which had indeed grown over the years of the Synod.

The paper industry which had developed during the Synod remained. Taking advantage of the water power available from the Birs and the Wiese, it had been founded by Councillor Heinrich Halbysen during the Synod and was taken over, after his death, by Italian entrepreneurs. Under their direction, Basle paper became world famous. Thus, papermaking, and its associated activity, printing, became the industrial activity which continued and grew long after the economic stimulus of the Synod had disappeared.

Another and very important activity was to continue in Basle even to the present time. The secretary to the Synod was the great Italian Humanist, Aenea Silvio Piccolomini. In this office he had taken an important part in the selection of the counterpope, Felix V. When he himself became Pope Pius II in 1458, he received the congratulations of the city of Basle along with a request that a university be funded in Basle to serve the city and the surrounding community. Accordingly, the new Pope replied to the request with a papal bull and the University of Basle was inaugurated in the Munster on 4 April 1460. Thus, Basle became an important centre of learning through the centuries.

Another event of some significance which followed the Synod was the Basle fair. The pope, as Piccolomini, had served as secretary to Felix V, and after the deposition of Felix moved to the court of King Frederic III. When Frederic became Emperor, and after Piccolomini became Pope, the guilds of Basle requested that a fair be inaugurated in Basle to be held twice a year. The request was granted by an Imperial decree in 1471 and Basle then became a commercial centre as well as a centre for learning. Once more, the town was able to take advantage of its experience of the Synod to advance itself still futher. Not only was merchandise sold duty-free under the terms of the decree but the development of banks, taking advantage of the credit payments which the fair required, was encouraged. While the Basle fair never achieved the greatness of those in Frankfurt or Geneva, it nevertheless was an important part of the ensuing prosperity of the city.

In the meantime, political events began to overtake the city. Basle had always been part of the Empire, yet its proximity to both Austria and the Swiss Confederation meant that it could hardly avoid being drawn into the conflicts between states. The defeat of the Duke of Burgundy at Grandson by the Confederates and another complete rout of the Duke's army later at Morat by a force from Zürich proved that the Swiss Confederation had become a major power in central Europe. Finally, when the Swiss emerged victorious from the Swabian War, fought against the Emperor Maximillian and the Swabian League, Basle's future was sealed. The Peace of Basle in 1499 ensured that, in fact, the Swiss Confederation was now independent of the Empire, and both Basle and Schaffhausen joined the Confederation in 1501.

These events ensured an environment of peace and stability, necessary for the development of banking institutions. The new university made possible the academic atmosphere within which banking ideas and skills could grow, and the commercial activity brought by the fairs created the necessary demand for banking services. Still, however, much ground had to be covered, for despite the experiences of the Synod and the regulations of coinage which were developed at the time, there were many grievances, real or imaginary, voiced by both townspeople and peasants regarding the maintenance of its monetary system by the money changers, despite the reputation for high quality enjoyed by Basle coins.

It is not difficult to understand the nature of these grievances and why they would exist at the time. We recall that the mediaeval just price system prevailed: that is, prices would not change appreciably in the short term without considerable social dislocation. This meant that any 'real price change' would occur not by means of nominal prices but by a depreciation (or appreciation) of money. For instance, a depreciation of money, in terms of its gold or silver content, would initially be the equivalent of a decrease in prices of goods. This follows from the fact that more money in circulation (due to a reduced content of precious metal) would be available for the purchase of a fixed amount of goods at constant goods prices. On the other hand, both the wages of workers and the prices of agricultural commodities to farmers were also stable. The extra money, in other words, was not available to these working classes; they did not share in the benefit of 'falling' prices.

In a similar fashion the traders and merchants had every reason for complaint regarding the increased amount of the currency because they too experienced 'falling' real prices. Those who benefited were the merchants, who exchanged better quality foreign coin (which they earned from exports) for the trivial or 'bad' money which could be used for domestic purchases. In effect, a redistribution of real wealth took place, with the disadvantaged traders and farmers objecting to the process. Thus, 'daily greater injury to the townspeople and the small farmers from the trivial and bad money' was heard continuously – a commonplace objection to the operation of Gresham's Law.

THE BANK IN BASLE

In response to this situation, the town council of Basle in 1504 established a town exchange, a public institution which included a municipal share of 600 florins 'for the common good'. From here it contracted with the leaders of the money-changers guild (Heinrich David and Andreas Bischoff) for the foundation of an open money exchange, to include members other than those of the guild. In addition, the market was to be completely cleared of 'bad' money through the process of exchanging foreign money for domestic. Also, and this is the important point, the acceptance of deposits was provided for and the money changers themselves were excluded from the deposit taking business on their own account. Loans were made with guarantees 'against good gold and silver pledges' only in amounts of over 100 florins, and the ban on interest was relaxed sufficiently to permit the town exchange to charge loan interest and thereby earn a profit. Such profits accrued to the town but the administrators of the exchange were responsible for losses.

In other words, the first halting steps were being made by the city of Basle itself toward the formation of a modern bank in the form of its town exchange. Further, these actions were taken in response to a situation which we might describe as the failure of a metallic currency system to maintain its intrinsic value, in the first place, and the relatively continuous increase in the wealth of the city which required a means by which the wealth could be utilised in the form of loans in the second.

To Basle, then, must be attributed the 'honour' of having the first bank in Switzerland. To be sure, the bank in Basle was not a private bank in the same sense as were the Geneva banks which arrived later on the banking scene. In effect, the Basle bank was a commercial bank, owned by the town, that transacted the necessary banking business that was typical of the banking requirements of commercial activity in the sixteenth century. It accepted deposits and made loans from these deposits largely for purposes of commerce, offering interest for deposits and charging interest for loans. It represented, in addition, the beginnings of the same capital market which existed in Basle well into the nineteenth century, and as such, its lending and deposit-taking activity ranged well beyond the borders of Basle into Alsace and the states of southern Germany.

Despite the absence of concrete historical evidence, the technique of sixteenth century banking was, in all likelihood, learned from the Italian bankers who were present in Basle during the Synod. We can assume this because the Basle money changers were still active for some thirty years after the founding of the Basle bank. The business of money changing alone, in other words, was a well-practiced art, but banking activity was not. Thus, the earlier presence of the Italians in Basle, combined with the growing sophistication and wealth of the city and the dissatisfaction with the existing currency system, resulted in the founding and development of the bank in Basle.

In the first period of the bank's existence (that is, the town exchange), the right of minting gold coins was granted again by Pope Julius II in 1512. Once more this was a happy circumstance, in that the Pope was most appreciative of Basle's assistance during his campaign against the French. This military campaign, incidentally, was a remarkable achievement for the Swiss, in that they proved themselves to be the decisive influence which saved Rome from the French advance. In the period preceding the Swiss intervention the forces of the anti-French Holy League had been defeated by the French at Ravenna in 1512, with the result that the conquest of Rome appeared inevitable. Or so it seemed until the news arrived that a force of 18,000 Swiss soldiers had crossed into Lombardy and were pushing back the French lines. This forced the French into a retreat. Thus, once more we find a connection between Swiss military successes and the banking and monetary system of Switzerland, in this case in the form of a grateful Pope Julius II!

Basle's new right of coinage was further strengthened in 1516 when the banker, Jakob Meyer zum Hasen, master of the exchange-house league, was able to win from the Emperor Maximillian the right of circulation of the coins throughout the empire. This was a considerable achievement because, instead of depending upon 'foreign coins' of doubtful quality, the city could have its own coins of guaranteed weight and fineness in accordance with the regulations of the town exchange. Such coins, since they were universal, could be required by Basle merchants for the payment of debts incurred outside of Basle in the states of the empire. Furthermore, and more important, the prestige in terms of weight and fineness of Basle's coins extended well into the states of Germany, adding further to the reputation of the town exchange which was itself in the evolutionary process of becoming a bank.

The town exchange existed side by side with private money changers for some thirty years. It acted as a regulator of the circulation of money and played such an important role in the finances of the city that in 1533 it obtained a complete exchange monopoly as a public (or state) institution. At the same time, its growing banking business meant that it was functioning as a cantonal bank.

In the granting of the monopoly there is scarcely any doubt that the highly profitable town exchange was an excellent source of funds for the city, but there were administrative considerations as well in the minds of the city council. Such matters as 'frivolous money circulation' and the 'secondary sale of gold and silver' as well as 'secondary money changers' (as decreed by the town council) were punishable as crimes since such activities were the right and privilege of the monopoly.

The question remains, and will always likely remain, what happened to the great banks of Venice and Genoa, as well as the Jewish pawn-broking banks? The whole process of Italian banking actually retrogressed from the period of the later Middle Ages, not to re-emerge until the beginnings of the modern era. Why were the great achievements and skills of the Italian bankers forgotten in Europe during the period when nation-states began their own process of evolutionary development? Indeed, one might expect, at first sight, that Italian banking could have greatly assisted the economic development of the nation-states of both France and England to become an integral part of the engine of economic growth. Such was not the case, and the answer to the question, we submit, lies in the dead hand of English mercantilism, Colbertism (or étatism) in France and the cameralists in Germany and Austria. While the general principle of mercantilism may have stimulated the growth of banking as a substitute for scarce metallic currency, mercantilism as practised in these countries actually *discouraged* banking.

The differences that existed among the three were merely those of emphasis. For instance, to the English mercantilists, gold and silver were at the focal point of the system. The importance here was that precious metals must not be exported to pay for imports; hence, the value of exports must always exceed that of imports. To the camera-lists, on the other hand, economic development of indigenous industry was most important – in this case sponsored by the State. Similarly, French Colbertism emphasised economic development but with the state as the engine of growth, étatism in its economic sense, to support the newly emerging nation-state. Thus, we would suggest, the growth and development of all three types of mercantilism was inimical to the banking process even though the inheritors of the Italian banking tradition existed and thrived in the cities of northern Europe and, of course, in Basle.

CONCLUSIONS

It is to the Italians that we owe the invention and development of banking as an art. Indeed, it was by way of the Italian branch banks that were established in Geneva, Basle, Hamburg and the Low Countries that the principles and practice of banking spread beyond Italy itself. When the Mercantilist philosophies became the accepted political doctrine in the rising nation-states of England, France, and Germany banks, though impossible to eliminate, became instruments of the state in France and a means of serving the needs of commerce in England. It was, however, not until after the great Smith *coup de grâce* in the *Wealth of Nations*, which effectively destroyed the mercantilist philosophy, that London banks began to achieve their supremacy in the same commercial bill of exchange that the Italians had invented centuries before.

In the meantime, the bank in Basle continued to grow and prosper, having learned its lessons well. In this instance, it was the occasion of the Basle Synod and its aftermath that offered the opportunity for its citizens to learn from their Italian teachers. Even though the neighbouring states of France and Germany had discouraged banks (except as instruments of the state) the need for banking services did not disappear. As a consequence the bank in Basle was able to extend its influence well beyond the borders of its own region.

We would suggest, therefore, that the lasting impact of the philosophy of mercantilism, for good or ill, was to influence the structure of European banking during the ensuing centuries. A banking specialisation amongst countries developed during that era which need not have occurred and which may be attributed to the mercantilist influence. For our purposes, it made possible a 'niche' in banking activities which the Swiss were able to exploit, even though a couple of centuries were to pass before the Swiss banks were able to realise fully that potential.

Notes

1. The name Basilea Civitas on the dinars of Burgundy attests to the activity of the Basle mint.
2. The Sieur de Malestroit wrote, in 1567, that currency is 'a mystery which few people can understand'. Braudel and Spooner, Ch. VII *Cambridge Economic History*, Vol iv, Cambridge University Press, Cambridge, 1967. E.E. Rich and G.H. Wilson, eds, p. 378.
3. 1168 pfennigs equal one rough mark. On the basis of one silver mark equals six pounds, the pfennig was 15 gms silver in weight. Bauer, H., *Vom Wechsler zum Bankier* (Basel: Friedrich Reinhardt Verlag, 1989), p. 29.
4. Ibid., p. 30.
5. It must be obvious to the reader that the 'just price' is really nothing more than a price which has been established by way of a time mechanism, that is, the principal variable is time alone. The question which could be raised, of course, is how did the specific item arrive at that price in the first place? Our only reply to this must be the supply/demand mechanism, which must have prevailed at some time in the past however dim and distant. That is, it must have been profitable, however small the profit, for peasants and artisans to produce specific items for sale in markets; otherwise, they would not have done so. In this way, the labour theory of value would come into its own. 'Just prices', therefore, would settle at a level just high enough to permit the production of specific items, and the profit would be just sufficient to sustain the worker in the business. There is no economic growth in such a system.
6. Smith, A., *The Wealth of Nations*, McCulloch's Edition, Adam and Charles Black, Edinburgh, 1889, p. 28. The market price, to Smith, could deviate from the natural price but would soon return to it, because factors of production would be attracted to the production of those commodities of which the market prices were above the natural price. This would force a return to the natural price because the natural price itself was determined by the 'natural price of each of its component parts': wages of labour, profits and rent. Of course, Smith recognised that

monopolies could keep markets continually understocked and thereby maintain the market price permanently above the natural price which was, incidentally, the price obtained under perfect competition.

7   This was the king of Bohemia who later became Emperor.

Part 2
The Roots of Swiss Banking

3 The Background

THE REFORMATION

In a Europe consisting of rising nation-states which had developed their respective mercantilist economic theories, the Swiss confederation and the powerful cantons of Berne, Geneva and Basle had little directly to contribute. What we find to be the 'Swiss contribution' was much more subtle and certainly of more lasting significance.

Mercantilism as a doctrine was ultimately doomed; it could not survive either empirically or philosophically because it was based upon the fundamental principle that foreigners must provide the necessary capital for the economic growth and development of the state. This arose from the fact that the mercantilist states strove to export more than they imported both by the creation of import-substituting industries and the encouragement of export industries. The resulting inflow of gold intended provide the necessary capital for economic development. Stripped of its non-essentials, the mercantilist philosophy, whether in England, France, or Germany, seemed to be hardly more subtle than this rather obvious principle.

In the smaller states of Europe, such as Hamburg, Geneva, the Swiss Cantons and Holland, there was another 'philosophy' which, though not of a purely economic origin, proved to be of much greater economic significance – the Reformation. It is in this great movement that the foundations of modern Swiss banking can be found.

Few today could doubt the truth of the assertion that the Swiss version of banking, as opposed to the English commercial banks, has its origins deep within the Swiss psyche. In searching for the origins of this peculiarly Swiss phenomenon, we discover that it was the Reformation that not only changed the structure of Swiss society forever but also laid the groundwork for the economic future of the Confederation itself. This is not so apparent to English understanding, conditioned as it is by the structural changes within the church wrought by Henry VIII as 'the Reformation'.

The idea that somehow the Protestant Reformation and the rise of capitalism are linked is by no means recent. In the seventeenth century the fact that England and Holland were commercially successful, even though engaging in mercantile wars, was linked with their respective Protestant faiths. Obviously, as has been shown by several modern

45

historians, such a linkage is entirely too facile to be of significance. The early Protestant religious reformers of Plymouth in Massachusetts, as well as the Calvinists of Geneva, could hardly be considered as fertile ground for the development of commerce, banking, or any other of the essentials of capitalism. Conversely, commercial activity can hardly be considered to be a cause of Puritan dogma, and Luther's thundering references to the Biblical prophets can hardly be seen as a source for capitalism.

In the Reformation we can find two principal developments which have been significant for the growth of capitalism. The first was the breaking up of the religious and social structure of the Roman Catholic dogma which stood between man and God. This structure, though important enough for man's salvation, had tended to condition man into a particular calling. With divine sanction, man's only need was to serve God within the social structure, and, when the time came for his passing, the church saw to it that his sins were appropriately disposed of. Since the church stood between man and God, the satisfaction of the church's requirements, which were clear enough to all men, was also the satisfaction of God's requirements.

Protestantism took away this cushion. Man was now responsible to God through his own conscience. His works and deeds would be judged under a Calvinist interpretation of God's terrible justice or, according to Luther's hope, in the ultimate goodness of God. In both cases, gone is the church as an intermediary between God and man. The direct outcome of this new direct relationship between man and his God was that man had become free. Responsibility to his own conscience meant that numerous courses of action were available to him and he was now free to choose among these courses according to his own conscience.

In this sense, (as H. Luthy argues) the Protestant Reformation was actually no different from all the other aspects of Renaissance Man. The awakening of the human mind and spirit which led to Columbus and the explorations of the New World, to Galileo, and to the beginnings of modern science was the driving force behind the Reformation as well. It followed directly from this that capitalism, loosely defined as the accumulation and the use of capital in science and discovery, was not simply a by-product but a necessity for the successful growth and development of man in his new-found freedom.

The second development, and more significant for the development of banking, was the sanctification of the work ethic. This was particularly evident in Geneva and Zürich, where both Zwingli and Calvin recognised that religion could not be set apart from the business of government and industry. It was quite natural that Calvin would legitimise credit and interest, otherwise the city could not otherwise have prospered. But therein lies the new approach to religion. The ethic of work was expressed simply – with work there would be no poverty, hence no institution such as the church must stand in the way of industry.

While it is true that the monastic orders of Catholicism did stress both prayer and work, it became part of the Protestant doctrine that work would prevent the very idleness from which sin was bred. Satan could not penetrate the busy and productive mind. Similarly, Calvinism, of necessity, could not look upon wealth as a personal gain of worldly goods at the expense of the poor (hence to be dispensed with to gain salvation) but could only recognise wealth as the reward of both ambition and saving. So, when lent at interest, capital would beget additional wealth because it would be put to work to enrich society further. For these reasons charity had no place in Zürich and Geneva because there were no paupers. 'To work is to acquire the wherewithall to eat' was a simplistic union of economics and religion.

It is not so easy for the modern mind to grasp and appreciate the almost monastic fervour of the Reformation's principles, which spread well beyond Calvin's Geneva to Zürich, Basle, and St Gall. But, and here is the main thrust of the argument, its almost monastic fervour stopped short of the common ownership of property. Property was privately owned, to be used as the individual saw fit. The owner could either waste resources or husband them, but if the former, could hardly expect salvation. Religion and economics were thus linked, such that economic man was at the same time a devout man ensured of his own salvation. Instead of a Roman Catholic hierarchy of values – prayer, meditation, and charity – superimposed upon a foundation of economic men, the entire structure was unified as a single Christian life which openly embraced work and prayer as a joint process.

It must be obvious that such a value system, combining both economics and religion, must have had a degree of success with the public. Yet, at the same time, the reinforcement from religion for those who become rich (the rich *can* enter the Kingdom of Heaven after all!) could indeed give rise to the thesis that the rise of capitalism and the Reformation were so closely related as to be a joint process. Alms-giving, and the fact that Jesus himself was born in extremely poor circumstances, no longer appeared relevant. It was the poor themselves who were truly responsible for their own state of existence because they were not in God's favour – to work is to pray. The new doctrine was not only satisfying but comforting to those successful merchants, bankers, and so on because they could at last rest easy enough in their comfortable beds.

Clearly, though, if the poor are not to receive charity, pure and simple, they must be provided with the opportunity to work. This was the responsibility of those with property: people with available capital must make available to the poor work of *some* kind, however menial. In this way the capitalist could acquire favour with God. This is quite different from the idea that the poor must be given charity: any type of work, however hazardous, arduous or badly paid, could be offered and still remain within the dictates of conscience.

Along with the Reformation of Luther and Calvin, another, equally important, development took place in France – the revocation of the Edict of Nantes of Henri IV. While the actual 'revocation' itself was a lengthy process which gradually reduced the privileges of the Huguenots, it was the final 30 years of the reign of Louis XIV which brought together the persecution and arrests, that made the life of the Huguenot intolerable in France. Calvin's Geneva was but one of the several refuges for these people. London, Holland, and North America benefited considerably from the absurd set of French laws and regulations which were arbitrarily and sporadically enforced by Louis.

It was this scattering of the Huguenots, we would argue, which proved to be the most significant, and propitious, event in the history of continental banking. Until that time, banks were, firstly, money changers which had become sufficiently sophisticated to accept deposits and issue credit albeit in rudimentary forms. Secondly, there were highly developed commercial banks (those of Italian origin and inheritance) that expedited the flow of commerce by means of the instruments of banking such as the bill of exchange. These were located principally in the Low Countries as well as in Italy itself. Thirdly, there were wealthy individuals and families who loaned money to princes and emperors, accepting both interest and titles in return. The Fuggers were the obvious examples of these. Fourthly, there were the Jews and Lombards who made loans at high interest rates to individuals who were (so they hoped) temporarily out of funds – the equivalent of pawnbroking. Finally, a new type of bank was emerging, the Protestant bank which not only had the capital but also the expertise to assist the development of industry in a newly emerging capitalist era.

Before attempting an analysis of this 'new' bank, one should consider once more the impact of the Reformation within both Zürich and

Geneva, as well as in other cities which were to become part of the Swiss Confederation. As noted above, the structure of the Roman Catholic church was broken by the Reformation such that nothing really stood between the conscience of men and God. At the same time, to work was to pray, and the material success which accompanied that work was simply God's reward for it. This was a reform of men's thinking of substantial proportions. That is, instead of the church requiring alms-giving and ministering to the poor, the poor themselves were considered responsible for their own miserable state, from which they could escape by exerting themselves in work. Therefore, so it follows, assistance to the poor in any form but the offering of employment opportunities was not only unnecessary but quite incorrect.

Yet, one must ask oneself, is this truly the philosophical foundation for the beginnings of capitalism? Could capitalism not have developed with just as much vigour in Roman Catholic countries? If we accept the modern historical thesis that Reformation man was really a part of a larger 'creature' known as Renaissance man, then we are forced to recognise that the Reformation alone was not a sufficient reason for capitalism. But to do so would, we suggest, underestimate the impact of the Reformation upon the Swiss themselves.

The Calvinist capitalist, in other words, was a different creature from his economic equivalent in Britain, France, or Germany. He was an active capitalist who administered his own capital, both putting it to work for his own profit and giving employment to workers. There was no room here for wealthy stockholders in corporations, as in England, who would prefer professional management to administer the companies, thereby freeing them from the onus of administrative responsibility and, plainly, work. To the contrary, the Calvinist capitalist actually put in longer hours than his workers. The reason for this was simple. The responsibility for the enterprise rested entirely with him – and his God, of course, to Whom he looked for guidance.

In other words, there was no room for the Roman Catholic church's objection to usury, meaning profit as well as interest. Since the capitalist worked along with his workers, he was entitled to his own reward, profit. Then the question of what is 'excessive profit' becomes a matter of an arbirary distinction and a subject which could be argued *ad infinitum*. Similarly, the matter of interest and what is the correct level of interest rates became impossible to determine.

But one must avoid attributing to the church's stand on usury the importance of an actual restraint upon the development of capitalism. Already, by the time of the Calvinist Reformation, the church's position had been by-passed, evaded, or just plain ignored. This was certainly true in Geneva, a city which had long ago, in the days of the fairs, learned to evade usury by means of various commercial stratagems. The prohibition of usury was, therefore, by the time of Calvin only an incidental, a position which could not be accepted by the early capitalist.

At the same time, we suggest, Calvin's thought lay far from the advantages of worldly success. To him it was a matter of the salvation of mankind and his soul which mattered – the other-worldly achievement of grace. But here we find a remarkable historical coincidence, nothing more: the alignment of moral reasoning, Calvin's true objective, with economic reasoning. By emphasising the importance of work and saving so as to gain God's favour, Calvin served the objective of capitalism without consciously being aware of his ambivalence. Similarly, by permitting the use of interest, albeit at a moderate level, he laid the foundation for the Protestant bank which later was to develop into the modern banks of France, Germany, and Switzerland.

We should also note the direction of causation. Here was a philosophy which was built upon the discipline of work, not the 'work' of bureaucracy, law, the church, and so on, but work built upon custom, tradition, and, ultimately, salvation. It comes directly from within the minds of the population itself, as opposed to Colbertism, for instance, which had imposed work upon the French people by the authority of the state, from above. It was a new, and inverted, value system which ignored religious holidays, pilgrimages, and alms, all of which had acted to discourage work.

One might imagine how Colbert himself would have longed for just such a system within the economy of France. In Colbert's case, a massive bureaucratic machinery had to be substituted for a philosophy, a system which was certain to fail eventually. His use of monopolies, privileges, and capital supplied by the state, along with the inevitable regulations in their use, provided just such examples of attempting to force an economic development upon a disinterested populace.

HUGUENOT BANKING IN GENEVA

It was precisely this 'world' of bureaucracy, tradition, and church custom in which the Huguenots found themselves, virtually as aliens after the revocation of the Edict of Nantes. As early capitalists their emphasis upon work and saving meant that an accumulation of capital was taking place, yet there existed no practical outlet for this capital. They were excluded from the financial offices of the *ancien régime*, those tax farmers and speculators who made loans to the state, at interest, of course. In addition, the Huguenots, by the circumstance of history, found that they were forced to leave their homeland to seek refuge in the Low Countries, England, Geneva, and even in the New World. However, their connections of property and capital, it appears, were not completely severed. Thus while they loaned their surplus capital to foreign countries, they also were able to continue the practice of commercial and industrial lending in France itself.

Foreign lending (that is, lending to countries other than the residence of the Huguenot), necessarily meant the exchange of one currency into other currencies, and this brought the fledgling Protestant banker into direct contact with the already well established banking system. As we have already argued, and as Raymond de Roover has so eloquently shown, the practice of money changing and commercial banking via the bill of exchange had been in existence since the early Middle Ages; indeed, Basle itself was a well-known banking centre of this type. From these beginnings an international Protestant banking system emerged in the form of a network of contacts which grew and developed among the Huguenot settlements as refugees. The network grew outside of France in particular for the reason that there was little or no opportunity for Protestant banks within the structure of the *ancien régime* for the financial transactions which are so necessary to the success of investment banking.[1] Important to this network was Amsterdam, the great capital market for western Europe at that time.

Geneva, therefore, became a major focal point of the Protestant banking network. Indeed, the wars of Louis XIV were partially financed by Geneva bankers.[2] Since loans to the royal monarch were loans in perpetuity, never maturing, they were the equivalent of rent. As such they were good investments so long as the interest on the loans was paid. It is, however, not at all difficult to imagine the consequences of waging costly wars during the days when mercenaries were the principal source of military manpower. Debts upon debts piled up until the inevitable consequence of bankruptcy.

The method of finance used by the typical Geneva Protestant banker, Jacques Hugetan, was to secure funds from Swiss depositors at a lower rate of interest and re-lend these funds at a higher rate to the French Minister of Finance. The profit margin was assured just so long as the French monarchy could honour its interest payments. The interesting question was: whence came the Swiss funds for deposits in the first place?

The answer to this question lay in one of the more significant features of Swiss history, already introduced in Chapter 2. Switzerland, (that is, the three cantons, Uri, Schwyz, and Unterwalden which formed the original Confederation in 1291) was a region which produced families just as large as in other European regions. However, in such mountainous areas, inhospitable to agriculture, there was little for the male children to do other than to cultivate the arts of war.[3] The result, in brief, was that the Swiss became unusually efficient soldiers that not only fought for their own independence but actually became a balance of power during the French wars of conquest during the fifteenth century. More to the point, Swiss mercenaries were eagerly sought after by both sides during the wars of religion between Charles V and Francis I.

The method by which the mercenaries were recruited was to request from the regions of Switzerland a certain quota of soldiers. The heads of the regions would be paid (in the best of gold coin) and the soldiers recruited with an offer of money. Not all the money, however, went to the soldiers; much was retained as pensions by the city governments which did the recruiting. In effect, the system became an export of fighting skills for which 'hard currency' was paid. The result was a massive build-up of investible funds seeking an investment outlet.

In a word, the Swiss had become a nation of relatively rich, wealthy classes with ample funds (this does not include, of course the ordinary peasants who provided their own sons to fight for foreign kings and princes!). It was these funds which found their way to Geneva to be used by the Protestant investment bankers, who were not really 'bankers' in the ordinary sense of commercial banking, but rather deposit bankers who simply collected the funds for re-lending to the French monarch. The bankers used their own good name and reputation as security for the depositors.

The inevitable end to the process of Geneva Protestant banking which elected to lend its funds to Louis XIV meant bankruptcy for Hugetan and the other participating bankers. Nevertheless, we can imagine the balance sheet of these bankers as consisting of deposits (liabilities) and bonds as assets. Liabilities would equal assets, but there were little or no actual liquid funds to protect depositors in the event that they wished their funds to be returned to them. The crisis of 1709, in which the French government became insolvent, meant that Geneva's bankers would also become insolvent. Many of them were actually suspended from the governing Geneva Board of Two Hundred by reason of their inability to honour their obligations. The result was that some of them moved to Paris hoping to recoup their losses. In the end, they become well-known names in French banking.[4]

In this rather ignominious way, Geneva's first banking adventure came to its early end. We have no historical record of the amount of losses sustained by the Swiss investors, but we can assume that it must have been considerable because the entire town of Geneva was severely affected. However, it is likely that the lesson was not lost on these bankers, for not until the years immediately preceding the French Revolution do we again find such a concentration of investment in one country.

ZÜRICH

The history of banking in Zürich, though relatively late in developing, is actually more instructive than that in either Basle or Geneva, since the market forces of supply and demand for funds can be more readily identified. As we have already observed, the age of discovery and expansion brought to Europe the turmoil and upheavals characteristic of more rapid economic change than had been known in the past. The city of Zürich experienced these changes just as elsewhere; indeed, the result was that Protestant Zürich, like Roman Catholic jurisdictions, was forced to come to terms with these new economic conditions.

While the interest prohibition of the church had remained in force throughout the Middle Ages, the recognition on the part of the church that risk was involved in credit, and must be rewarded, proved to be the 'thin edge of the wedge' which was to break down the moral position held by the church dignitaries. Indeed, the so-called 'rotation costs' by means of which a charge for credit was made as a recompense for the lender, meant that the shorter the loan the greater the amount (per annum) of additional charges could be earned. Thus, while the excess charge was not interest *per se*, the fact was that credit granted for shorter periods could bring in considerable reward. Such charges were permitted by the church.

It was the risk factor, however, which proved to be the more important. (In an empirical sense we may argue that a risk theory of interest was the first to appear in economic science.) Thus, should anyone not be willing to incur any risk in lending his life savings, he would be forced to keep his money safely in a chest. But, and here is a most interesting point in early Zürich banking, an individual could actually purchase an annuity by surrendering his capital and thereby be guaranteed a stream of income for the remainder of his life. Should he not wish to surrender the full value of his capital in order to leave some as an inheritance, he could have a diminishing stream of income – discounting in a modern sense – through time. The 'rate of discount' was, of course, the rate of interest, but it too, along with interest as the reward for accepting risk, was quite acceptable to the church. In this sense interest crept in 'through the back door'.

The annuity concept was a somewhat curious form of credit. The recipient of the credit, those who received the life savings as a capital sum, were mostly cities or princes. Zürich, for example, was quite eager to engage in this particular form of contract with those of its citizens who were elderly or frail. In this way, the rather large balance of unpaid capital, which was certain to arise in such instances, became the property of the city. We can only imagine how the city's finances must have been considerably enhanced by such transactions.[5]

Perhaps more to the point is the fact that the interest rate on such transactions as annuities was actually quite low, about 3 per cent. This suggests that the annuity was a popular form of 'investment' for Zürichers during the Middle Ages. It was popular because it was allowed by the church. Thus, those (states, cities, or other public authorities as well as the private sector) who could guarantee a stream of future income could receive credit in the form of a capital sum. Those, perhaps unfortunates, who could not guarantee such an income stream were forced to resort to pawnbrokers for their credit needs, and here the interest rate was quite high because the risk factor was also high. The church excluded Christians from such lending, permitting only Jews to participate in this. (Later, the Lombards were also included with the Jews.) Thus, a high risk coupled with a scarce supply of funds inevitably produced the highest of interest rates; indeed, it was unlikely that debtors could ever repay their debts in full. It was for this reason that pawnbrokers were required to collect their interest at short periods, to avoid the enormously high interest charges which would result from multiplication by the factor of time.

It is interesting that the pressure of economic events, following upon the great events of exploration and discovery of the New World, actually forced society into a recognition of both the existence and the necessity for interest. Initially, there was considerable opprobrium attached to transactions involving interest. There was no end to the slander and ridicule hurled by the conservative social classes against the usurers. Even the great reformers, Luther and Zwingli, severely censured the 'new' movement in business which involved both profit-taking and the use of credit and interest. In Zwingli's case, however, the compromise between the divine rule in which no interest could exist and the sinful worldly affairs of men was necessary. He recommended, therefore, an interest rate of no higher than 5 per cent, based upon the curious, almost Wicksellian, idea that a 'natural' interest as distinct from a 'money' interest existed. This was despite the fact that no professional banking (in the sense of collecting capital for the purpose of its re-lending) existed in Zürich until very much later.

The absence of professional banking did not mean that Zürich was undeveloped in any sense of the word. Quite the contrary, it was a prosperous centre for business activity. Zürichers did, however, lack that particular psychology which would permit them to use the capital of others instead of their own. They simply preferred their own capital and property for business activity.

It was not that capital was plentiful within Zürich; foreign capital from Augsberg, Nuremberg, and Frankfurt, among others, was used in the city for a lack of available domestic capital. It was rather the fact that the idea of mobilising the resources of society for the purpose of establishing business ventures via a banking institution had not yet arrived. The merchant guilds, for instance, strongly opposed such a means of capital accumulation and actually defeated any attempt to establish a bank for that purpose. To put it again quite simply, Zürichers preferred the use of their own capital generated from their own savings when possible, and it was not until the nineteenth century that this psychology began to lose its force.

While a psychology such as this may seem strange to modern perceptions, we might do well to recall the Anglo-Saxon Puritan background to which many of us owe our own pre-conceived notions regarding borrowing and lending. Living beyond one's means, that is, enjoying a standard of living which is unwarranted by income, is certainly frowned upon by society as a whole. This is the over-use of consumer credit. 'He who goes a-borrowing goes a-sorrowing' said Poor Richard. So it was with the typical Züricher businessman. He too must live, i.e. invest, to expand his enterprise from his own resources and within his own capacity.

The Leubank of Zürich

But the curious feature of Zürich and its citizenry was that these rather excessively Puritan concepts did not apply to *all* the public, and certainly not to the city. The city government initially was a heavy borrower, but from the mid-seventeenth century on it began to accumulate its own capital surplus. This surplus was used not only in times of emergency but also for lending to individuals, for the financing of raw material purchases, for construction, and for the all-important mortgages.

Eventually, under the regime of mayor Hirzel, the construction of a new state treasury was begun in 1647. The project prospered and sufficient budget surpluses were collected that the city actually became a major source of lending to the private sector, in other words, a state bank which satisfied the minimal banking requirements of the time. For a short period following 1649, an exchange bank existed for the purpose of changing money and otherwise eliminating the inferior coins which had come into Zürich during the period of the Thirty Years War. It lasted only five years, principally because it was used, rather cautiously, for borrowing foreign capital to assist in the Peasants War. The money thus received was turned over to the government, but since the interest paid by the bank was so very much less than that paid elsewhere (capital was in short supply), the bank proved to be unsuccessful. It was liquidated in 1655.

The Zürich experience with an exchange bank contrasts sharply with the bank in Basle. There, it will be recalled, the strength of the bank lay in the right of coinage as well as the learning of banking techniques from the Italians during the great Basle Synod. This experience was not shared by Zürich, where the art of both money changing and commercial banking which accompanied it was still quite foreign, though, we might suggest, the beginnings in the form of the state bank and foreign borrowing had already been made.

In actual fact, it was the Thirty Years War and the enormous profit earned by Zürich business enterprises which encouraged economic growth in the region. When combined with the principles of the Reformation, which attributed to profit the reward of divine sanction, the result was 'electrifying'. Zürich's capital increased enormously during the period, all from the fortunate combination of the German recovery from the War and a Puritanism which was not confined to Zürich but was general throughout Europe. Germany's princes began seeking credit from Zürich's successful businessmen to make possible, for the first time, a foreign outlet for a surplus of Zürich capital.

A second war, the Seven Years War which ravaged France, added further to the already heavy demand for Swiss products. In this case, it was France which experienced the consequences of war and its industry was simply not capable of meeting the enormous demand for goods which the war required. Germany's factories were not yet ready to meet this excess of demand, with the consequence that Zürich's factories once again found themselves in a position of attempting to meet a demand situation without an adequate supply. This resulted in a massive transfer of capital from commercial and wholesale activities into factories.

At the same time, the capital surplus pressed upon the interest rate forcing it below the 'normal' mortgage rate of 5 per cent, much to the dismay of the city government. The city council feared that excessive debt on the part of the general public would follow from low interest rates, with the consequence of rising prices of land and property. The council even attempted to prohibit interest rates lower than 5 per cent, but to no avail.

Under ordinary circumstances, we would have expected that a general rise in the price level of all goods would have followed from the unusual inflow of funds into Zürich. Aside from land values, such was not the case. Fortunes were accumulated, both private and, of course, for the city of Zürich. Guilds also experienced considerable increases in their treasuries. Thus, instead of attempting to spend in futile consumption, Zürichers preferred to save and when insufficient outlets for investment relative to the savings existed, fortunes simply grew as hoards. The abhorrence of consumption for consumption's sake was recognized in the futile attempt on the part of the city council to maintain, by decree, interest rates at the 5 per cent level. To permit lower levels would encourage the people to consume for the purpose of outdoing their fellow parishioners.[6] Such consumption would only lead to excessive debt even for their successive generations! Apparently, it was the preference on the part of Zürichers for modest and restrained living, a characteristic that can be observed to this day, which was instrumental in avoiding the worst effects of the Quantity Theory of Money.

The surplus of capital was even augmented by savings in Winterthur and Schaffhausen, with the result that a most important event in Swiss banking history took place – the appointment of a commission in 1747 to consider the possible solutions to the problem of lower interest rates. In essence, it was to look into the possibility of establishing a fund for the investment of capital outside of Zürich, a 'non-local fund'. This would relieve the pressure of local investment demand.

The result was the establishing, at the suggestion of Johann Konrad Heidegger, of a bank which would accept the funds of local people not experienced in the arts of investment or banking so as to invest these funds abroad, that is, outside the Zürich area, 'as far as human insight stretches'. Adopted by the Zürich council on 11 February 1754, the result was the Leu and Co. bank, so named for the budget-master of Zürich who was the company's first president. Since the government did not wish to appear as the actual entrepreneur in this case, it used the new bank as a medium through which funds were accepted in the form of 'city-hall obligations' and thereby attracted a great deal of capital. By 1798 the Leubank already had placed some three million florins in the form of foreign funds in London, Paris, Vienna, and Hamburg. These were actually used for the purpose of public loans to the states of Germany, Denmark, Austria, England, France, Wurtemburg, and Saxony.

The significance of the Leubank, then, ought not to be overlooked. It is not a matter of Protestant banking, as in Geneva, or purely commercial banking as in Basle, but rather an actual excess of funds which required an outlet. Most important is the fact that the funds were the property of many private individuals in Zürich who used the banking method as an outlet, and the final outlet, in this case, was foreign. Deposits, albeit 'obligations' of the city, were collected to be invested by experts on behalf of the public. Thus, it was no longer a question of individual Zürichers speculating on risky stock exchanges, as in the infamous John Law scandals, but one of surrendering their right to control their own funds, accepting instead the obligations of the bank backed, as it were, by the city's opulent treasury.

Iklé suggests that Geneva may well be called the oldest banking centre of Swiss cities.[7] We might also suggest that Basle was the first city to have a bank in the sense that, like other centres in the Empire and in Italy, Basle's bank evolved directly from minting and money-changing activities, the antecedent of commercial banking. Zürich, on the other hand, could lay its claim to fame in having the first *modern* Swiss bank. We use the term 'modern' in the sense that a surplus of Swiss capital existed first, to become Leubank 'deposits' which then sought foreign assets. Even though the Leubank itself came to grief in 1799, it was still a first, for the history of banking in all countries consists of as many failures as successes. (Very few banks of Europe were able to survive the tremendous social and economic upheavals wrought by the French Revolution.) This is a quite different banking function than that of the Protestant bankers of Geneva who simply administered funds on behalf of clients.

Zürich's first private bank appeared in 1786 in response to the fact that the Leubank was, literally, unable to accommodate all the available capital. It arose as a direct outgrowth of the success of non-local private bankers in selling foreign securities in the city. Accordingly the firm of Usteri, Ott, Esher, and Co. was formed for the express purpose of investing funds in Swiss firms located in Paris.

Zürich's move into international banking, which had showed great promise in the beginning, suffered greatly from the massive upheavals of the French Revolution, and even Leu and Co. was forced to default on its bonds in 1799. The French invasion under Bonaparte simply impoverished a great community which had built up considerable capital over a two-century period. Even the local industry suffered from the lack of capital and the collapse of foreign markets during the era of the Napoleonic wars.

THE SWISS BANK, THE BEGINNINGS OF A TRULY UNIQUE INSTITUTION

Readers may find the use of the word 'unique' to be somewhat of an exaggeration; however we would suggest that such is not the case. Only in Basle does one find commercial banking *per se* which was the logical outcome of the money changing and minting processes which were the integral parts of monetary transactions in mediaeval times. In Geneva, on the other hand, we find that Protestant banking meant the actual lending of 'pre-accumulated' capital. (We have the capital so what can we do with it?) The Protestant bankers offered the investment outlet which was required. The fact that the 'investment' happened to consist of the purchase of perpetual French government debt, and hence was doomed, is not so important as the fact that the Geneva bankers served as intermediaries. We would suggest (without further intensive research into the matter) that this was the first time in modern history (excluding the Italian banking experience) that the intermediation function of banking was so used. Certainly the intermediation process of the early Geneva bankers left a permanent mark on Swiss banking.

Perhaps the most interesting of all, however, was the Zürich experience. Here, the accumulation of funds from abroad, as a result of the huge amount of import requirement due to both the Thirty Years War and the Seven Years War in France, meant that Zürich was experiencing an embarrassment of riches. Further, true to Keynes' argument some three centuries later, there was a tendency for interest rates to become lower as a consequence. This would mean, so it was feared by the authorities, that Zürichers would be tempted to borrow money for both speculation and mortgage purposes – beyond what the economy could safely sustain. Industrial expansion was already at its limit and had spread beyond its borders into Winterthur and Schaffhausen.

The result was that, contrary to the experience of England and Holland which had deliberately put mercantilist doctrines into practise, Zürich experienced mercantilism unwillingly. The circumstances of the time had imposed the best of mercantilism traditions, a surplus of foreign funds, on Zürich and its people. The question remained, then, if we do not want interest rates to be lowered and we cannot utilise the existing capital within the region of Zürich, what is the next logical step? Here we find the beginnings of the most outstanding characteristic of Swiss banking – the export of surplus capital itself. For this purpose, the Leubank had its beginnings.

CONCLUSION

We cannot emphasize too strongly the sharp difference between early Swiss banking and, say, English or even Scottish banking. While the English banks were in the real sense of the word commercial banks and the Scottish banks were deposit banks, Swiss banks were formed as an outlet for a pre-existing supply of capital. They did not 'double the effect' of coin (as expressed by Petty) nor did they increase the availability of credit to result in an increase in the supply of an exchange medium. They learned to act as intermediaries to channel existing funds in the direction in which funds were in short supply. The important question of risk and the consequent possibility of losing the entire amount of the funds so invested was something which was to be answered with both time and experience.

Underlying the entire process of Swiss banking activity, we can hardly overstress this important point, is the Reformation and the complete philosophical change of life experience which occurred at that time. Consider, for instance, the value structure that a mediaeval Zürich society might have held had there been no Reformation. An 'embarrassment' of wealth resulting from a surplus of Zürich exports to the German states, and later to France, would have meant that alms to the poor could have been increased to such an extent that there might have been no poor at all. Interest rates, and the possibility of their falling due to an excessive supply of capital, might not even exist because the church forbade usury. More important, the bulk of the wealth surplus would surely have eventually become the property of the church and been used to expand landholdings and so on, as a result of the desire on the part of a mediaeval society to ensure salvation for itself.

All this was not the case, because of the Reformation. Capital (that is, the surplus wealth that accrued to Zürich), was to be used to employ the poor in order that they themselves might cease to be poor. After all God recognised the importance of work and rewarded those who diligently applied themselves. But now, as both Calvin and Zwingli had recognised, interest must be considered as legitimate because, since capital was used to employ workers, it earned a reward and those who lent at interest were entitled to at least some of its fruits. Most important is the fact that a surplus of funds can exist and be used in other ways than alms-giving. Indeed, such a surplus *must* have an outlet, either in domestic investment, at lower rates of interest, or in foreign investment at existing higher rates. Zürichers chose the latter.

In a larger sense, we would agree with Luthy in that the Reformation and capitalism were both actually a manifestation of a much larger development in human history – the Renaissance. Thus capitalism can be found in countries, such as Italy, where the Reformation never really appeared. However, in Switzerland it is certainly true that the principles of modern capitalism were reinforced by the Reformation. Profits were, to say the least, attractive. Revenues for the cities were likewise attractive. Interest earned by lenders of capital was also attractive. All of these were made considerably more desirable when God approved; indeed, even more so when God looks with favour upon the new capitalistic phenomena.

It was within this fundamental drive that we find the origin of Swiss banking. Banks developed as a partner, and an equal one at that, of industrial enterprise and entrepreneurship. Their function was not to expand the money supply by making loans, as in England, nor to serve the interests of an outmoded economic philosophy like mercantilism. We cannot repeat often enough that Swiss banking was an independent entity in the economic system of central Europe. Its function was to intermediate, not to provide credit for exchange purposes, but to channel the surpluses of capital possessed by the cantons toward some profitable objective. When this objective was the development of industry, not only was a vital service being rendered, but the future structure of Swiss banks was already being foreshadowed. The nature of this structure and service is the subject of the following chapters and is the most interesting single aspect of the development of modern banking.

Notes

1. It should be made quite clear that the French Protestants, the Huguenots, were actually more than a mere religious movement. They had already achieved, by the time of the revocation of the Edict of Nantes, a considerable political force within France itself, especially under the influence of Calvin. Thus, the nationalist movement of the nation toward a unified state could not tolerate such a political counter-force and it chose the method of religious differences to eliminate it. This 'nationalist force' took the form of the person of Louis XIV who was particularly determined to crush all political opposition. Luthy, H., *La Banque Protestante en France* (Paris: S. E. V. P. E. N., 1959) p. 12.
2. Max Ikle notes that by 1709, nearly a dozen bankers were found in Geneva, the names of which were to become famous in the financial history of Geneva. Ikle, Max, *Switzerland, an International Banking and Finance Centre* (Stroudsburg, PA: Dowden Hutchison, and Ross, 1972) p. 5.
3. The Swiss soldiers developed an extraordinary skill with the halberd, a pole culminating in a hook-shaped axe head and a point. When the knights on horseback, the mediaeval version of the modern tank, charged the Swiss line, they faced the halberd point with the other end of the pole braced against the ground. Should the point miss its target, the hook of the axe head could grapple the knight, pulling him off his horse. Once dismounted the knight was at the mercy of the halberdier and the axe head finished the task. The Swiss soldiers never took prisoners. It is remarkable, though true, that the arts of war directly contributed to the evolution of Swiss banking.
4. Ikle, *Switzerland, an International Banking and Finance Centre*, p. 6.
5. Leo Weisz, 'Der organisierte Kredit in Zürich von der Reformation bis zum Jahre 1835', *Geld und Kreditsystem der Schweiz* (Zürich: Schultheiss and Co. AG, 1944) pp. 135–156.
6. Weisz, 'Der organisierte Kredit', p. 146.
7. Ikle, *Switzerland, an International Banking and Finance Centre*, p. 5.

4 The Dawn of Modern Switzerland

INTRODUCTORY

We have attempted to uncover those roots of the Swiss banking system which lie deep in the history of Europe. In this sense, the Swiss and their banks share the common political and economic ground of all Europe, except for that unique position of the Swiss which developed after the disastrous 1515 defeat of the Swiss army at Marignano – its famous neutrality. There is yet another root, a philosophical background, which has its own origins and which was also influential in determining the unique character of the Swiss banks. Once more, though, we should stress the substantive difference between the Swiss bank of the nineteenth century and the 'credit banks' which had developed so extensively in Great Britain, because it is precisely this difference that is the distinguishing characteristic of Swiss banking. This will become clear in the following pages.

THE TRANSITION PERIOD

The years of turmoil which affected Europe during the end of the eighteenth and the early years of the nineteenth centuries were not without purpose. There was a dismantling of not only the society but also the structural underpinnings of the old orders, making way for a new era which would belong to the new century, in brief, the culmination of the Renaissance period. With economic and social systems in a state of flux, the like of which had never before been seen, it was almost to be expected that new and different ideas and thought structures would accompany the collapse of the old orders.

Such was the nature of that age of transition. Without delving into Swiss history excessively, we should point out that the old Confederation, which had served the Swiss through the centuries since 1291, was simply no longer equal to the task. The old order of aristocracies in the cantons crumbled at first before the onslaught of the French Revolutionary armies. The result was the proclamation of the Helvetic Republic on 29 March 1798. Of course, such a change from confederation to a centralised republic was excessive for the cantons that had known independence for so long, and the Republic was doomed. Only the military power of the French armies could sustain the new system.[1]

After the withdrawal of the French troops in 1802, the Helvetic Republic was driven back by force of arms. The federalists, those who favoured the former confederate system, were proving to be too strong for the unitary, or Republic, party headed by both La Harpe and Ochs. Again Napoleon intervened and, to his credit, recognised that Switzerland (it is interesting that the name 'Switzerland' was then used for the first time as referring to this new Confederation) with its peculiar structure should indeed have a federal system somewhat akin to the old. Accordingly, in 1803, a new constitution was created which involved the old cantons just as before but with an increase in their number to nineteen; thereafter the Swiss enjoyed ten years of peace and prosperity under the protection of the Emperor.

Once it became clear that Napoleon's power was waning, Switzerland's status again became precarious. When Austrian and Russian troops crossed the Swiss frontier at the end of 1813, it became necessary for the Swiss Diet to declare the 1803 Constitution invalid, once more throwing Switzerland into turmoil. The quarreling between the parties was so bitter that many questions in dispute had to be referred to the Congress of Vienna for settlement. After considerably more strife, another Constitution was finally agreed upon by all the cantons except Nidwald which, after the threat of armed force, was pressured into entering the agreement in 1815. Such was the state of transition of the Swiss during the early decades of the nineteenth century.

While it is simple enough to recount these facts from Swiss history, it is not so easy to appreciate the re-awakening of old passions and jealousies among the cantons, the strength of resurgent religious differences which dated from the Reformation, and the inherent conflicts of differing political structures within each of the cantons. Indeed, it would be virtually impossible, from the standpoint of the twenty-first century, to enumerate all possible sources of conflict amongst the many cantons which were forced, first by the Helvetic Republic and then by the new constitution of 1803, to live together in some kind of amity. Then, to complete the indignity, only to discover that the end of the Bonaparte era meant that since the Swiss were on the wrong side the process of constitutional struggle would have to begin anew.

Despite its 'foreign origin' (having been guaranteed by Bonaparte himself) the constitution of 1803 served the Swiss well. Peace and prosperity were the general rule. Pestalozzi and Fellenberg first developed their theories of education and Escher constructed the embankment of the Linth in Zürich. Industry, particularly silken goods (ribbons, and so on), which had been established by the Huguenots, thrived during this period, and cotton manufacturing, begun as early as the fifteenth century, developed even further. Of course, watch-making in Geneva had already been introduced and had progressed to the level of a mature industry well before the French Revolution. (It should be noted that Geneva was not a part of the Swiss Confederation until 1815.)

The cities, however, were small; only Zürich, Geneva, and Berne could be considered as genuine 'cities', though their populations were hardly more than 50,000, if that much. The Swiss population was mainly rural, with agriculture, utilising about 25 per cent of the land area, the principal occupation. This meant that the Swiss farmers, or 'peasants', were the mainstay of the economy of the entire country. Given their strategic importance, what were the Swiss farmers *really* like during the early decades of the nineteenth century?

John Stuart Mill, in his Principles of Political Economy, gives us an excellent picture of the state of Swiss agriculture during the early nineteenth century by quoting from the distinguished Swiss economist de Sismondi – well-known for his theory of interest and as the founder of the Lausanne School of Economics. The quote which Mill found so trenchant is as follows:

It is especially Switzerland which should be traversed and studied to judge of the happiness of peasant proprietors. It is from Switzerland we learn that agriculture practised by the very persons who enjoy its fruits, suffices to procure great comfort for a very numerous popula-tion; a great independence of character, arising from independence of position; a great commerce of consumption, the result of the easy circumstances of all the inhabitants, even in a country whose climate is rude, whose soil is but moderately fertile, and where late frosts and inconstancy of seasons often blight the hopes of the cultivator. It is impossible to see without admiration those timber houses of the poorest peasant, so vast, so well closed in, so covered with carvings. In the interior, spacious corridors separate the different chambers of the numerous family; each chamber has but one bed, which is abundantly furnished with curtains, bedclothes, and the whitest linen; carefully kept furniture surrounds it; the wardrobes are filled with linen; the dairy is vast, well aired, and of exquisite cleanness; under the same roof is a great provision of corn, salt meat, cheese and wood; in the cow-houses are the finest and most carefully tended cattle in Europe; the garden is planted with flowers, both men and women are cleanly and warmly clad, the women preserve with pride their ancient costume; all carry in their faces the impress of health and strength. Let other nations boast of their opulence, Switzerland may always point with pride to her peasants.[2]

These are idyllic, as well as eloquent, words; indeed, they may appear excessively so to our modern and somewhat cynical eyes. Nevertheless, we must not overlook what is important for our purposes – the important groundwork for nineteenth century Swiss banking which distinguishes it from the British credit banks. We note, firstly, that Swiss farmers are proprietors who work for themselves and, since they enjoys the fruits of their own labours, they prefer their independence (that is, to own their own land). This means that they are likely to be in debt. Such is the case for the rich canton of Zürich which was reported by Gerold Meyer von Kronau in his *Historical, Geographical, and Statistical Picture of Switzerland* as 'the indebtedness of the proprietors in the flourishing canton of Zürich borders on the incredible; so that only the intensest industry, frugality, temperance, and complete freedom of commerce enable them to stand their ground'.[3] Fair enough, and we might ask to whom are the farmers indebted? The answer, as we shall see, is the banks, for it was precisely in such financing of debt (that is mortgage debt) that cantonal banks had their beginnings.

But Mill was much too scientific an economist to accept everything in Switzerland as perfect, so he notes that Berne was 'burthened with a numerous pauper population because of the worst regulated Poor Law administration system in Europe'.[4] Nevertheless, he makes reference to an English traveler and writer, H. D. Inglis, who reported in the most glowing terms regarding the Engadine where farmers produced virtually everything possible in the most adverse conditions where the 'lowest part is not much lower than the top of Snowdon.'[5]

The success of the Swiss farmers, which entranced observers and writers of the time, certainly must have been founded upon a principle, that of proprietorship. The metayer (or sharecropping) system which was common in France stands in sharp contrast to the rural Swiss proprietors. Metayers had an interest, to be sure, in the increase in the amount of output and, therefore, an increase in their share. However, to quote Adam Smith, 'It could never, however, be the interest even of this last species of cultivators (the metayer) to lay out, in the further improvement of the land, any part of the little stock which they might save from their own share of the produce...'[6] In other words, only the landlord could afford to make capital expenditures of any kind on the land, and since the cultivator was best equipped to judge the nature of the expenditure required, a fundamental inefficiency existed. This inefficiency was not shared by the Swiss farmer.[7]

As a proprietor, the Swiss peasant had every incentive to increase the output of his land and to increase, whenever it be appropriate, the size of his farm. This is why we can say that the first use of industrial credit in Switzerland was not that of manufacturing but of agriculture. A demand for credit existed not just in the towns but in the rural areas which were just about everywhere cultivation could exist. It was only a matter of meeting that demand with supply. Most important, the single proprietor could establish his own level of agricultural efficiency. In many instances, this meant, according to the reports of the day, the use of every conceivable space for cultivating some crop. Thus, an intensive type of agriculture was developed with the peasant profiting entirely from his labours without the requirement of sharing his crop with a landlord.

HENRI DE SAINT-SIMON AND THE SAINT-SIMONIANS

During the post-Revolutionary transitional period in the history of Europe, there appeared on the scene a most extraordinary philosopher and thinker, Henri de Saint-Simon. He had an unusual career, having been born in 1760 into one of the most ancient families of France. He fought in the American War of Independence with some distinction, and, returning to France, became a man of peace. With the outbreak of the French Revolution, he renounced his title and proceeded to make his fortune by speculating in church lands.

His writing, or philosophical, career can be characterised as reflecting a society in transition: governments and social structures were crumbling, to be replaced with something – precisely what was that 'something' to be? He envisioned what, to us, borders upon the nonsensical: a replacement of politicians, parliaments, and so on with a government of the intellectual aristocracy. There was to be a Council of Newton consisting of scientists, mathematicians, and artists. Spiritual matters were to be the responsibility of learned men (*savants*). It was the responsibility of the electorate to select these members (twenty-one in all) of the Council of Newton.[8]

All this is nonsense, of course, and serves to suggest, as noted above, the lengths toward which the philosopher would go to re-order a society which was already in a state of flux. The surprising outcome of his many pamphlets and letters was a following of scholars, bankers and engineers (including Auguste Comte) which he inspired. They formed themselves into a 'school' and continued writing and publishing long after the death of the master.

What interests us here is the new concept of banking which emerged amongst the Saint-Simonian school. To the Saint-Simonians, banks, or rather the banking system as they knew it, occupied a strategic position. Instead of the usual mediation function in which the owners of the 'instruments of work' have the same interest as the distributors of these instruments (the bankers), there was to be a great central bank which would have as its assets the entire 'fund of production' of the nation (in modern terms, presumably, the Gross Domestic Product).

From this great central bank, there would be 'secondary banks' which would be 'merely extensions of the first', or central, bank. In another passage, the Saint-Simonians make reference to the liabilities of the central bank being the assets of the secondary banks; hence we may assume that the entire banking system was to be linked in this way. The assets of the secondary banks would be the loans and credits granted to industry as well as to increasingly specialised banks within the territory of each of the secondary banks.

It is interesting that Saint-Simonians conceived of their banking structure as fundamentally different from that which existed in reality. What they saw in the real world were bankers, the distributors of capital, attempting to maximise their earnings from the workers, hence the interest charged to the workers was always high. Similarly the owners of capital, those who entrusted their funds to the bankers, enjoyed the highest rate of interest which the bankers could pay. There was, thus, an inherent conflict of interest between those who borrowed and those who owned. In the Saint-Simonian system this conflict would be resolved because everyone would have a stake in the increase of production which was the sole source of interest as a payment to owners of capital.

This somewhat socialist view of society depended upon the appointment of the highest quality of the intelligentsia to positions of responsibility. At the same time the leadership of society, the ultimate leaders of this vast workshop, must be those who are most trusted and loved.[9] (At the risk of straying from our subject of banking, we might query such a doctrine by suggesting that a beloved leader means followers who, presumably, are willing to tread any path the leader suggests. Many of our generation may recognise here the later *Fuhrerprinzip* with its tragic consequences.)[10]

Readers familiar with the English system of banking will note that the banks which existed on the Continent during the early nineteenth century, and the somewhat naive banking version of Saint-Simonians, is one of pure intermediation. The deposits of those who have are made available to bankers for investment in the form of loans to those who have not and who also desire the use of such funds. In this way savings of society are channelled, hopefully, into investment, but, as Saint-Simonians noted, the social benefit of investment may be quite different from the private gain therefrom. To correct this discrepancey was the objective of the 'new' banking structure which they had conceived.

What is most interesting (and remarkable) is the fact that the Saint-Simonians themselves eventually dispersed to become engineers, bankers, and railway administrators, all in the 'ordinary business of life', but by no means *ordinary*. They all distinguished themselves in their respective professions so that France, in the final analysis, owed a great debt to the Saint-Simonian school. Thus, what had its beginnings in such nonsense as the Universal Law of Gravitation (which would attract all economic activity in harmony), a new 'religion' based upon science, industry and politics as one and the same, and so on actually made a distinct and unique contribution to society.[11]

THE CREDIT MOBILIER

At first sight it is difficult to relate the financial institution developed by Isaac and Emile Pereire, two Saint-Simonians, with the extraordinary banking concept of the master. However, if we hive off the grandiose scheme of a central bank using the Gross Domestic Product as assets and bank credit for liabilities, channelled through a pyramidal structure to industry, and reduce the concept of investment banking to its fundamentals, there is, to be sure, a kernel of truth remaining. If we imagine investment projects which we would today refer to as 'economic infrastructure' so glaringly obvious as to be bottlenecks to economic growth and development, and if we believe that in the long run such projects must become self supporting, we will have served two Saint-Simonian objectives. The first is the building and development of the investment project itself which will unleash the pent-up flood of potential production which is otherwise unrealisable. The second is the actual service rendered by the project itself which is valued as the revenue produced therefrom. It is here that we find in *laissez faire* economics the closest approximation to Saint-Simon's vision of harmony. It is not the direct service rendered by the infrastructure which is important in itself but the service of infrastructure in cooperation with industry, which is enhanced thereby, which matters.

Accordingly the Credit Mobilier of France was formed as a joint stock company in Paris in November 1852, under the lead of the Pereire brothers (based upon the principle of limited liability) for the purpose of transacting general banking business, to facilitate the construction of public works, and to develop internal industry.[12] It had a capitalisation of 60 million francs divided into shares of 500 francs each. The company was authorised to hold public and other securities (assets) and to issue bonds of its own to an amount equal to both its subscriptions and purchases of its own shares, and after the entire amount of original capital was taken up by the market, the bond issue could be *ten times the amount*: 600 million francs![13]

While the mania of launching new companies continued (this was the characteristic of the second Empire in France as well as in other countries), there was a huge profit to be earned by the company; indeed dividends of 41 per cent were declared in 1855, rather considerable for a company just three years old. When we realise that it would have been impossible for it to earn 'legitimate' profits, that is, a return on fixed investment in so short a time period, the profits must have come entirely from speculation on the stock market as well as excessive promotion charges. Speculative profits would arise from the purchase and sale of securities which were held as assets and which rose in value on the market.

The practice of the Credit Mobilier at that time was underwriting, instead of outright lending, loans from existing credit banks. These loans from credit banks were secured by the stock of the newly formed companies (underwritten by the Credit Mobilier) so that when it became clear that profits from the new ventures were not forthcoming until after a long gestation period (if at all) the Credit Mobilier found itself with a large quantity of depreciated or unsaleable stock on its hands. At the same time the inevitable collapse of speculation restricted a source from which earlier profits had arisen. The world financial crisis in 1857 contributed, of course, to this situation as stock markets reacted sharply to a general loss of confidence. The rates of dividend and, consequently, the prices of the stock of the Credit Mobilier fell as quickly as they had risen before.

By 1867, having paid only slight dividends for some years, the company's stock fell to just 28 per cent of its par value, and it went into liquidation. The managers became exceedingly wealthy from their investments in the company; however the High Court of Appeals decided in 1868 that the Pereire brothers and other managers should recompense stockholders for their losses. The extent to which such payments were actually received by the stockholders remains unknown.

While the Credit Mobilier was considered to be little more than a gambling casino (as it indeed was) by veterans of the Paris stock market, it did manage to serve some of its original purpose. Among the enterprises which it helped to finance were the Paris Gas Company, the Paris Omnibus Company, the Maritime Company of Clippers, the Grand Hotel du Louvre, and some large loans to French railway companies as well as railways in Austria, Spain, Russia, and Switzerland.

In its simplest terms, it is the intermediary's obligations (stocks and bonds) which the public is willing to purchase rather than the assets of the actual project, which may be fraught with excessive risk or excessively long in maturing. The public gains a degree of liquidity in the sense that the intermediary's obligations can be readily sold in the aftermarket, in the first place, or the value of the obligations might be underwritten by some other agency (the government, for example) in the second. This is important because it unlocks the savings of the public to be used for a necessary social investment.

The Pereire Credit Mobilier was a pioneering effort, to be sure. It was able to take advantage of the circumstances of the time when construction and development projects had reached a manic stage. Being a Pioneer, it could require heavy promotion charges and investors could enjoy the high profit and correspondingly high dividend distributions which resulted.

The Credit Foncier in London had a similar history. The introduction of limited liability gave a powerful stimulus to this institution and the results were quite similar to the Paris experience. Large sums of capital were locked into hopeless undertakings such as the Imperial Land Company of Marseilles and the Santiago and Carril Railway. Thereafter the Credit Foncier, just as any other bank in London, structured its assets toward short-term low-risk investments.

THE BEGINNINGS OF BANKING

Despite the obvious weakness of the Credit Mobilier (it accepted no deposits and derived its funding from the sale of its bonds) its important function as an intermediary was not lost on the Swiss. It was, therefore, during the early nineteenth century that modern Swiss banking actually began. As we have seen, this beginning was really the logical outcome of a series of both natural and historical circumstances, ultimately culminating in the most extraordinary banking structure in the world. These circumstances can be readily summarised as follows.

The Swiss had been fortunate in the sense that they were able to avoid the stifling hand of feudalism which had oppressed the French, the English, and the Germans. The defeat of the Hapsburgs, the Duke of Burgundy, and the French, at the hands of the Swiss armies, ensured the freedom of the cantons and their territories and, lastly, their ultimate neutrality. But, curiously, the avoidance of a feudal structure did not mean that the Swiss were a 'free' people. The ruling classes in the cantons, harsh as they were with respect to the peasants within their territories, were also the business class. Those who were successful in business became members of ruling councils, reflecting, incidentally, the influence of Saint-Simon in his use of 'experts' in his system of government. At the same time there was little or no opportunity for the Swiss themselves to establish a useless landed gentry, as was the case in other countries, for the very simple reason that there was insufficient land worth owning and controlling. The energies of the ruling classes were directed to business instead.

This alliance of government and business meant that the Swiss were able to avoid that drain of wealth to support the leisured (or warrior) class which plagued all of Europe, especially during the Wars of Religion. Quite the contrary, the export of Swiss mercenaries during those wars enriched the ruling classes of the cantons, which became such because of their success in business enterprises. All this meant that Zwingli and Calvin, with their doctrines of the blessedness of work, gave the stamp of divine approval to an existing order. The Swiss were, and still are, pragmatists. To put it in lay terms, it is nice to have theory and practice reinforcing each other, but if theory is absent and practice happens to work, so be it.

The strategic position of Switzerland, particularly Basle at the headwaters of the Rhine, must not be overlooked. This gave an unprecedented opportunity for the development of commercial and financial activity in currency exchange, discounting, factoring, and so on, all related to the transshipment of commodities between northern Germany and the great Italian city-states. This advantage, we would argue, was more than mere happenstance. Basle as a bishopric, then a state, was small. Progress in economic activity meant an introspective development of skills and arts rather than the territorial expansion which was so characteristic of feudal societies. The University, printing, the minting of coins to precise specifications, skills in banking and finance, all suggest that Baslers were living and growing by their wits, not by a sterile force of arms. At the same time, the capacity to learn from the Italian bankers during the great Basle Synod suggests that Baslers had a great advantage in not having to start afresh to learn by their own experience alone. It is this recognition of the importance of the 'headstart' which again suggests the importance of the capacity to use their brains rather than their brawn.

History has its own way, so it seems, of evolving as it should. Suppose, as an example, that the Swiss army had not been soundly defeated at Marignano in 1515. Suppose further that success in military adventures had encouraged the Swiss to annex some of the neighbouring territories in an expansionist move. This would have required military leadership and, what might inevitably follow, a hereditary feudal class precisely the same as in other countries. Most important, the energy of the Swiss would have been redirected into a useless pursuit of selfish, and temporary, gain, for always there would have been some other power which would eventually have triumphed in the end. This is why, by turning inward toward the pursuit of neutrality and the development of their own skills and arts, the Swiss achieved a much more lasting 'conquest': economic growth to an extent that was the envy of all Europe.

The absence of feudalism had another result which gave rise to the glowing account of Sismondi regarding the Swiss farmers. Rural Switzerland includes a quite considerable area which is 'productive', 71 per cent of the entire land area.[14] This means that there was considerable scope for individual intiative since the farmers themselves own their own land. They could increase the size of their farms by borrowing, by means of mortgages, whenever an increase in agricultural efficiency so required. Similarly there was every incentive for intensivity of cultivation because the entire output of the farm belonged to the farmer. There was no feudal obligation to share or to rent. Thus, as a follow up to von Kronau's coment quoted above, a genuine economic rationale existed for the high mortgage demand we find amongst the early cantonal banks. Likewise, as he noted, indebtedness spurred farmers to their greatest efforts. It is in this sense, therefore, that we can say that Swiss farming in the early nineteenth century achieved a level of efficiency unequalled in all of Europe, all the while serving as an important demand for the assets of a new banking system.

At the same time we might ask: whence came the liabilities? The answer lies in the genuinely Swiss habit of businessmen providing for their own growth and expansion from their own savings. This was the 'Protestant ethic', so-called, which encouraged frugality. (Actually, one might even argue the other way round, that the Swiss habit of frugality was justified by the Protestant ethic!) Whatever the source of the saving, religion or the Swiss psyche itself, it was very real. The consequence was the establishment of industry quite early in the Confederation. Silk had already been produced in Zürich and Basle during the latter half of the thirteenth century, and was re-introduced by Protestants in 1555. Ribbon weaving came later, with the Huguenots. During the latter half of the nineteenth century, this industry became a major employer. Cotton manufacturing began during the fifteenth century and the power loom was introduced in the 1830s, utilising the abundant water power which was available. Similarly, food manufacturing, embroidery, and straw plaiting were major export industries. Of course, the great watch industry introduced by the Huguenots in 1685 should also be mentioned, especially around the area of Geneva.

There is a fundamental characteristic amongst these industries which ought not to be overlooked. With practically no raw material of its own, the country was and still is entirely dependent upon the process of upgrading commodities to the highest value possible. These are then exported to yield a balance-of-trade surplus. This suggests once more the application and utilisation of skills which have been developed either through education or tradition. Watches are an obvious example of items with the absolute minimum of raw material input relative to the value of the output. The service of international banking is another. Here there is no commodity input at all, but the value of the output is considerable. To this we can add insurance and financial services of all kinds, all of which are based entirely upon the wit and wisdom and native intelligence of the Swiss. It was industries such as these which were created and developed by Swiss entrepreneurship and, most important, with their own capital.

There were, however, limits to the capacity of individual entrepreneurs to finance, from their own savings, the great world-class industries for which Switzerland is now so well known – electricity, chemicals, engineering, and so on. More than the savings of the individual is required; in fact, it is the mobilisation of the savings of many concentrating on the establishment of a single industry that is required. Ultimately the savings of the entire nation are necessary for the building of monumental tasks such as railroads. It is in this huge task, the mobilisation of savings of the Swiss public, that the Credit Mobilier appeared to have the answer.

Whether or not the Credit Mobilier in the French version is used as a 'model' is immaterial. The principle of a joint stock company was finally acceptable to the conservative Swiss business mind, and, furthermore, the idea that bonds as well as shares can be sold to a public which has ample idle savings added to the possibilities inherent in the mobilisation of savings. All that is required is that the bond issue not be excessive (10 times the amount of paid-in capital) but some reasonable amount such as equal to the value of the capital stock.

It was Alfred Escher, businessman, statesman, politician, and member of the new Federal Council of 1848 who first recognised the great potential in the modern Credit Mobilier type of bank. He had the vision to recognise the strategic position of Zürich in the new Europe connected not by the river Rhine, as in Basle, but by rail across, or through, the St. Gothard Pass. In order to realise this dream it was necessary to concentrate huge amounts of capital on a single objective, the construction of the rail link.

The new Swiss Credit Bank which he formed was capitalised at 15 million francs, one-half purchased by a German firm, and the other half taken by Escher and his private group (3 million francs) and the Zürich public (4.5 million francs) during a massive sale of bank stock on a memorable date in Swiss banking history, 17 July 1856.[15] What is important in this remarkably successful venture is that the savings of many small businessmen in Zürich were at long last released to be used for investment in a venture not directly related to the business activity of the share purchasers.

The new Credit Mobilier type of bank entered a Switzerland which was already 'banked' in the sense that banks existed which served the needs of business enterprise in its existing form. They were conservative (although not backward-looking) yet capable of satisfying the demands made upon them by the economy, particularly agricultural, of the time. Already, the Kantonal Bank von Bern, founded as a state bank in 1834, had been issuing bank notes, a practice well established in Great Britain for centuries. Similarly, the Bank in Zürich, opened in 1836, and the Bank in St. Gallen, opened the following year, 1837, had also been issuing bank notes. These banks, referred to as 'Credit Banks', followed the principle outlined in the theoretical model of the Credit Bank. They accomplished two objectives: first, they permitted an expansion of the means of payment via the issue of banknotes – an elastic currency; and second, they established a deposit mechanism whereby Swiss savings could be used for investment. Investment in what? Agricultural mortgages, of course, for these were in greatest demand.

In Basle, still the great commercial centre of Switzerland, there were sixteen banks engaged in the discounting of bills, exchanging currency, and any other bank service which would satisfy the credit needs of relatively small enterprises in the area served by the city.[16] These banks were following a tradition of Basle banking which had already been well established over the previous five hundred years. Thanks to the efforts of Johann Jakob Speiser, an enterprising and promising young banker who had observed the banking practices of England and Holland, a new bank based upon the syndicate principle was formed. It was a combination of some 16 individuals and bankers in Basle who conceived of the idea of extending bank services beyond the traditional forms of lending to the area of actually making payments for business enterprises following the British model. This resulted in the establishment, on 1 January 1844, of a syndicate, the Giro und Depositenbank, which was followed in 1845 by the Bank in Basle with Speiser himself as manager. This latter bank became the fourth note-issuing bank in Switzerland (after the banks in Berne, Zürich, and St. Gallen). Thus true commercial banking, in the form, we might add, of joint stock banking, had entered Switzerland precisely at the point where commercial activity was its greatest, Basle.

The problem here, just as in all countries where commercial banking is generally practiced, is that the commercial bank's welfare depends entirely upon the welfare of the business activity with which it is closely bound. So it was that the crisis of 1848 in Paris seriously affected the banks in Basle. Since Swiss foreign trade was still very much tied to France so that the trade bills issued by the Basle bankers to their clients became uncollectable. Speiser himself developed a kind of 'credit union' of all bankers which cancelled debts against credits and only required a loan of 800,000 francs to balance the two – a true stroke of banker's genius.

With the formation of the new Swiss federal state in 1848, cantonal barriers to trade were broken down and a new era of Swiss commercial banking began. At the same time the new concepts of protectionism swept into France and Germany, the traditional Swiss trading partners. This had the effect of forcing Swiss manufacturing not only to turn inward toward its own federal cantons but beyond to Russia, England and to the United States.

As the push for further large-scale industrialisation and the development of railways to accommodate the transport requirements of the new trading markets grew, it became clear that the existing Swiss financing structure was unequal to the task. It was here that the Credit Mobilier type of bank, Alfred Escher's masterstroke in Zürich, entered into Swiss banking and finance. Escher was not the first, however. The credit for being the Swiss pioneer in this area must belong to James Fazy, who founded the Banque Generale Suisse de Credit Foncier et Mobilier in Geneva in 1853.

The Basle bankers, still the conservatives, reacted to the new development in banking in their own way. Just as they had formed a syndicate to establish the Giro und Depositenbank, they formed *another* syndicate for the purpose of financing projects which none of them alone could handle. This became the Bankverein, a name which appeared in the early documents concerned with a loan to the canton of Fribourg in 1860 to finance the railway from Lausanne to Fribourg.

It is curious, in retrospect, that the Basle intellectual elite should have looked upon such a new banking facility as the Credit Mobilier with suspicion. Such is the nature of Swiss conservatism and pragmatism, which shows little interest in a new and different approach to new situations. One almost has the feeling that the Swiss must have been the originators of the famous mechanic's rule, 'if it works, don't fix it'. So it was that the *Baseler Nachrichten* noted in its issue of the day, 'We frankly admit we see neither the advantage nor the purpose of these new institutions for the provision of credit . . . that is what banks, that is what private bankers were there for, and these have so far always been anxious to do business wherever an opportunity has been afforded to do so on a solid basis.' And again, 'On the one hand we see at the head of industry and other branches of business well-endowed firms which work entirely with their own capital and yet can also put out a considerable portion of their funds at interest. On the other hand we find in our city an extensively developed and generally accessible credit system such as can probably be paralleled in no other place in the world . . . If, then, there is any place where an actual credit institution may be regarded as absolutely superfluous, it is here.'

It is this very Swiss conservatism which also worked to the advantage of the Swiss banking system, because there was still another influence which was pushing for recognition. This was the fact that since the Credit Mobilier type banks had already opened in Geneva, St. Gall, and Zürich, why continue along the same line when ample supplies of capital were available to industry already? There was logic in this argument. How many such banks did Switzerland need (given the circumstances of that particular time)? In such an argument there appeared another function of banks which was to prove most important in the future.

There were considerable deposits available to the banks of Basle – that was obvious. But in deciding on the question as to what to do with these deposits, there were the obvious differences between domestic government and real estate bonds which paid an interest rate of 3 per cent or 4 per cent as against American bonds which paid 6 per cent, 7 per cent, or more. In other words, Basle, still the financial centre of Switzerland, could find its most profitable, risk-free, and still liquid (because bonds could be readily sold in the US bond market oftentimes at a profit) form of assets by purchasing foreign securities.

We can recognise at once a situation which was rapidly developing in Switzerland and was to shape Swiss banks well into the future. Domestic investment opportunities within the geographically small and already relatively 'overbanked' cantons were already being filled up. The encouragement, therefore, was to place their assets in foreign securities where interest rates were higher. At the same time, by going further afield than the immediate area of Europe around Switzerland, the uncertain political conditions which plagued France and Germany could be avoided.

We can recognise also in the newspaper reports and minutes of bank meetings a slow, but sure, decline in the importance of Basle as the financial centre of Switzerland. This was almost to be expected, for the reasons already suggested – a large per capita savings rate amongst the Swiss and the importance of a finance industry which utilises no imports of raw material but which requires native intelligence. In a word, regions other than Basle, Zürich in particular, wanted a piece of the action in a world which was desperately short of capital for investment purposes. Twenty to thirty banks and lending agencies, a dozen industrial companies, fire and life insurance companies all competed against one another on the capital market and prepared to 'cook their hare before they had caught it.'[17] Two new banks of the Credit Mobilier type, and twenty two others – mortgage banks, cantonal banks, as well as commercial banks to make a total of twenty-four – appeared during the year 1861. In addition, the Basler Handelsbank, which began business in 1863, was an attempt, though unsuccessful, to continue the preeminence of Basle as a commercial banking centre.

In a larger sense, this flurry of activity in the banking and finance sphere was laying the foundation, within the context of free enterprise, for a modern credit system. It was at this time that the principle of economic liberalism, in the tradition of Adam Smith, reached its zenith in the English Manchester School. To put it simply, the best way to order an economic system, in a pragmatic sense, was to have'... liberty to choose one's employment, free competition, free trade outside as well as inside a country's boundaries, free banks, and a competitive rate of interest; negatively it implied a resistance to state intervention wherever the necessity for it cannot be clearly demonstrated, as in the case of protective or parental legislation'.[18] Thus, while many of the Swiss banks formed during this period were destined for bankruptcy, it mattered little because this was the free enterprise system's method of clearing out the inefficient.

At the same time a peculiarly Swiss problem emerged. Even though the modern Swiss Federal State had come into existence in 1848, this did not mean the end of cantonal, and regional, rivalries. These were far too deeply rooted in history to be expunged by a single act of federalism. An interesting, and amusing, example of just this peculiarly Swiss rivalry can be noted in the proliferation of banks during the mid-nineteenth century. There was an attempt on the part of the Basler Bankverein, the loose association of six private banks, to establish a joint stock bank in Zürich, which was fast becoming the major banking centre for Switzerland. This was to be accomplished with the aid of a Zürich private banker. The attempt, unfortunately, died in the process of negotiation in 1863, apparently because of the intense opposition from the Swiss Credit Bank as well as other potential competitors. Later, in 1865, J. Riggenbach, a member of the original Basler Bankverein, displayed his pique in a letter which read as follows: 'I should like to tell the gentlemen in Zürich that Basle does not feel itself called upon to help them out of the impasse in which their own pride has landed them.' The 'impasse' referred to here was the heavy burden of railroad financing which the Zürich banks, under the leadership of Alfred Escher, had undertaken.

THE RAILWAYS

The financing of the railways, in which the banks participated so heavily, stemmed from the Federal Law of 1852 which, despite opposition from many experts in the field, authorised the construction and operation of railroads to be in the hands of both the cantons and private enterprise. It also meant that the Swiss capital market, as well as foreign markets, became flooded with Swiss railway securities. On the strength of these securities the railway companies borrowed heavily, using bonded loans from the banks.

Cantons also sought their own piece of the action by borrowing for their own participation in railway construction. So heavy was the debt load on the railways that 'In 1861, out of a share capital of some 167 million francs invested in 611 kilometres of railway line, 100 million francs was paying no dividends.'[19] Very many of these shares were owned, of course, by foreigners, and since most of the debt was owned by banks and since 'the total proceeds of all the companies did not suffice to cover completely the interest payable on the debenture capital; at an average rate of interest of 15.022 per cent , there was a shortfall of SF1,388,108.'[20] This shortfall was considerable for the banks at that time and foreclosures became inevitable.[21] Fortunately, many of the more prominent banks did not rely on railway construction alone for their lending. It was these banks that survived to grow, to absorb their less fortunate competitors, and ultimately, to prosper.

There is one other factor which should be mentioned regarding the excesses of railway financing that took place during the period: a surplus of world bank liquidity. During the mid-nineteenth century, there were gold discoveries in California and Australia. These discoveries had the result of expanding the world's money supply. As imports into the US and Australia tended to be financed by the export of gold, the commodity exporting countries, mostly Europe, received additions to their monetary reserves of gold. At the same time, the exporters of commodities received additional purchasing power in their own currencies. These could be, and were, used for purchases of shares on the stock market, particularly those shares which were 'good buys'. The result was an inflated price level for speculative stock.

At the same time that stock prices rose in Europe, gold prices in gold-producing countries such as Australia fell rather considerably. It became profitable, then, for gold to be shipped from Australia to London or Paris (assuming price differentials were outside the gold shipping points, which they indeed were) directly from Australian banks to European banks. This enhanced the liquidity of European (including Swiss) banks, making possible an increase in lending for railway construction. In a word, as the demand for long-term credit increased, so did its supply because of the fortunate circumstance of an increase in the world's supply of gold.

Another factor in this particular episode was the fact that as the gold reserves in France increased, the French government reduced the gold/silver ratio to 1:15.5. Since Switzerland was on a silver standard (even though using the French franc system) *and* the Swiss did not adjust the silver ratio until 1860, it meant that a drain of gold coins from France to Switzerland was inevitable.[22] Furthermore, since France began the issue of 20 and 40 franc gold coins, there was an ample supply of coins. Swiss banks of issue, as well as other banking and commercial firms, accepted these coins in exchange for their own notes. What was obviously a source of embarrassment, as well as a source of important bank liquidity, finally came to an end with the establishment of the Latin Monetary Union in 1865. This union, including France, Belgium, Italy, Switzerland, and Greece, lasted until 1926.

CONCLUSION

In retrospect, we can recognise the evolving of modern Swiss banking from the European turmoil of the mid-eighteenth century. History converged on this particular period at the same time that demand for investment capital, both domestic and foreign, increased as never before. As far as the Swiss were concerned, the banks' development took the form of a method of intermediating between the supply and the demand for capital.

The ultimate form that Swiss banks would take was not at all clear in the nineteenth century. A more protracted evolutionary process was required before their shape could emerge. The Credit Mobilier type, though popular enough, had not yet been completely established, and the highly profitable practice of concentrating assets in foreign bonds and securities was still in its infancy. Commercial banking, on the other hand, had centuries of development behind it, especially in Basle where money changing, factoring, and the more modern bills of exchange were common. Finally, the practice of utilising deposits to finance mortgages, which had become quite common amongst cantonal banks and savings banks, grew and developed over the earlier decades of the nineteenth century.

At this point, however, we would do well to recall the four 'roots' of Swiss banking which we have identified:

1. The Italian commercial banking practices introduced by the Basle Synod.
2. The accumulation of capital due to the fighting skills of Swiss mercenaries.
3. The Protestant Reformation.
4. The banking philosophy of Saint Simonian banks (Credit Mobilier, etc.).

All four of these roots can be recognised in the continuous interplay of financing and re-financing, the formation of new banks, and the bankruptcies of some of the old, all in a swirling mass of bank intermediation which was characteristic of the nineteenth century. From this financial turmoil, the unique Swiss banking system was to evolve, capable of taking its place amongst the great banking structures of the world.

We might close this chapter with a repetition in the form of an answer to just one more question. What was the driving force which motivated the Swiss both to create and to hone their banking skills at that time? We would assert emphatically that in a small country possessed of the minimum of natural resources, banking and finance was the general field of economic activity which could be developed effectively and which could sustain many thousands in gainful employment. In so doing, it only required the use of the native intelligence of the population.

As a further caveat to this general observation, we would suggest that it was also the free market economic climate which prevailed throughout the country as early as the middle of the eighteenth century which suited the Swiss temperament admirably. Picture the pragmatic Swiss, the product of Zwingli and Calvin, at his best. He was free to develop his own talents in industry, including banking, not for the purpose of achieving his own 'glory' in the form of feudal titles or honours but to work both for himself and his fellow Swiss, all the while serving God in the manner that he saw it. It is precisely this traditional Swiss characteristic, we would suggest, which not only distinguished the Swiss from other Europeans but laid the foundation for the future of the nation.

Notes

1. The original forest cantons did, in fact, rebel, but to no avail because they were put down by the French army.
2. 'Studies in Political Economy, Essay III', quoted in Mill, J. S. *Principles of Political Economy* (London: Longmans Green and Co., 1902) p. 157.
3. Ibid., p. 159
4. Ibid, p. 159
5. *Switzerland, the South of France, and the Pyrenees in 1830*, Mill, *Principles*, p. 158.
6. McCulloch, J.R., *The Wealth of Nations* by Adam Smith, (Edinburgh: Adam and Charles Black, 1889), Book III, Chapter II, p. 173.
7. The criticisms of the *metayer* system by Arthur Young, McCulloch, and many other English economic writers are so many that it would be superfluous to attempt to list them here. Suffice it to say that wherever the system was practised poverty was the general rule.
8. Saint-Simon, *Lettres d'un Habitant de Geneve. Oeures Cloise's*, Vol. 1, p. 12., taken from Gray, Alexander, *The Socialist Tradition* Longmans Gran & Co. London, 1947, p. 140. There is no evidence to suggest that Saint-Simon had ever resided in Geneva; however, he did appear to be influenced by the somewhat Calvinist philosophy of Switzerland. His Socialism suggests that the poor should labour for the rich who, in turn, will use their brains to direct the poor, thus rendering a consistency in the obligation to be useful to humanity.
9. In an industrial society, conceived as such, one will always see a leader and inferiors, bosses and dependants, masters and apprentices. Everywhere legitimate authority exists because the leader is more capable; everywhere there is free obedience because the leader is loved; there is order everywhere. No worker lacks guidance and support in this vast workshop. All have instruments they know how to use, work they love to do. All work – no longer to exploit men, not even to exploit the globe – but to embellish the globe by their endeavors, and to adorn themselves with all the riches the globe can give them. *Ibid.*, p. 106.
10. On the other hand, it must be conceded that the Swiss democracy bears an extraordinary resemblance to what Saint-Simon originally had in mind. Swiss politicians, before they enter politics, must distinguish themselves in other lines of activity such as business, law or academic. This contrasts strongly with our western system which encourages those who are singularly undistinguished, if not failures, in their respective fields of endeavour to enter politics as a last resort. The result is mediocrity with all its consequences in our governments.
11. Prof. Gray in his charming book, *The Socialist Tradition*, suggests that Saint-Simon's writings are a confused jungle... 'He was always writing to catch the post.' These phrases are apt and certainly catch the hodge-podge which Saint-Simonians were teaching. Nevertheless, one ought not to forget the times in which they were living, that is transitory society groping for new solutions. Whether we characterise their writings as the beginnings of Socialism or the *Furtherprinzip* is immaterial; the fact is

that they were well ahead of their time. Gray, A. *The Socialist Tradition*, Longmans Gran & Co., London, 1947, p. 138.

12. There is a confusion here between the terms Credit Foncier and Credit Mobilier. The former has reference to the provision of credit for construction of fixed assets in general, whereas the latter, as the title suggests, is for the finance of movable assets. In practice, the terms have been loosely applied to either type of asset. It is interesting that the Credit Mobilier of America was patterned after that of the original Credit Mobilier of France for the purpose of constructing the Union Pacific Railroad during the American Civil War. See Crawford, J. B., *The Credit Mobilier of America* (Boston: C. W. Calkins & Co., 1880).

13. Modern readers may well be surprised at the liberality of the legal limit of debt permitted by the law at the time. Certainly the Credit Mobilier was doomed, as it were, to collapse in a tangled mass of debt and scandal.

14. There is a considerable discrepancy here. Fehrenbach mentions only 7 per cent of the land area as 'farmable', without a definition of the term. The 71.7 per cent referred to must include livestock grazing and so on, which, when defined as 'productive', can include the mountain sides. Forests and vines are also included as productive. Thus 'unproductive' land means land under buildings, towns, glaciers, lakes and rivers. Encyclopaedia Britannica, Ninth Edition, Vol. XXII, p. 776.

15. Hans Bauer, *Swiss Bank Corporation, 1872–1972*, Swiss Bank Corporation, Basle, 1972, p. 26.

16. We must always remember that the Basle area consisted of Alsace and neighbouring southern Germany as well as Switzerland; hence the Basle bankers referred to in the text were by no means 'small', only relatively so in the sense that alone they could not grant loans for the construction of railways or other very large-scale enterprises which were becoming the 'in thing' by mid-nineteenth century.

17. Ernst Blessing, Freiherr Friedrich von Rothkirch, 1826–86. This statement aptly expresses the mania of finance company formations during the early part of the decade of the 1860s. Bauer, *op cit*, p. 38.

18. Gide C. and Rist C., *A History of Economic Doctrines*, (London: Harrap and Co., 1948), pp. 362–3. On the Continent, the term *Manchesterthum* was applied to this particular doctrine by its socialist critics.

19. Bauer, Hans, *Swiss Bank Corporation, 1972–1972*, Swiss Bank Corporation, Basle, 1972, p. 39.

20. Ibid., p. 39.

21. One should add that the construction of railway lines in Switzerland, doubtless as elsewhere, reached the stage of a mania. Thoughtless construction of lines, not only between cities but *outward* from cities into the countryside, without a population centre as a terminus, took place.

22. It is always worthwhile to be precise on these points. Suppose the ratio in Switzerland is 1:16. A gold unit can be exchanged for 16 silver units in Switzerland, then, purchasing another gold unit for 15.5 silver units in France yields a 0.5 silver unit profit. The process can be repeated endlessly, until no gold is left in France or either the ratio or the exchange rate is changed.

5 Savings Banking and the Industrial Revolution

The nineteenth century may be characterised as not only the flowering of the industrial revolution but also the development of modern banking to the effective and efficient institution for the transmission of payments that we know today. In this the British certainly led the way, to be quickly followed by other countries in Europe and North America. From note-issuing banks in the earlier years of the century to cheque accounts and demand deposits, the banks proved themselves to be both at the centre of economic development and necessary to the efficiency of the growing economies of the world.

It has been asserted by many, including Franz Ritzmann, that Swiss banking was late in arriving on the European scene of banking development, not becoming mature until the mid-nineteenth century. We would argue that this depends entirely upon the definition of the term 'banking' which happens to be generally accepted. In previous pages, we have shown that under the old Confederation, as well as during the Holy Roman Empire, Basle, in particular, was at the forefront of monetary and financial development and was the major source of supply for the money requirement of the day. If Swiss banks were relatively late in evolving, the reason surely was that the economics of Swiss society did not require their services. It was as simple as that.

By the year 1840, Basle had sixteen bankers, active in the process of acquiring capital where it was in surplus and lending it to where it was in demand. Were these institutions 'banks' in the modern sense of the word? Hardly. However, we can readily identify their influence in the development of the modern Swiss bank, especially the private banks.

As a financial centre for long term borrowing and the investment of capital, Basle had achieved a high degree of efficiency. The 'partial loan', whereby an individual lender need only supply a part of the borrower's loan requirements, was a Basle development. The Basle bankers were arranging and combining these partial loans into the one large loan which the borrower required, thereby acting as true intermediaries between the borrower and groups of lenders. They were, in effect, merchant bankers similar to the great modern merchant banking houses of England. As such they provided the capital for the development of industry in Alsace and southern Baden as well as in Switzerland itself.

The Basle bankers were not the only merchant bankers in Switzerland. There were many in Geneva, the forerunners of the well known private bankers who are still very active in Switzerland today.[1] They were indicative of a society that was rich in capital and which sought its outlet in the foreign sector for the simple reason that domestic investment possibilities were just not sufficient.

In a Europe in the throes of an industrial revolution, struggling to locate capital as well as the savings to provide the capital, Switzerland stands out in sharp contrast. Switzerland was a creditor country and had been for the two centuries or so preceding the industrial revolution. It would be no exaggeration to suggest that Switzerland was the equivalent of Japan in our modern era.

We have already noted the considerable amount of gold brought into the old Confederation by the pensions and the soldiers themselves. In addition there was the unfortunate circumstance, though fortunate for Switzerland, of the Thirty Years War from which the Confederation greatly profited through its exports. Indeed, there must been a considerable surplus in the balance of trade for the Swiss Confederation during those early years.

Under these conditions, is it possible for banking, as we know it, to develop? Banking, as Bagehot had suggested, is productive when the deposits of the nation are applied to a developing industry for which the marginal product is high – higher than the marginal product of an industry for which, without banking, the deposits (or wealth) would have been used. The interest rate charged to the developing industry for bank loans was determined largely by this higher marginal product; whereas the interest rate on deposits reflected the marginal product for wealth which would have been invested elsewhere without the intermediation of banking. The force of competition from these sources of alternative demand for investment ensured this.

Already Switzerland had achieved one of the highest levels of industrial development in Europe. (This, we recall, was prior to the arrival of the industrial revolution to Switzerland and, of course, the railroads.) The populations of the cantons could not furnish a demand for domestically-mass-produced goods which were already forthcoming from English factories and were being exported to the Continent.

Ritzmann notes, as an exception, the establishment by public law in 1752 of a cloth savings bank in St Gallen, to assist the linen industry which was suffering from excessive competition from abroad. The additional capital pumped into the industry at that time was successful in bringing back the industry to health, so much so that another cotton cloth savings bank was established in 1788. This second bank, however, fared much worse than the first because its resources were just not required. The industry preferred its own private funding, and the bank had little opportunity for alternative domestic investment of its own funds.

In general, this was true of most banks in the old Confederation. There was a surplus of funds relative to domestic investment possibilities and this resulted in banks seeking outlets in other countries. The marginal product of capital, hence the interest rate, was higher in other countries than within the Swiss cantons themselves. This is why the early Swiss banks, particularly the private banks, became hardly more than investment houses channelling surplus Swiss capital to those areas outside Switzerland where investment opportunities were more profitable.

Public funds in Berne and Zürich cantons were also invested in this way, with the result that an inflow of interest returns took place which made possible a number of public undertakings within those cantons. This is the consequence of an amount of capital which is large relative to the size (population and area) of the canton which invests it. Banking in the old Confederation, just as in England, sought the highest marginal product, and since this lay outside Switzerland, the result was not an expansion of Swiss domestic industry but a return inflow of interest payments into the cantons which became sufficiently great as to make the cantons truly prosperous. Swiss banks were thus forced into learning the techniques of foreign banking which were to make them, in this aspect, second to none in the world.

When reference here is made to 'Swiss banks', it must be kept in mind that only a relatively few (relative to the population) bankers became proficient in the art of investing the wealth of the wealthy ruling class. Their location was Switzerland but their activity was investment abroad. Banking was not yet the prerogative of the masses. Nor did these bankers assist in the movement of goods by means of short-term credit as had been the practice of the English banks since the time of Queen Elizabeth. Banks in England had attempted to alleviate a shortage of money by means of transferring the ownership of deposits (primitive cheque accounts) thereby making possible an increase in commerce which could not have occurred otherwise. Business transactions had taken place in this way which would not have been possible on the basis of a purely gold specie transfer.

This was not true in Switzerland. Any shortages of coin were accommodated by debasement – a rudimentary method at best – to be adjusted once more when gold became more abundant. What credit requirements were necessary in trade were taken care of by the merchants themselves.

The Banks of the Masses, the Savings Banks of Switzerland

Into this banking structure were introduced the savings banks, somewhat late in the post-Napoleonic period.[2] It appears that a writer, Jeremias Gotthelf, was particularly eloquent in praise of the ethical aspect of the savings bank '... in order to provide this beneficial institution with still greater beneficial extension and effectiveness among the poorer classes, in order to save many of the silver coins which run down the throat or evaporate in the wind, so that they proliferate and grow into francs...'.[3]

There is an extraordinary, almost innocent, lack of knowledge of the banking processes in all of this. We can understand the concept of savings banks in England, France, and Germany, but we are hard put to explain the logic of collecting the savings of the masses without any objective for their investment. Without a shortage of capital (to the contrary a surplus) what are the savings for? The only real purpose served by such an accumulation of capital was to apply downward pressure on domestic mortgage interest rates, the only outlet for the capital of savings banks being mortgages, and thereby to encourage a still further outflow of capital abroad.

But this is surely a short-term, relatively narrow point of view. More importantly, a banking habit was introduced to the general public and encouraged by these institutions. With the emphasis placed upon the liabilities of the savings banks, the advantages in terms of security and interest earned could offer the poor the opportunity to take charge of their own destinies, something denied them heretofore. It was this, we would suggest, rather than the capital accumulation *per se*, which was the greatest contribution of the Swiss savings banks. In other words, the emphasis of the early banks lay in the insurance aspect; deposits, either obligational or just encouraged, were easy to place into the banks but difficult to remove. In this way the thrifty habits of the poor were encouraged.

Savings banks in Switzerland first orginated in the towns. For example, Niklaus Tscharner, a member of the ruling elite of Berne, was the acknowledged 'father' of the Dienstentzinskasse. This bank, founded in 1787, was designed, firstly, as a means of relieving the welfare rolls and secondly, to provide a pension to ease the burden of labour during old age. It was a bank for servants and manual workers employed by the citizens of the town. Rather curiously, the amounts deposited had to be regulated and depositors identified so as to eliminate the deposits of the more affluent citizenry who also found the savings bank a useful device for their own savings. These additional deposits of the affluent were considered to be a 'burden' to the bank since they necessarily involved some kind of placement in investment which would yield a return greater than that of the interest rate paid on the deposit.

The savings bank in Zürich, founded in 1805, is the oldest still in existence. Its original objectives were precisely the same as all other similar banks and it was patterned after the Hamburg bank. It provided for capital subscriptions and a reserve fund from which losses could be made good and deposits thereby protected. Small weekly contributions were the general rule, but, and this is the important point, withdrawals required six months notice! Even after the lapse of six months, a complicated arrangement of visiting the receiver, the bookkeeper, and the teller, all of whom lived in different areas, followed.

The complex procedures designed by the wealthy to look after the savings of the poor was formidable. Twenty directors, of whom two were Schlüssler (to guard the cash box), a teller who had to be 'guaranteed' by two worthy citizens, and a bookkeeper were members of the board. Noting that all these services were unpaid, purely voluntary, so that administrative costs were absolutely minimal, we can recognise the spirit of paternalism involved in the establishing and operation of these banks. Indeed, this was the characteristic of all such banks that were established in Swiss towns. The depositors were largely servants, workers, small merchants (Kaufleute), employees, and the like which were the poorer people of the towns. Always the objective of the savings banks was in the forefront – the more these people could look after themselves through their own savings, the less would be the burden upon the welfare system of the community. In the countryside, savings banks did not make their appearance until somewhat later, about 1815, after the most powerful revolutionary change Switzerland had ever experienced.

One can appreciate the extent to which some 'federalist' Swiss might have welcomed the change to the revolutionary Helvetic Republic, for the old Confederation had already outlived its usefulness. But the Helvetic Republic had moved too far in the direction of centralisation, and to find a median was not easy. The violent discussions which ensued were an attempt at just such a restructuring of Switzerland, and finally resulted in the Act of Mediation in which Napoleon outlined the basic structure of a new Confederation, the fundamentals of which had a strong influence on the future of the nation. Once again the privileged classes were removed, the subject lands were eliminated, and the right of settlement anywhere in the country was assured. Also, of course, a close alliance with France was included in the Act.

Guaranteed by Bonaparte, the entire fabric of the new constitution depended upon his fate; therefore, with the fall of Napoleon, reactionary forces could re-assert themselves once more in the Constitution of 1815 in which the Congress of Vienna acted as arbiter between the conservatives (Berne in particular) and the more progressive majority headed by Zürich. Once again a new constitution was accepted by the Diet, this time with a return to the lines of the old constitution, particularly regarding cantonal rights. When compared to the Napoleonic constitution of 1803, however, this new constitution was definitely a victory for reaction.

These were certainly trying times for the Swiss masses – rights were granted to them, then removed a decade or so later. Further, much of the common lands were eliminated by the new constitution, thereby removing an important source of income security for farmers. Thus, while freedom was gained, to be sure, there was a price, that of security lost.

But there was another, perhaps more important, feature of the Swiss economy of the day which must be carefully considered. This was the Swiss farmer's independence of the market place, as eloquently described by Sismondi (see Chapter 4). Farmers raised their own food, prepared their own dairy products, and were generally self sufficient and, of course, independent.

The Swiss farmers of the day must surely have been the most successful of all their counterparts in other countries in achieving this independence of the market place. At the same time, however, as we noted in Chapter 4, many of them were in debt to the banks for their land. This meant that some cash must be provided for in the farmers' alternative activity which was generally hand work such as embroidery, wood carving, straw plaiting, and the like. Indeed, such industries as these were important exports of early Switzerland.

Such industries as these required a use of cash, and since note-issuing banks did not arrive in Switzerland until the decade of the 1830s, specie was the only form of cash which was acceptable. We can readily perceive the result. Farmers, the economic mainstay of the entire confederation, had to use their own cash boxes, until the arrival of the savings bank which could provide a much more secure method of holding surplus cash. Furthermore, the possibility of interest being earned on deposits must have seemed attractive so that farmers had every reason *not* to hold their cash in their own boxes.

The arrival of the industrial revolution in Switzerland, unlike that in England, began in rural areas, valleys, and villages. Along with it came a monetised economy – a shift from Sismondi's description of a direct consumption-type agriculture to the production of a surplus for sale on the market. This agricultural surplus was required to satisfy the needs of the growing numbers employed in mechanised silk and cotton mills.

Monetisation, or the introduction of money and markets, necessarily involves a quantity of money to circulate from hand to hand. Without note-issuing banks in rural communities, the currency system is inelastic, incapable of expansion. The savings bank offered an alternative to this inelastic currency, and we find that after 1815, during the political turmoils of the post-Napoleonic era, the savings banks proliferated throughout the countryside. Instead of hoarding specie, farmers could return the coins into circulation by acquiring savings deposits, which in turn were used to finance mortgages so that the same farmers could expand their land area to increase production. In this way, a re-circulation of specie, the combination of mortgage debt and savings deposits, relieved a shortage of currency.

At the same time, the pressures of politics, the loss of common lands, and the desire for new machinery to increase the output of cottage industry all conspired to expand the number of savings banks throughout the Swiss countryside. In effect, the propensity to save was being increased by both political circumstances and the forces of economic change. It also helped to explain the large numbers of deposits in Switzerland relative to note circulation.

Under these circumstances, the success of the savings bank movement throughout the countryside of Switzerland was understandable. It must be noted, however, that the spread of the banks was largely in Protestant Switzerland: the northern cantons. We find them concentrated in St Gall in the east, Zürich canton, Aarau, the northern half-canton of Appenzell and fairly evenly distributed throughout Berne and the cantons of the west. Curiously, the Catholic regions did not accept these institutions to the same extent. We have little rational explanation for this aside from the Protestant ethic suggested in Chapter 3.

If the argument that the Protestant ethic lent itself to saving be accepted, it suggests that the savings bank movement as a whole did less to increase the propensity to save, it rather liberated existing savings from the strong boxes (or whatever) of farmers and factory workers. The cash was put back into circulation by the loans and investments of the savings banks. On the other hand, to the extent that the savings bank movement followed the growth and spread of factories, it is quite possible that the propensity to save was indeed increased. Factory workers, who became a 'landless proletariat', were given an opportunity to provide an estate of sorts for their own social security, and like their English counterparts would be less of a burden on the community than would otherwise have been the case.

BANKING, AN OUTGROWTH OF CIRCUMSTANCE

The success of the savings bank movement in Switzerland during the early years of the nineteenth century contrasts sharply with the failure of the 'commercial bank': the note-issuing bank which had found such fertile ground in the English economy. There are two fundamental reasons for this. Firstly, there was a political system based upon autonomous cantons, with limited movement of citizens from canton to canton. We can visualise such a situation. Should a potentially successful businessman wish to establish himself in a neighbouring canton and thereby spread his talents more widely than his own limited home territory, he would find it difficult to do so (not completely impossible, however). This restriction meant that one potential demand for bank credit was severely limited by the political circumstance of the time. By being thus restricted, his ambitions for expansion were limited to his own narrow region and to his home plant; consequently, his own savings were quite adequate and credit which could have been made available to him from domestic savings were unnecessary. In this way an important outlet for domestic investment was simply not available.

Secondly, each canton, before the establishment of a common currency after the coin reform in 1852–3, had its own preferred currency. This further restricted the possibility of investment for the simple reason that a rate of exchange intervened in any transaction should an entrepreneur wish to expand production in a neighbouring canton.

During the period of the Helvetic Republic, a common currency, the franc, was introduced into all of Switzerland. Regretfully, however, the cantons refused to accept this important innovation and proceeded to return to the issue of their own currencies after 1803 with the result that surpluses of crowns (fractions of francs) were circulating uselessly and were finally destroyed in 1830. Effectively, the cantons had opted not for a modern world of finance and commerce but for a continuation of the monetary chaos of the old Confederation which made it impossible for commercial banking to develop. We might even suggest further that trade and commerce could only suffer as well.[4]

The circumstance of a completely disunited (disunited in every sense of the word, including currency) Confederation, and, at the same time, a people who had already developed a strong propensity to save, accounts in large measure for the growth of the savings bank movement, on the one hand, and the failure of note-issuing banks on the other. The savings banks, established by prominent persons and/or welfare societies with well-known individuals as functionaries, gave the saver a measure of security which would otherwise not have existed.

BANKS OF NOTE-ISSUE

Still more difficult was the lot of the note-issuing bank. It was Walter Bagehot who had argued that the right of note-issue is the necessary forerunner of the deposit mechanism. Granted that notes were lighter and more easily handled than coin, the problem that remained was in which of the cantonal currencies would the banknote be issued? But more importantly, since the French experience with the Law scheme as well as the Revolutionary *assignats* was bitter enough, and the Swiss by nature were (and still are) conservative, how does a bank encourage the public to accept its notes? It is, after all, the Swiss workers, farmers, and so on who must, in the last analysis, accept banknotes in payment for their labours, and this was not an easy adjustment.

Nevertheless, the course of events appeared to move in the direction of bringing the Confederation into the nineteenth century, albeit 'kicking and screaming'. Swiss exports were increasing, especially to more distant markets such as Great Britain and the United States. The traditional export market, Germany, had been discouraged by the high German tariffs under the influence of Friedrich List, forcing Swiss exporters to go further afield for their markets. In this sense, and in this sense only, there appeared to be a shortage of the means of finance, such as trade bills and discount facilities, which the exporter could use to expedite commercial activity.

Under ordinary circumstances, the Swiss exporter would have presented a trade bill, drawn on London, for discount at the local bank, thence to be paid in the banknotes of that bank. This was the normal practice of any commercial bank. However, issuing notes (which are merely an extension of the bank's credit facility) by discounting trade bills is one thing – payment in specie (which is not credit) is quite another. Since exporters preferred coin to paper, the inability to extend short-term credit facilities through banknote issue certainly must have retarded commercial banking development for many years. The reason, as observed above, was that there was no shortage of money (coin) and the average Swiss was reluctant to accept notes in lieu of coin.

The first bank of note-issue in Switzerland was established in Berne as the Cantonal Bank of Berne in 1834. It was a government bank which, because Berne was not yet ready for such bank facilities as discounting and note issue, languished for two decades with little activity. Both note issue and lending were too small to be of consequence. It was followed by the Zürich bank of note-issue which was begun in June of 1837. Here again the purpose was to serve as a discount bank as well as issuing, notes in order to facilitate domestic payments transactions. The third bank of note-issue appeared in St Gallen in September of that same year; in this instance, the purpose of the bank was to assist the textile industry in its export activities. In both cases, Zürich and St Gallen, foreign participation (relative to domestic) was strong.

Somewhat later, and quite different from these two banks, the Bank in Basle was formed in 1844, though technically not named the 'Bank in Basle' until the year following. In the case of this bank it was the monumental efforts of one man, Johann Jakob Speiser, that eventually succeeded in establishing the bank despite the opposition of the existing bankers in Basle, the leading financial centre of the Confederation at the time. Speiser had gained considerable knowledge of the operation of commercial banks in England and Holland and recognised the advantages to commercial and business enterprise of these institutions. Considering the fact that Basle had 16 active bankers in 1840, with a population of just 24,000, any contemporary might have considered the city to be 'over-banked'. Speiser's argument, familiar enough to our modern eyes, is best summed up in the following quotation:

The heavy monetary turnover required by thriving trade, the frequent cash transactions in the form of both receipts and expenditures, and the necessity of carrying money about on the person, put a businessman to expense in keeping a staff to deal with all these aspects, without considering the losses that might be incurred. The safekeeping of the money also involves trouble and calls for installations which are not always proof against care and anxiety. A bank relieves commerce of all such burdens. England and Holland have had favourable experience of these institutions for centuries, and it is partly due to them that these countries and their industries have made such enormous advances. Recently all French commercial cities have followed one another in setting up banks; the results in terms of soundness and usefulness, and profit for their operators, are well known.[5]

The modern researcher has the impression that Speiser literally had to 'squeeze' his banking philosophy into the Basle banking community. Conservative as a rule, most bankers of the time perceived the new bank to be a potential competitor because its operations, similar to the other two private banks in Zürich and St Gallen (excluding the Cantonal Bank of Berne), embraced the discount of local bills, Lombard loans, note issuing, non-interest-bearing sight deposits, interest-bearing time deposits, purchase of giro and collection of accounts, and, of course, the covering of all deposits with reserves. We note that most of these activities, which are really quite familiar to the modern mind, are simply the functions of a typical commercial bank already well developed in England. The Basle bankers, however, did not conceive of such a bank as anything but competition for them. '. . . industry and commerce find an abundance of capital in Basle and, indeed, foreign industry draws upon it daily'. 'After all why start a discount bank when the people who are expected to implement or support this project are the very ones who would lose their living?'[6]

Despite the opposition, Speiser was able to set up the Giro und Depositenbank in 1844, a year later to become simply the Bank in Basle. The bank's funds came from paid-up capital of 118,000 French francs, later raised to one million, but due to the declining economic conditions which preceded the upheavals in Paris in 1848, half the capital was repaid because the amount of capital relative to the small amount of business transacted was too great. Like the other two private banks, the Bank in Basle was ahead of its time. Discounting business was sluggish, and note issuing was small. All three of them became hardly more than local lending banks, relying upon their own funds for their loan finance.

In suggesting that the three banks arrived too soon, we are also suggesting that the economic and political conditions of the old Confederation were not conducive to the development of commercial banking. This, of course, contrasts sharply with the British banking system which had already achieved a high degree of perfection. The money and banking system of Britain had proven itself to be a flourishing productive industry making a major contribution to British industry. Paper money in Great Britain was already declining in relative importance and the cheque account, which utilised (and still does, of course) the services of the clearing banks, was the principal means of payment. In Switzerland, by contrast, cantonal barriers to trade still existed, both by customs barriers and by 'hidden tariffs' in the form of differing cantonal laws, literally awaiting the the establishment of the new Swiss Federal State in 1848. Under such conditions, an efficient commercial banking system had no purpose, no *raison d'être*.

Indeed, in a larger sense, the Swiss were really not much different from the rest of the Continent. Everywhere there was a surplus of coins. Protective tariffs in France and the Zollverein in Germany had already discouraged Swiss imports as well as imports from other neighbouring countries. In other words, throughout the Continent the necessity for a modern commercial banking system had not yet arrived. Certainly not in Switzerland.

Probably most important of all, however, in Continental countries as well as in Switzerland, was the absence of central banks which were capable of managing government debt, on the one hand, and the note issue on the other. Once Peel's Bank Act of 1844 was introduced, which limited the note issue of the Bank of England, it was a small step for British banks to introduce a substitute for bank notes, the cheque account. Following Bagehot's principle, the banks had used their own banknotes to facilitate commerce, then when the banknotes became limited, they developed their own substitute which proved to be much more efficient than the banknote system.

In a capital-rich country such as Switzerland, there was ample opportunity for industry to develop within small regions. We recall that Switzerland was, during the seventeenth and eighteenth centuries, the most industrially developed country of Europe. For the Swiss, the industrial development of the previous centuries, such as it was, combined with a capital surplus, became an industrial launching platform, awaiting the establishment of the new federal state in 1848.

CONCLUSION

This brings us to the important point: did a Swiss banking system truly exist prior to 1848? The answer, we would argue, is definitely yes. Banks not only existed but performed very well given the constraints of the old Confederation. Similarly, with the advent of industrial growth and development, Swiss capital was very important to the region of Alsace, southern Germany, and France. The Swiss bankers that provided the capital, however, were private bankers who were scarcely more than 'investing houses', many of them Protestant bankers whose ancestors had escaped from France to Geneva.

In the matter of credit between cantons (that is, from those with capital surpluses to those with shortages) Swiss bankers effectively made the transfer, and contributed mightily toward holding the Confederation together. Thus, the true function of the early Swiss banker was one of acting as a conduit transferring capital surpluses to shortages. This was the only banking function available to them. This same function, the conduit, appears in the Swiss banking system even today, and the skills and knowledge required for the complex international banking system which we have in modern times were gathered long ago.

In a word, the Swiss banking system had progressed just as far as it could within the political and economic constraints imposed upon it both within the old Confederation as well as outside it. We would again stress the point made in the preceding chapter: the Swiss genius lies in the ability to utilise its indigenous resources, whatever they may be, to the maximum. In this case, the banking industry had developed to its maximum utilising the native Swiss intelligence, and capital surpluses, which were available to it. It only remained for the constraints to be relaxed, in this case the establishment of the new Confederation, for the banking industry to move forward and to develop its own unique characteristics.

Notes

1. Just prior to the French Revolution, Geneva banking houses were particularly strong in France, financing international trade and payments. In Paris, Geneva houses were represented by Jacques Mallet, Paul-Henri Mallet, Girardot, Haller and Co. and Etienne Delesselt. In Lyon, there were Benjamin Delesset from 1725, and Phillippe Gaillard, Grenus and

Co. and in Rouen, Lullin, Lemaire and Co. In London there were also Mestrezat, Rilliet and Co. and Liotard, Aubertin and Revier – to name a few. Usteri, Ott, Escher and Co. in Zürich should also be mentioned as the first private bank to carry on international business. These firms were practically showered with capital for foreign investment purposes even though at considerable risk, as subsequent events bore out, to the contributors and the bankers. Ritzmann, Franz, *Die Schweizer Banken* (Berne and Stuttgart: Verlag Paul Haupt, 1973) p. 21.

2.　　Daniel Defoe, in 1697 was, to the best of our knowledge, the first to conceive of the savings bank. The earliest institution of this type, the *Sparkassen*, or *Ersparungskasse*, appeared in Brunswick in 1765, to be followed by one in Hamburg in 1778, and at Oldenburg in 1790. A *caisse d'epargne* was formed at Loire in 1792 and the Basle regional mortgage bank in 1794. In 1797, Jeremy Bentham revived Defoe's original concept as 'Frugality Banks' and in 1799 the Rev. Joseph Smith opened one in Wendover. This was followed by many others throughout Great Britain and by legislation regulating them in 1817.

3.　　Ritzmann, *Die Schweizer Banker*, p. 23.

4.　　Ritzmann notes that when currency reform was finally introduced and the old currencies called in for exchange purposes, a total of 319 domestic coin types were discovered. He mentions a few: Dublonen, Ducaten, Gulden, Gold und Silberfranken, Batzen, Kreuzern, Schillingen (the more familiar issues in the cantons), Neutaler, Sonnentaler, Adlertaler, Diken, Boecke, Biesli, and Bluzger. The accounting problem involved in dealing with such a bewildering set of currencies is suggested by a handbook issued by the bank in Zürich suggesting that paper currency be used as an alternative to the expensive transport of metals. 'If merchant A received in payment for goods a barrel of money of about 20,000 florins, he would then have it taken immediately to the bank by the cart driver. There the money is counted and credited to Merchant A in the bank's books, while he quietly applies himself in his writing room to his other affairs, and does not have to trouble himself with either the counting or the safekeeping of this large sum. The bank gives him a pretty little book in pocket form (a passbook); he sends it, if his servant has something to arrange in that district anyway, to the bank, and there the 20,000 fl. are written in his little book as a credit.' Ritzmann, *Die Schweizer Banken*, p. 42. This is an argument for the use of paper currency by a note-issuing bank. We may imagine the problems involved when merchants must use coin only. They would of necessity have to employ people simply to move money, count it, and provide for its safe-keeping quite apart from the actual function of the merchant in moving goods.

5.　　Quoted by Hans Bauer in *Swiss Bank Corporation, 1872–1972*, pp. 20–21, Published by the Swiss Bank Corporation on the occasion of its centenary.

6.　　Bauer, *Swiss Bank Corporation, 1872–1972*, pp. 21–22.

6 The Development of a New Swiss Banking System

INTRODUCTION

Most of us are accustomed to think of the supply of money as an important economic variable within a complete macroeconomic system. This money supply, combined with the availability of bank credit, is a principal determinant of economic activity. By affecting the amount of credit (or its cost in terms of the interest rate) made available by the banking system, the central authority (or the central bank) can implement its monetary policy objectives as far as the economy is concerned. Moreover, when bank credit is translated into loans and deposits, the money supply is correspondingly affected. In this way economic activity can, supposedly, be controlled.

It is obvious that the supply of money, which today consists mostly of bank deposits, must be at the focus of attention as far as modern economies are concerned. Whether we adhere to a strict quantity theory of money in terms of either the Fisher or Cambridge version or a more modern Friedman approach, the fact remains that during our current years, at the close of the twentieth century, money supply, money and credit markets and the monetary policies followed by central authorities are the most significant discretionary variable in the control of inflation and/or unemployment.

This was not true during the middle years of the nineteenth century. To be sure, Great Britain had already had several experiences with the business cycle during which the money and credit supplied by banks had become 'misaligned', as it were, with the requirements of business activity. The result was the cycle of boom and slump precipitated, generally, by the banking system's failure to satisfy the need for credit at precisely the appropriate time. The key to this was the fact that business activity in Great Britain was already based upon the credit system which, in turn, is based upon confidence.

Confidence in the value of one's own capital is considerably more tenuous than one might expect. For centuries, gold had served as both an exchange medium and a store of value (capital). To shift, therefore, from gold to paper, which only promises to pay in gold, requires a considerable psychological adjustment. It was precisely this shift, from gold hoards to bank deposits for which the savings banks had been preparing the Swiss public for some fifty-odd years prior to the introduction of the new commercial bank. The banking habit was then, and is now, slow to acquire, but it is essential to a modern banking system.

One difficulty lay in the simple fact that Switzerland was not yet a federal state, only a confederation of independent cantons. To be sure, the agreement of 1815 had provided for a federation with a federal budget supported by customs duties and contributions from the cantons. However, with the passage of time and inevitable change, the cantons themselves had assumed increasing responsibility for economic development as well as for the infrastructure necessary for economic growth. This meant a growing need for cantonal revenues which took the form of tithes, royalties, customs duties and turnpike tolls. Twenty-two sovereign cantons within a relatively small area, each responsible for the welfare of its citizens, as well as infrastructure, meant that economies of scale, so absolutely vital for a modern banking system, were not possible.[1]

With the adoption of the new federal constitution in 1848 and the establishment of a federal state, many of the responsibilities of the individual cantons were turned over to the new state. Such tasks as the conduct of foreign policy, customs duties, postal services, weights and measures, coinage, and the defence of the cantons became the prerogatives of the new federal government. In the area of the protection of human rights, political and religious freedoms, and so on, the cantons retained their traditional role. At the same time, the cantons had to find new forms of taxes to support their own budgets, having surrendered much of their traditional sources of revenue to the federal state. But most important, as far as the banks were concerned, was the fact that banks could now cross cantonal boundaries and identify investment opportunities in other cantons without being subject to either a different set of taxes or a different monetary system. The scale economies which the federal state now made possible could at last work to the advantage of banks within Switzerland; hence the building of domestic bank assets could be just as advantageous to them as their portfolio of foreign assets.

THE SWISS BANKING MILIEU AT MID-CENTURY

It is not easy for us to transport our minds and attitudes back into an era long past, a century and a half ago, and into an environment of which we were never a part, but let us try. We recall that the Swiss were a people that had already raised themselves to the highest living standard of any in the world, and that they had done so entirely by their own efforts. Industry had grown and developed by means of the savings of entrepreneurs who had returned their profits to the business. Such a practice, laudable enough in itself, serves its purpose but fails in one important respect, that of developing a viable credit market. Thus, when the time finally arrived that it became sufficiently obvious that a requirement for credit existed, there was no market to handle the task of credit allocation.

When working efficiently, capital markets are extremely valuable to an economy. But the question remains: how is it possible to separate the practice of investment in one's own industry from investment elsewhere by way of a capital market? This is particularly difficult for entrepreneurs who believe fervently in the practice of self-finance. It is the interest-rate mechanism, the reward for loan of capital, which is the reward necessary to entice entrepreneurs to invest elsewhere. They recognise that by lending their own capital they can earn at least as much as they would by employing it themselves without, it should be added, the risk and trouble involved in using it themselves.

At the same time that bank formation after the fashion of the British was very much in vogue on the Continent, railroad building had likewise become popular. The underlying logic of the situation was quite simple; industry had already grown to such an extent that an improved and more efficient means of transport of both raw material and finished product was essential. In the Swiss case, it was even more important because the traditional north–south trade route was in danger of being by-passed should the Swiss not undertake the task of railroad construction.

But all this required considerable amounts of capital. The traditional Swiss business method of providing own capital from retained earnings was simply not adequate for the task of railroad construction. The only answer was a capital market which could allocate savings to the most advantageous use, in this case a highly capital-intensive method of transport. To be sure, the returns on such infrastructure would be long in coming, too long for many Swiss investors; nevertheless, the development of adequate transport facilities was an essential for further industrial progress in Switzerland. Some type of Credit Mobilier bank was the only reasonable method of collecting the capital, on the one hand, and allocating it to its most avantageous use on the other.

A UNIQUE INSTITUTION, THE BANKVEREIN

In Basle, the centre of Swiss banking and finance in the mid-nineteenth century, a group of private bankers had already agreed to form a joint stock company (1844), for the purpose of financing the manufacture of gas for lighting in the city. For some reason, we have no information as to why, the project did not proceed beyond the provisional agreement stage with the civic authorities, hence the immediate result was zero. It did prove, however, that private bankers could *in fact* cooperate in a financing venture of sorts, a 'first' in Swiss financial history.[2] This had occurred during the same year that Speiser's Giro und Depositenbank had opened for business in Basle (that is, 1844).

Even though the gas project had failed, the bankers were determined to continue their cooperative efforts at the same time that the Speiser bank was in operation, though, to be sure, hardly thriving. In other words, they perceived the new bank as a threat to their established positions and, to meet this new threat, it was to their advantage to cooperate rather than continue to compete amongst themselves. In this spirit of cooperation, rather 'un-Swiss-like' in character, they formed a Credit Mobilier type of institution, preferring the title Bankverein, purely as a defensive measure against Speiser's new bank.

The formation of the Bankverein, amidst the circumstances surrounding its inception, suggests an interesting characteristic of the Swiss psyche itself. While not attempting to seek explanations which are excessively 'romantic', it would seem that the very act of cooperation in the face of a joint threat to their existence is reminiscent of an earlier period when Swiss farmers, faced with a common enemy, cooperated with each other in battle. Or the willingness of cantonal governments to lend money to other cantons which happened to be in financial need, or the formation of a federal government involving the surrender of some privileges of independent cantonal governments, these also seem to be typically 'Swiss'. Such cooperation, however, takes place only when confronted with a common 'foe'; otherwise cooperation is unthinkable.

Considering that bank formation patterned after the British model was in vogue throughout Europe, Speiser's bank was actually a spearhead of this movement, which happened to be aimed at the very financial centre of Switzerland. The defensive reaction, of the bankers, therefore, was precisely as might have been predicted by any contemporary who understood this Swiss characteristic. Yet, the Basler Nachtrichten, the influential newspaper of the day, actually saw no reason for a Credit Mobilier type bank which the bankers were forming as a consortium.[3] In the face of influential opinion to the contrary, the Bankverein moved forward to identify and exploit, without being aware of its significance, a niche in the capital market which up to that time had not been occupied. It was this niche which proved to be the true demand for a new institution which was to become not just another Credit Mobilier but a world class Swiss bank. No one, certainly not the bankers who organised themselves into the consortium, could have foreseen the future development of their efforts. Nevertheless, it was the Bankverein itself, a typically Swiss defensive reaction, which lay at the beginning of the modern Swiss bank.

The success of the Bankverein, it would appear, was due to its *not* becoming a Credit Mobilier at the outset. Six private bankers merely combined their resources so as to finance considerably larger undertakings than would have been possible by each one separately, no more. As an example, we have the following five million franc loan to the Canton of Fribourg in 1858. It was distributed as follows:

Bischo zu St Alban	650,500
Ehinger & Cie	386,000
J. Merian Forcart	426,000
Passavant & Cie	2,722,500
J. Riggenbach	393,500
von Speyr & Cie	421,500
Total	5,000,000[4]

Each of the six members was to place these sums with clients. By holding rigidly to the loan business in this way, the Bankverein avoided competing with other private banks, maintaining its own unique position in the credit market. The Basler Handelsbank, on the other hand, consistently competed with the private bankers both through its commercial credit services and in larger scale lending, and this ultimately led to its downfall.

The Bankverein was always an extremely cautious group, scrutinising its loan applications with the greatest of care. Indeed, it demonstrated even further caution by not proceeding with the formation of a joint stock bank on its own; it preferred to wait until world conditions (that is, the American Civil War and the European quarrels of the 1860s) were settled. Amongst its more notable Swiss loans was included a loan to the Gotthard Railway in 1871. In all, between the time of its inception and its dissolution, some forty loans were granted by the *Bankverein* from the many proposed by the members, all carefully considered as to their credit-worthiness.[5]

Before it became a joint stock company, the Bankverein proved to be an excellent example of combining the resources of the six members to achieve economies of scale in financing. Joint administration of the group's lending meant that individual members were relieved of the onerous responsibilities which would be attendant upon all of them separately had they not been organised. That, plus the careful screening of loan applications, was the major reason for its success.

From the side of demand for loans, which had grown enormously because of Swiss industry and railway development, loan requirements had reached the point where small loans from individual private bankers were simply no longer feasible. Further, since foreign lending was not possible because of world events, the lending opportunities lay within Switzerland, and these the Bankverein used to its advantage. By avoiding the pitfalls of commercial banking and note issue, leaving those to the Handelsbank and Speiser's Giro und Depositenbank, it built upon a foundation of not only what it could do best but also of what Switzerland then needed most, an available source of capital.

It is interesting that with the beginnings of both the industrial revolution and the construction of its capital intensive railways, Switzerland had been transformed in scarcely more than two decades from a capital-rich country into one of acute capital shortages. The Switzerland of the old Confederation, with its small scale, highly skilled, craft industry, had already become past history. In this sense, 1848 was a watershed year both politically and economically, for from that year forward the demand for capital investment greatly exceeded the supply. In mobilising scarce capital resources to be used for economic growth and infrastructural investment, the Bankverein discovered its important position in the capital market as referred to above.

THE SWISS CREDIT BANK

Unlike the Bankverein, which was a cooperative effort of bankers with common cause, the Swiss Credit Bank had originated with the express purpose of becoming a Credit Mobilier in the true sense of the word. Again, unlike Fazy's Banque Generale, the objective of the Bank was much more modest, more realistic, more appropriate to the time. Indeed, the only thing the two institutions had in common was that they were led by men of considerable vision and prominence. We might include here that in Switzerland 'men of prominence' did not mean just industrialists or financiers but politicians as well.

Alfred Escher was one of these. He realised the importance to Switzerland of maintaining the transport route via the St Gotthard Pass through Ticino to the Lombardy plain. The achievement of this monumental task required credit which only a Credit Mobilier type of bank could mobilise. But most important to Escher was the fact that the Swiss must remain in control of such a bank. In 1856 he approached the Rothschilds of Paris for financing assistance, but because of the French insistence upon control, the negotiations failed. It was at this point that Escher decided upon the Credit Mobilier. He managed to gain the 50 per cent participation of the new Allgemeine Deutsche Kredtanstalt of Leipzig without any attempt at control. Of the balance of the total of 15 million francs, 7.5 million francs, 3 million was for Escher's own group, and 4.5 million francs for the government of Zürich and the public. When the government refused to participate, the entire 4.5 million francs worth of shares was offered to the public. To the surprise of Escher (and everyone else) the offering was greatly oversubscribed.[6]

The astonishing success of the initial offering is suggestive of two important factors: the first is the great availability of funds which had been amassed by Zürich business enterprise over the years; over and above, we might add, their own business requirements. It is suggestive of the prosperity enjoyed by the Swiss during their early years of growth and development. Secondly, the Paris Credit Mobilier itself was still enjoying considerable prestige with prices of its stock rising; hence the idea of a Swiss counterpart must have been seen as an attractive investment, even for the conservative Zuricher.

Still, one cannot but admire the vision of Escher, who not only conceived but planned his bank in such a way as to avoid the mistakes of the Periere brothers. In particular, instead of an overextension of bonds sold to the public to a value many times that of shares, as was the Paris case, the Swiss version was restricted in its bonded debt to an amount equal to its subscribed capital. In addition, the early bank practised strong risk diversification tactics, more so than other banks of its type. Short- and medium-term credits occupied some considerable amount of its balance sheet structure along with the development of other long-term industrial activities. Significant also was emphasis upon the participation of the bank in developing enterprises; to take them over, if necessary, and to be involved in their administration.[7] Eventually, the bank undertook a complete universal banking program involving bond issues to the value of shares, the establishment of affiliated institutions, branch banks, partly owned subsidiaries, deposit banking, bill discounting and brokerage, and trade in securities and precious metals.

When comparing the activities of this bank with that of the Periere brothers or the original Saint-Simonian concept of a universal bank, it is difficult to recognise that they could possibly have shared a common origin, the notable exception being the Swiss Credit Bank's heavy involvment with the building of railways, the Nord-Ost Bahn in particular. But so was the Bankverein; indeed, railway construction was an investment of top priority in Switzerland at the time.

As might have been expected during the bank's earlier, formative years in the 1860s, there was an inevitable excess of investment of assets in railways as well as in other industrial undertakings both at home and abroad. This necessitated a realignment of industrial risk in those areas other than railroads and which took the form of more investment in less risky food and machinery and reduced investment in greater risk textiles. This was particularly important because it prepared the way for withstanding the very heavy financial responsibility for the St. Gotthard. As the decade of the 1870s emerged, it was clear that the Swiss Credit Bank was actually emerging as a truly Swiss Universal Bank (or Credit Mobilier if that is what the term was supposed to have meant). Escher himself lived to see his bank through its period of *sturm und drang*, for he died in 1882.

SWITZERLAND AND THE EUROPE OF THE 1860s

The Swiss did not develop their financial institutions in a vacuum; otherwise there could have been no development at all. Early nineteenth century Europe was a ferment of industrial activity determined, as it were, to catch up, if not surpass, the lead of Great Britain. Long before Escher's masterstroke in Credit Mobilier banking in Zürich, the Belgians had established in 1822 (even before the Belgian independence from The Netherlands) the *Société Générale pour favoriser l'industrie nationale*. This was a bank, complete with note issuing powers, which was the custodian of savings bank funds and, most important, invested in industrial enterprises. In other words, there was a Credit Mobilier with the right of note issue which existed some 30 years before the Pereire brothers' own efforts. Whether or not the Société Générale was a Belgian concern or Dutch (King William was a principal shareholder) the fact was that it became Belgian after 1830. With the Société Générale and the Banque de Belgique, which rivalled it with note-issuing of its own, and the other banks, the Bank of Flanders and the Banque Liégeoise which followed shortly thereafter, the Belgians were well prepared, in terms of finance, to undertake the great railroad building efforts in which they were truly pioneers.

The fact of the matter was that the Continental banks of the early nineteenth century became absolutely vital as far as industrial growth was concerned. It is interesting that both history and theory are in complete agreement here, for it was the joint-stock method of industrial organisation which made possible, first, the development of banks, then, through the banks, the financing of actual producing companies or projects. The problem lay in the high risk factor involved in forming new endeavours during the period.

Adam Smith made this very clear in his argument concerning joint-stock companies and monopolies. Because of the high risk involved, joint-stock companies formed for commercial purposes must have a monopoly granted them for a period of time only (not in perpetuity) in order to compensate investors for the great risk of loss of their capital. Indeed, and we quote:

> The only trades which it seems possible for a joint stock company to carry on successfully, without an exclusive privilege, are those of which all the operations are capable of being reduced to what is called a routine, or to such a uniformity of method as admits of little or no variation. Of this kind is, first, the banking trade; secondly, the trade of insurance from fire, and from sea risk and capture in time of war; thirdly, the trade of making and maintaining a navigable cut or canal; and, fourthly, the similar trade of bringing water for the supply of a great city.[8]

The key word here is, of course, the *banking trade*, which to Smith was a 'routine' activity. The reason for this, as he saw it, was the established rules of operation which could not be departed from except with great peril to the firm. On the other hand, banking required great capital which would, at times, be required for lending to the state in anticipation of tax collection; hence the joint-stock method of company formation was used by the 'principal banking companies of Europe' as well as the Bank of England.

In point of fact, the continental joint-stock method was developed from the French Commercial Code of 1807, the société anonyme, and was the basis for the company laws of western Europe, including Switzerland. Limited liability could be provided for, depending upon the constitution of the particular company. It was such companies as these which proliferated during the first half of the nineteenth century. There was an important reason for this. During the eighteenth century, private capital had learned, to its regret, that lending directly to governments or to enterprises such as the South Sea Bubble and the like, was fraught with risk. Indeed, many of the Swiss private banking houses had come to grief through excessive lending to the French government. By channeling private capital through a joint-stock bank société anonyme, much of the risk could be eliminated. Since the bank would follow the relatively simple rules of operation, just as in Smith's day, the investor's capital would be relatively safe.

When the bank undertakes the process of note issuing, it enters into quite a different activity, that of the production of money, which Smith did not consider. In this case the bank is engaging in lending just as normally, but the borrower receives banknotes which are the equivalent of gold or silver. The borrower, in turn, passes these notes on in discharge of debt, to make a purchase, to pay an expense, and so only so that the notes move into circulation to perform the function of money. Instead of the precious metals, we have paper which is the equivalent of precious metals since the bearer is entitled to receive a fixed amount of the metal merely by returning the note to the issuing bank. The paper, in this case, is redeemable in specie.

Since, during the period which is under consideration, any bank could issue banknotes merely by satisfying whatever loose or stringent government regulations were imposed, it follows that there could arise considerable competition amongst note-issuing banks. In a word, some banknotes could be preferred to others depending upon the reputation of the bank. In the event of an over-issue of banknotes by a specific bank, concern as to the redeemability of the notes could spread; hence the notes would be returned to the issuing bank for specie. After some unfortunate experiences with such over-issues, banks learned to regulate the amount of their banknotes that they handed over to their customers.[9]

THE BRITISH CASE, THE SUCCESS STORY OF THE NINETEENTH CENTURY

There was, and indeed has been until the present time, hardly a better example of checking the over-issue of notes than the Bank Act of

Sir Robert Peel, passed in 1844–5. The Act effectively limited the amount of notes in circulation to the exact amount of gold bullion in which the notes were redeemable on demand, with the exception of an amount of notes issued against securities.[10] All banknotes issued in addition to that amount had to be equal to the amount of gold in the Issue Department of the Bank of England. At the same time by limiting and gradually reducing the banknote issue of Provincial banks, the banknotes in circulation became the responsibility of the Bank of England.

The separation of the Issue Department and the Banking Department proved to be the masterstroke in limiting the over-issue of banknotes.[11] The day to day business of the Bank of England was confined to the Banking Department which had no control (or influence) whatsoever over the Issue Department. Thus, the twin objectives of Peel were partially served by preventing the possibility of excessive inflation such as had occurred during the Napoleonic era.

The other objective, that of stabilising the discount rate, or reducing the degree of variation of the discount rates, was by no means achieved. This was the responsibility of the Banking Department which had control, in the usual manner, of the credit system of the country. That is, the bank directors may lend or not lend precisely as they wish at whatever rate of interest or discount they deem appropriate.

The equilibrium between the supply of banknotes and the economy was achieved by strict adherence to the principles of the Bank Act. Thus, suppose an apparent 'shortage' of banknotes, relative to economic activity, happened to be observed. This would be the equivalent of an increase in the value of money with prices, generally, falling. Merchants, money changers and bankers, could realise an instant profit by presenting gold bullion to either the Mint or the Bank of England Issue Department, depending upon whether they wished notes or coins or both, and thereby increasing the amount of money in circulation. Should the domestic supply of bullion be inadequate to address the shortage, an inflow of bullion from abroad would take place to purchase relatively cheap British exports.

Of course, should an excess of currency exist, a corresponding export of bullion would take place and the difficulty would be corrected. Most important of all, the government, under the Bank Act, was completely removed from the matter of the amount of money in circulation. Only in matters of extreme urgency has it been necessary to suspend the Bank Act and permit the Banking Department to have access to the gold in the Issue Department. It was England under the Bank Act of 1844 which had so influenced Speiser in recognising the value of a bank which would assist in the transactions of traders, for having been severely restricted in the issue of banknotes, the English banks had turned to the development of the current account to accomplish the business of transactions on behalf of their clients.

Central to the current account is the Clearing House. This institution, which leant its name to the Clearing Bank, was established in 1775 as a substitute for the somewhat awkward practice of clerks being sent by banks to other banks to collect amounts which were payable to them. Not only was there a waste of time but there was also the danger of loss of money as well as the extra cost of transport. The result was obvious enough – to have a central meeting place for all clerks to exchange their cheques and bills payable.

While first confined only to private bankers, the Clearing House was later extended to include joint-stock banks. It was further observed that just a few clerks working jointly for all member banks could more expeditiously handle the payment of cheques for all the members so that the banker's clerk need only hand over all the instruments of payment to these 'common' clerks. The result was astonishing. When Mr Babbage analysed the statistics of the Clearing House, he discovered that the amount of cash that passed from one bank to another was often less than 4 per cent of the value of the total transactions.[12] A still further degree of perfection in the operation of the Clearing House consisted of the elimination of payments of coin, to be substituted by the accounts at the Bank of England. Finally, in 1858 the services of the Clearing House were extended to the country banks in England.

THE BANK OF FRANCE

Second only to the Bank of England in importance, the Bank of France must have been considered to be the most successful of European banks. Established in 1800, and revised in 1806 with a larger capital base, the Bank of France had a monopoly of note issue in Paris. This same monopoly was extended to other parts of France by means of taking over the joint stock banks of the larger centres, Lyons, Marseilles, and so on. This was effected in 1848 by the simple expedient of exchanging the shares, one for one, of the Bank of France for the local joint-stock banks. The result was that the prestige of the Bank of France, and the right of note issue, was increased to embrace the entire country. In this way a uniform currency in circulation was attained fairly early in the nineteenth century, a considerable achievement at the time.

Throughout the stormy period of 1848 and the financial crisis of 1864, the Bank showed remarkable skill in maintaining its reserves. The crisis of 1864 appeared as the consequence of the speculative fever accompanying the Credit Foncier and the Credit Mobilier, both of which had used their funds to invest in projects which were either excessively long-term in fruition or were destined never to earn a profit. Since the Bank had been authorized to make advances on railway shares, it was directly affected by the collapse of the speculative boom. It was, however, not until the war with Prussia in 1870–1 that the Bank of France became a means by which the war could be financed through an inflationary increase in the supply of money. Before the war, the amount of currency in circulation had been 1,400 millions of francs. This had increased to 2,400 millions by the end of 1871. The metallic reserve of the Bank had also decreased from 1,318 millions of francs in June 1870 to 505 millions by the end of that year.[13]

What proved to be the most impressive achievement of the Bank of France was the securing of a monopoly of the right of note issue early in its existence. In this, like the British Bank Act of 1844 which secured the note issue for the Bank of England, it seized upon the most important function of a central bank at the time. In doing so it made possible an increase, or decrease, of the money supply so as to assist the government in its finances by lending to the government at low rates of interest (3 per cent as against 6 per cent for other advances, as authorised by a law passed in 1857). Yet we do not find the rigid structure of the gold–banknote relationship which was so characteristic of the Bank of England. Franc banknotes could be issued by the Bank of France at will just so long as the redemption in silver did not become excessive. An excessive drain in silver did, in fact, occur during the Crimean War and later in 1870–1. Banknotes in those cases became non-redeemable. Nevertheless it was to the credit of the Bank of France management that the banknote issue was, in fact, sufficiently restrained.

The fact that this increase in the money supply did not result in something similar to the great inflations of the twentieth century is due, in the first place, to the relatively modest increase, in the second, to the pre-existence of a shortage of money, and, in the third, to the capacity of the French economy to increase production. Indeed, it was the latter, the extraordinary resilience of the economy in the face of adverse conditions, which seemed to be at the heart of the matter.

These were the banking circumstances of western countries which had so inspired Johann Jakob Speiser. For Speiser, who returned to Basle in 1843 prior to the 1848 takeover of the departmental joint-stock banks by the Bank of France, the French banks of issue were an example to be followed in Basle. Similarly, the London Clearing house must have been a model which he saw to be a useful means of making payments amongst traders. The fact that the existing system of bankers and banking in Switzerland did not recognise the usefulness of Speiser's new Giro und Depositenbank at once was the result not so much of an inherent excessive conservatism on the part of the Swiss bankers but of the success of the Swiss and German structure of banking without the use of cheque clearing which had proved itself over the years since the Napoleonic Wars.

It should be added that Germany also had had a successful history of banking which followed the boundaries of the German states, each of which had its own separate banking laws. Of course, the venerable Bank of Hamburgh, established in 1619, had been highly successful, just like the Bank of Amsterdam, the model for the Bank of Hamburgh. It had served as a deposit bank which transferred sums from one deposit to another in discharge of debt. It was not until the rise of Imperial Germany that a single note currency was established to circulate throughout the entire empire.

CONCLUSION

We may conclude, then, that the success of the banking equilibrium in Switzerland and Germany, combined with the apparent predilection of the Swiss for self-financing of industry, meant that the capital market which modern banks could provide was superfluous until a large scale demand for capital developed. To recapitulate, the economic function of a capital market is to allocate capital where it is in surplus to areas of industry where it is in short supply. This increases the efficiency of total capital utilisation. Swiss entrepreneurs on the other hand, had already achieved a high degree of efficiency by concentrating their surpluses, which were their capital, within their own industry. In other words, there was no shortage of supply of capital until the era of railway building and the system of large factories necessary for heavy machinery production arrived. To be sure, this was not long in coming and both the Bankverein and the Swiss Credit Bank proved to be highly successful in undertaking their task of mobilising capital.

With both these banks, we can be certain that the modern era of Swiss banking had begun.

Notes

1. This is not to suggest that the cantons themselves opposed progress. The Paris revolution of 1830 had its repercussions in the cantons, and many reforms and needed structural changes took place within the cantons. Such barriers to freedom of trade as tolls, poor roads, and poor postal communications were eliminated. All these were within each canton, not between cantons. Ritzmann, Franz, *Die Schweizer Banken* (Berne and Stuttgart: Verlag Paul Haupt, 1973).
2. The bankers were Bischoff zu St Alban, Passavant & Cie, J. Merian-Forcart, Ehinger & Cie, E. La Roche Sohn, and von Speyr & Cie. In the later agreements, J. Riggenbach takes the place of E. La Roche Sohn. The quarters of J. Riggenbach were the initial meeting place for the six bankers. Hans Bauer, *Swiss Bank Corporation*, 1872–1872. Swiss Bank Corporation, Basle, 1972.
3. 'On the one hand we see at the head of industry and other branches of business well-endowed firms which work entirely with their own capital and yet can also put out a considerable portion of their funds at interest. On the other hand we find in our city an extensively developed and generally accessible credit system such as can probably be paralleled in no other place in the world ... If, then, there is any place where an actual credit institution may be regarded as absolutely superfluous, it is here.' Ibid., p. 31.
4. Ibid., p. 40.
5. As an example, a municipality in a canton (unnamed) applied for a loan of 800,000 francs to be guaranteed by the canton. The reply was; 'Bankverein has no mind to entertain the business in view of the disrepute into which ... the railway and government finances of this canton have fallen'. Ibid., p. 41.
6. Fehrenbach, T. R., *The Swiss Banks* (New York: McGraw Hill, 1966) p. 27.
7. Ritzmann, Franz, *Die Schweizer Banken*, Verlag Paul Haugt, Berne and Stuttgart, 1973, p. 63.
8. Smith, Adam, *The Wealth of Nations*, McCulloch's Edition Edinburgh: (Adam and Charles Black, 1889) p. 340.
9. An excellent example of just such competition was the 1838 presentation of 2,500,000 francs worth of Banque de Belgique notes by the Société Generale for encashment. The Banque survived but continued to 'war' with the Société until both were caught by the difficulties of 1848. Both had to suspend payments in that year. Clapham, J. H., *Economic Development of France and Germany, 1815–1914*, Cambridge University Press, Cambridge, England. 1961, p. 128.

10. The original Act permitted an issue of banknotes against government securities to the amount of 14,000,000 pounds. That amount had been subsequently raised by Orders in Council (at the time of Bagehot's Lombard Street) to 18,450,000.
11. In actual fact the idea of separation between the two Departments was presented by Lord Overstone in tracts published in 1837 and 1840 as well as to a Committee of the House of Commons in 1840.
12. Courtney, Rt. Hon. Leonard H., 'Banking', *Encyclopaedia Brittanica*, Ninth Edition, Vol. III. p. 328.
13. Ibid., p. 338.

7 The Banking World of the Nineteenth Century

INTRODUCTION

In terms of modern banking, Swiss bankers entered an international world of banking and finance which had already been developed, and there was really nothing they could do about it. Leadership in the banking industry had shifted to Great Britain where the banking system had reached a stage of maturity which was both domestically and internationally well advanced. In the first place it had raised gold to the level of an international currency, and in the second, it had placed its own bank reserves securely on a gold foundation. This it had done through, firstly, the institutional mechanism of the Bank of England and, secondly, the Bank Act of 1844 which strictly limited the issue of banknotes to the amount of gold in the Bank's reserves. Thus, unless the Bank Act was suspended, which was only resorted to in times of emergency, every pound note was, for all practical purposes, the equivalent of gold.[1]

Another factor of considerable importance was the development of the joint-stock company. This had the effect of mobilising capital under the terms of limited liability, a principle which quickly spread to continental banking systems. The société anonyme was adopted fairly early in Belgium and France and later in Germany.

In Switzerland, joint-stock companies were formed just as in other countries when it became obvious that more modern industrial undertakings were entirely too capital-intensive to be financed by individual entrepreneurs alone. Banks in particular took advantage of this form of organisation as they sought additional capital for investment purposes. While the legal basis for these companies depended upon each individual canton, there appeared to be little or no objection on the part of federal public authorities to this form of business organisation.

An important outgrowth of this rush toward the formation of joint-stock companies was the broadening of stock exchanges to include stock price quotations and to provide for the buying and selling of shares for all industrial companies, not just the railroads or utilities for which the exchanges had been used heretofore. This meant that the shares of many companies were not only available for purchase by investors but could also become vehicles for speculative buying and selling. Furthermore, since these exchanges were open to anyone, both foreign and domestic, they became truly international, and prices on the exchanges tended to move in tandem. Additionally, the growth of investment bankers, the outstanding and most successful being the famous Kreditanstalt of Vienna, which used these exchanges for the purpose of investing in securities, meant that deposits in these investment banks could also be owned by foreigners. Such deposits were used to finance the purchase of shares in various companies – railways, industrial, and commercial.

The recurrent economic cycles of boom and collapse, so characteristic of nineteenth century banking, do suggest that something was indeed very wrong with the banking and monetary systems of Europe, particularly the banks of Great Britain which were the world leaders at the time. The British banks had sought security in a rigid structure of short-term assets, the commercial bills of exchange. Additionally, there was a powerful secondary bill market in London which added further security. At the base of the entire system was the Bank of England itself. Still, with all this security, the banks were still subject to the great psychological weaknesses with which all humans have been plagued and which still generate the boom–bust cycle.

We might ask ourselves at this juncture: where, precisely, did the new Swiss banks fit into this entire system? What was their real economic function? There are a number of factors involved which we should like to enumerate as follows:

1. The Swiss banks, led by the Schweizerische Kreditanstalt and the Bankverein, had developed the technique of minimising total risk, so necessary for successful banking, by spreading their individual credit risks over a broad spectrum of banking activity. This contrasted strongly with the British technique of acquiring, so they hoped, the same degree of risk minimisation by short term lending against commercial bills of exchange, the misuse of which was largely responsible for the banking panics of the nineteenth century. The difference is obvious. Banks that have structured their assets so as to minimise their risks have a portfolio of secure assets to balance the more insecure, hence a banking panic through bank closures, due to a concentration of loans in a single asset, becomes much less probable. Much of this bank security rests upon adequate reserves of cash or cash equivalent, and this the Swiss banks learned very early in their modern history.

2. Following directly from the first point, we note that a loan granted by a Swiss bank tended to be 'better' than a loan from, say,

a French bank of the day. The word 'better' is used here only in the sense that the borrower had to be of higher quality to satisfy the stringent requirements of the Swiss banks so as to acquire the loan in the first place, hence achieving a greater measure of security for the bank. At the same time the loan to a higher quality borrower was a wealth-creating loan as opposed to a loan for commercial purposes only.

We might argue even further that money thus loaned was 'upgraded' from the banks' more liquid liabilities, consisting of the deposits of Swiss banks owed to the public, to a higher quality, illiquid asset which took the form, generally, of fixed capital – railroads, factories, and the like.[2] This is what bank intermediation meant.

This is an important part of the intermediation function of banks. By intermediating between the depositor and the borrower, the bank 'bridges' a gap which is impossible to cross by the ordinary individual as an investor. The bank offers its good name and reputation along with its liquidity to depositors, then lends to borrowers to assume any risk which the depositor alone could not possibly accept. This 'upgrading' function of Swiss banks was responsible for investment which would otherwise not have occurred.

3. In contrast to the British banks, as well as other continental banking systems, we find no evidence, at this mid-nineteenth century juncture, of genuine money 'creation' by the Swiss banks. The exception to this are those note-issuing banks which were fortunate to have their notes accepted by the Swiss public. While the British banks were engaging in deposit creation by increasing deposits which were created against the bills of exchange as assets, the Swiss were utilising these deposits (those deposits the ownership of which had been transferred to Swiss banks) not to further expand the European money supply but to put these existing deposits to work.

4. We would offer the hypothesis that the young Swiss banks actually helped to reduce the severity of European bank panics with their consequent bankruptcies and personal tragedies. The degree to which they contributed to this is impossible to measure, but the fact that they were able to compensate for some of the loss of liquidity during bank panics by drawing upon their own liquidity stores suggests that the hypothesis is likely to be true.

A further extension of this idea was the tendency for Swiss banks to seek foreign investment outlets at higher interest rates as opposed to domestic investments at lower interest rates. Swiss banks, seeking better interest rewards outside Switzerland, were able to lend to worthy foreign companies that could not be accommodated by their own banks within their own countries because of the lack of liquidity. Foreign lending by Swiss banks became a substitute for domestic banking services in those countries outside Switzerland which suffered severely from banking panics.

THE SWISS ECONOMIC CIRCUMSTANCE

In Switzerland some rather subtle changes were taking place within the economy. The decade of the 1860s was characterised by considerable upheaval in such industries as cotton, principally due to the American Civil War. Prices of raw cotton rose to reach exceptionally high levels in 1867, then fell in 1868–9. Manufacturers found themselves in the unenviable position of having to sell at prices lower than the costs of their replacement inventory of raw material. The flax industry, which had developed during the American Civil War as a substitute for cotton, suffered also with the return of lower cotton prices at the end of the decade. There was an overcapacity in terms of flax spindles as a consequence, and the price of the manufactured product (linen) fell at the same time that the cost of the raw product, flax, remained high because of the short supply of the raw material.[3]

This particular situation in Swiss manufacturing emphasised both the structural weaknesses of Swiss industry: its dependence upon imports of raw material, and the simultaneous dependence upon exports. In terms of purely domestic markets, world class industries in Switzerland could not be sustained. Scale economies, in such small markets, were simply not possible. Silk production suffered as well, and demonstrated even more the dependence upon imports for raw silk and exports for sales of finished products. Strong international competition from German manufacturers and the exclusion of Swiss products via the Zollverein meant that only the London and New York markets were available. But in the United States the sale of ribbons depended upon the dictates of fashion and in London the preference seems to have been in favour of the French silk ribbons compared to which the 'ribbons of Basle show great inferiority...'[4]

It was becoming quite clear, as a careful reading of the economic history of Switzerland during this period demonstrates, that Swiss textile entrepreneurs, in order to survive, were being forced into the production of a higher quality product in order to meet the growing competition. Indeed, they were identifying a particular niche in textile manufacturing that the watch industry had already discovered for itself. This niche was characterised by a high value added to an imported raw material of relatively low value. The only way to achieve this was through a recognised level of quality which was higher than inferior competitors.

The watch industry is the most obvious example of this high value added. While the cost of the raw material is low, the value of the finished product is very high due to the application of skills and technology which are second to none. As early as 1839 Leschot had introduced standardised parts into the industry (specifically Vacheron & Constantin Co.) making possible a much quicker assembly of standardised watches but in different models. However, in the latter quarter of the nineteenth century both the Americans and the Japanese were developing strong capabilities in the watchmaking industry so that once again the importance of high quality became evident in the face of competition from these sources.[5]

The success of Swiss textiles and watches, with emphasis on higher quality, could only have been due to the general rise in the European standard of living which took place after mid-century. While industrial wages throughout Europe were undoubtedly low and the incomes of agricultural workers even lower, the fact that these incomes were rising above the subsistence level meant that a surplus, however meagre, existed for spending on 'luxury' goods. The 'Iron Law of Wages', propounded by Ricardo, which stated that wages could not be higher than that which was just sufficient to maintain a worker, was no longer valid. Incomes were rising and populations, and supplier of labour, were increasing at the same time.

Simultaneously with the growth of such industrial incomes, the incomes of the capitalist or entrepreneurial classes grew as well, and it was in this particular group that the market lay for the truly luxury goods. Thus, despite the adverse circumstances of the business cycle and world events such as the American Civil War, the Swiss textile manufacturers proved to be sufficiently adaptable to change. By adjusting to new conditions (such as the whims of fashion,) they were able to supply that unique portion of the market considered as luxuries. In this market, characterised by high value added with relatively low cost imports and high cost exports, they continued both to produce and to excel.

At the same time, the Swiss engineering industry, while it had its beginnings in the production of machinery for the textile industry, began to diversify. Machine tools, hydraulic turbines, presses, pumps, and milling machines were among the lists of production, not just for the domestic market but for export as well. This brought the Swiss into direct competition with other producers, particularly those industrial nations that possessed considerably greater resources within their boundaries. At the same time, this industry, a capital goods industry, was subject to the swings of the business cycle; nevertheless, the foundations of the modern, high quality engineering for which Switzerland is famous even today were laid at that time.

Without doubt, however, the greatest of Swiss engineering achievements was the building of the railway system. Railway construction began in earnest after the railway legislation of 1852. Ten years later, 718 miles had been finished; by 1872, the total mileage of 'ordinary' railways amounted to 1459, and by 1882, 2667 miles had been completed.[6] In that same year the St Gotthard Pass rail tunnel was opened, literally piercing the Alps to reduce a journey which had taken weeks at great risk to a matter of minutes. Most important, the railway systems of both France and Germany were connected via the Swiss system to the plains of Italy, no small engineering achievement.

Railway construction in Switzerland was much more than simply laying rails to connect points in the more or less populated areas of the country. Somewhat similar to the Belgian plan, Swiss railways were to continue the historic connecting link between the German states of the north and the plains of Italy in the south: instead of the great Rhine river passage, the railway would accomplish the same function. Already, by the middle of the century, threats to the strategic position of the Swiss had taken the form of the beginning of the Suez canal construction, the Brenner Pass railway and the Mont-Cenis tunnel in France. With these new routes, Switzerland could become not only bypassed but isolated as well. Thus the advantage of a strategic location (which the Belgians had long recognised) could be lost to Switzerland unless the St Gotthard tunnel could carry freight and passengers directly through the Alps. In that case, Swiss railways could connect the German railway system with that of Italy.

The crux of the matter proved to be the construction of the Suez canal. Prior to the Canal, ships travelling around the Cape had not only to withstand the hazards of long ocean voyages but also to allow for time-consuming journeys. This meant that cargo from the East had to be stored in English warehouses, to be financed by English banks, in anticipation of demand from the Continent. With the construction of the Canal, the entire travel time was reduced to some 30 days or less with corresponding stops at Trieste, Venice or Genoa, Marseilles, or Cadiz, depending upon the country of destination of the cargo. Most important, instead of anticipating demand, suppliers could provide for existing demand when it arose, all with considerably less risk and financing costs than before. Goods in transit to points in northern Europe would travel by rail from Mediterranean ports, hence the strategic importance of the St. Gotthard.[7]

Unlike the Belgians, the Swiss government, under the legislation of 1852, decided to leave the matter of railway construction as the responsibility of both the cantonal governments and the private sector. This somewhat unfortunate circumstance (as subsequent developments were to demonstrate) was attributed to the efforts of Alfred Escher, who was not only an engineer of considerable talent but also a politician. Still, one must credit Escher with an extraordinary vision. Landlocked, Switzerland could not possibly develop a modern industrial base without a railway system. Thus, to Escher, it was more than a matter of a mere connecting link in a chain of transport between neighbouring countries; it was also a means for the future economic survival of the new confederation. Escher recognised that Switzerland was already being by-passed by European commerce and it was vital that the country become part of that commerce. It was this vision which led (see Chapter 6) to the organisation of the Swiss Credit Bank, a remarkable achievement in itself.

The Basler Bankverein was also very active in its financing of railway development. Its share of the financing of the Gothardbahn was considerable, some 9 million francs of the total Swiss group's financing of 3.5 million francs. In addition, loans to cities were approved (some in Germany despite the initial agreement of 1854 which specified that only domestic loans would be accommodated), and to banks as well, particularly the bank in Winterthur. Approximately 40 of the many loans applied for were approved by the Bankverein.

The Bankverein, the original Basle bankers' syndicate later to be replaced 1870s, had the distinct advantage of growth and development during the establishment of the great free trade period known as the Cobden treaties. The result of the efforts of the remarkable Richard Cobden was both the repeal of the Corn Laws and the negotiation with France in 1860 of a tariff reduction of 30 per cent in much of England's exports to France and the abolition of all prohibitions. Britain, in its turn, abolished all duties on French manufactured goods and reduced the tariff on French wines. Since Britain made these tariff concessions universal, for the next 70 years Britain was a free trade country while France, under the influence of the writings of F. Bastiat, an ardent free trader, negotiated a number of reciprocal agreements with European countries, including Switzerland.

For the decade of the 1860s, then, despite the political upheavals in Europe and America (or because of them) commercial activity actually increased throughout Europe. Along with this increase came the corresponding increase in liquid funds, bills of exchange, and currency flows, so that banks had the advantage of ample reserves of cash-in-hand to be loaned at low interest rates.

The liquidity increase, due to enhanced commerce, was further strengthened by the formation, in December 1865, of the Latin Monetary Union which included France, Switzerland, Italy, Belgium and, later, Greece. This made possible the free circulation of the coins of the member states within each member state. Switzerland, in fact, had only a small portion of its currency minted in the Confederation. This pleasant circumstance of free trade and payments in the currencies of these countries continued until the Franco-Prussian War of 1870–1 when France placed an embargo on the export of gold coins and precious metals in general. The result of this embargo was a shortage of currency in Switzerland until the Federal Council made it possible for the English sovereign, as well as other foreign currencies, to circulate as legal tender.

While it is impossible to relate cause and effect with certainty, we do know that the decade of the 1860s, despite the American Civil War and shortage of cotton, was a generally prosperous one for European (and Swiss) industries. Expansion of output and the improved administration of industry, using the new joint-stock, limited liability methods, also required bank financing, particularly for the finance of circulating capital.

Further, since the financial capacity of single enterprises was insufficient to accommodate the new and more complex techniques of production, additional sources of funding were resorted to from new merchant banks in particular. These were international in character and involved payments of funds between countries in the form not of just cash or gold currency but as a cheque–a new means of payment for Europe, though long recognised in Britain. In a word, the gloomy predictions of those who opposed free trade were quite unfounded, though, we must repeat, it does not suggest that free trade was the sole cause of industrial expansion. We can only argue that it was a major contributing factor.

A SUMMARY OF THE EUROPEAN BANKING SYSTEM

It is a recurring theme of this book that the structure of banking adjusts and adapts to the circumstances which prevail. Banks, therefore, are never static; they cannot afford to be. Victorian banks, led by the British, had achieved a high degree of proficiency for the times. Indeed, banking panics aside, we cannot but admire the skill with which banks performed the task of providing an elastic money supply in response to the needs of trade, allocating the 'floating loan fund' (Bagehot's apt phrase) to its appropriate uses, transferring ownership of deposits in discharge of debt, and performing the important intermediation function. The fact that periodic panics occurred during the nineteenth century was likely due to an absence of external regulation and internal discipline which was yet to be developed. We might conclude this chapter with a summary of the principal points which we have developed to this stage.

The logical place to start is with the British banking system. Since the bill of exchange was a sound, short-term loan when backed by goods in transit, it would appear to have been a perfect method not only for securing commercial loans but also a means by which the growth of the money supply would remain in close relationship to the needs of trade and commerce. The Bank of France, however, was probably the most successful of the Continental central banks. It had achieved a monopoly of the banknote issue fairly early in the nineteenth century and had kept its issue well within reasonable limits relative to its cash reserve, with the possible exception of the year 1847 when the reserves were exceptionally low. The point is that the bill of exchange, discounted by the local bank on behalf of the exporter, is paid for with banknotes which, if the bill of exchange is a net increase in the local bank's assets, are an increase in the notes in circulation in France. Once more, the commercial bill of exchange serves its purpose, in this case increasing the level of the money supply in accordance with business activity. This follows because should the local bank be short of cash for its daily requirements, it could easily rediscount the bill of exchange with the Bank of France and acquire additional cash for its daily business requirements. Finally when the bill of exchange is due for payment, it is sent back to London to be presented to the original bank which guaranteed its quality for collection. The bank will then recoup its funds from the original importer.

It takes but little additional imagination to conceive of a multilateral trading system using the same bill of exchange. Thus a French importer could pay for Swiss exports since the Swiss exporters would discount the same bill with their bank in Switzerland. Similarly Swiss imports from Germany could also be paid by purchasing the same bill. In all cases, the money supply in the respective countries expands along with the needs of trade and commerce.

Furthermore, in the event that a specific country imported more in terms of value of goods and services than it exported (the balance of trade was 'unfavourable'), a shortage of bills would appear in the assets of the bank. In an attempt to purchase more, so as to accommodate its customers, the price of bills denominated in foreign exchange would rise as market demand exceeded supply. This would be a depreciation of the domestic currency making imports more expensive for the importer thereby tending to correct the original imbalance of trade.

To this point, trade requirements have determined the supply of bills and money within the respective countries. But when the accommodation bill (a method of acquiring long term loans by continuously issuing new bills to repay old bills as they mature) is introduced, the situation is reversed – the bills begin to determine the state of the economy. Ultimately, the British banks must find that they have as assets more bills than can be successfully used as sources of cash to satisfy the demands of depositors. Even the discount houses in London (such as Overend) and the Bank of England itself must eventually cease to discount bills when cash becomes in short supply. Foreign bills (those outside the United Kingdom as opposed to inland bills) will similarly be in surplus and banks will find themselves unable to exchange them for the necessary cash to honour their deposits. The bank panic ensues unless a continuous expansion in the supply of cash (beyond the needs of trade) takes place. It is the trade and commerce which suffers for the lack of adequate means of payment. The 'money supply' (good bills, banknotes, and so on) collapses and a business activity throughout Europe slackens.

The Swiss banking system may now be fitted into the entire European structure of banking. Noting the four points listed earlier, we can easily recognise the intermediating function of Swiss banks. Swiss exporters or other businessmen acquired the deposits which were created by the issuance of London bills of exchange. They were then loaned by their Swiss banks for capital creation purposes (such as railways and factories) just so long as the Swiss banks maintained sufficient liquidity to honour their obligations to the Swiss exporters, who owned the deposits in the first place.

Is this banking process a pure Credit Mobilier type institution, as many economic historians like to suggest? Certainly not. The Credit Mobilier of the Periere brothers and of the other continental institutions which are patterned after the original are quite different. These involve the acquisition of funds through the sale of bonds in money markets. They then loan these funds for long term project development, and in the event that the projects are successful, the bonds are repaid with interest.

Not so the Swiss banks. Here we find genuine intermediation as between short-term deposits and long-term financing. The success of such a process of intermediation depends upon adequate reserves and careful allocation of capital funds to those projects which have the least degree of risk. It is, in the final analysis, just such projects which must yield a return not only for the banks but for the payment of interest on deposits as well. Thus the practice of being sure of the quality of the investment project as well as the personnel who administer it was the single characteristic of Swiss banking which distinguished it from the Credit Mobilier. Frequently the lending of such funds for specific projects was accompanied by the actual placement of bank personnel on the board of directors to participate in the administration of the project, thereby ensuring that the bank would continue to minimise its risk.

So it was that from the beginning of 'modern' Swiss banking in the nineteenth century, a concept of banking quite different from either the British banks or the continental banks was emerging. Some might argue that Swiss banks were not really banks at all, just investment houses. But this is not correct either, because it ignores the important liquidity function in modern banking and this the Swiss were in the process of learning very quickly and very well.

Notes

1. In actual fact, the Bank Act permitted only £14 million of banknotes to be issued against government securities by the Issue Department, required gold bullion as backing. Orders in Council could, of course, increase the amount of sterling notes issued against government securities which has

indeed taken place. But without such authorisations, the Bank itself cannot increase note circulation without a corresponding increase in bullion.

2.   Readers may object to the use of the word 'quality' in a judgemental way here. It is only a means of distinction between deposits arising from commercial activity and assets which are essentially long term.

3.   'Depression in the Swiss Industry, 1868–69' Report by HM Secretaries of Embassies and Legations, (Parl. Papers, 1868–69).

4.   Ibid.

5.   Bergier, Jean-Françoise, *Wirtschafts Geschichte der Schweiz* (Zürich: Benziger Verlag AG, 1990) p. 231.

6.   Sime, James, 'Switzerland', *Encyclopaedia Britannica*, Ninth Edition, Vol XXII, p. 780.

7.   D. A. Wells, 'Recent Economic Changes and their Effect on the Production and Distribution of Wealth and the Well Being of Society' (New York, 1893). Pollard S. and C. Holmes, *Documents of European Economic History, Vol. 2.* (London: Edward Arnold, 1972) p. 142.

8 Swiss Banks Reach Their Formative Stage

A PERIOD OF DEFLATION

It is curious for us in this modern age to reflect upon the fact that the gold standard, as a means of national and international payment of debt, never really came into general acceptance until after the year 1870. Prior to that time, the world was on a bi-metallic standard with silver circulating jointly with gold. In the Latin Monetary Union, in which Switzerland had been a member from its inception, silver was the accepted currency with gold completely demonetised.

The difficulties inherent in a bi-metallic standard are not difficult to appreciate. Inevitably there must be an official exchange rate between the two metals if they are to circulate as money, and for this rate, the ratio of 1:15.5 was established in France. At the same time, along with the circulation of silver, 20 and 40 franc gold pieces were being minted. Now suppose the market price of gold falls (as it did because of the new discoveries of gold in California and Australia during the mid-century). It would be a simple matter to purchase gold on the market with silver at the market ratio, then exchange the gold for silver at the mint at 1:15.5, thereby realising a tidy profit. Gold, in this case the cheaper metal, would flow to France.

Similarly, the fall in the market price of silver in 1871 meant that silver flowed to those countries of the Latin Monetary Union, France, Belgium and Switzerland, which had a free coinage of silver at the specific ratio. The result was that free coinage became limited in 1873. Of course, national interests aligned themselves behind one metallic currency or the other. Those countries heavily dependent upon agricultural exports, such as the United States and eastern Europe, found that the cheaper silver was to their advantage because when prices of primary commodities fell in world markets, domestic prices, and farm incomes, could be correspondingly maintained with cheaper silver.

Ultimately it was the market oscillations of silver prices which proved to be the downfall of the bi-metallic system, so that countries gradually moved toward gold as their national currencies. The new

German Empire led the way, after the war with France, when the coinage of silver ceased in 1872. The transition was completed in two years with the calling-in of silver precisely when increasing world silver output (and falling silver prices) was taking place. This further decreased the price of silver through the selling of German silver on the London market.

The Latin Union, originally founded with the 5 franc piece as the official currency in the signatory countries, agreed in 1874 to place limits on the coinage of these pieces. Without a free coinage, for all practical purposes the silver standard ceased to exist, and in 1878, the minting of silver was completely abandoned. All of western Europe, therefore, including Switzerland, was on the gold standard by the end of the 1870s.

The interesting feature of this period, the decade of the seventies, was that it marked the beginning of a general fall in world commodity prices. There was a 'spike' of recovery in 1880–1 (which ended in France with the collapse of the Union Générale in 1881) but the general trend was downward to the end of the century. These two decades, 1850–70, were characterised by considerable increases in productivity because of the introduction of new machinery and equipment which, in turn, meant that the output of goods was rising.

At the same time that the gold standard was being adopted (the new South African fields and the cyanide processes were yet to be introduced), a massive deflation was occurring due to the abandonment of the bi-metallic system. To be sure, substitutes for gold, banknotes, bills of exchange, and cheques, were being introduced; however, these required an acceptance by the public in general, which was not yet ready for such an innovation. The result was a rising output of goods combined with a static (or even falling, in some countries) medium of exchange which resulted in a twenty-year deflation.[1]

From a more positive point of view, the constructive feature of that twenty-year period was the emergence of money substitutes, notably a banking system which could provide alternatives to cash. In a word, claims against banks might be used as freely as money; indeed, as the banking habit progressed, such claims against banks eventually became *de facto* money. As we shall argue in this chapter, this meant a gain in economic efficiency, in the first place, and the development of a monetary policy on the part of governments in the second. Most important, there was a further development of the Swiss banks which held great promise for the future.

THE ECONOMICS OF SWITZERLAND, MID-CENTURY

The interesting development in mid-century Switzerland was the transition from a capital surplus country to a nation of capital shortage. In this sense, capital shortages, Switzerland shared common ground with other countries during the industrial expansion of Europe. The combination of domestic economic expansion, fostered by the new economic and political relationships among the cantons and between the cantons and the federal government, and the necessity for the building of capital intensive railroads and industry proved to be too much of a strain on existing supplies of financial capital. It was this pressure of capital shortage which led to the establishment and growth of the Grossbanken for which the country is now so well known. It was these banks which were particularly suited to the import of foreign capital through the media of the Swiss stock exchanges. At the same time these banks were, in the tradition of the Credit Mobilier, engaged in the development of domestic industry.

This unique Swiss version of 'industrial banking', the outgrowth of the Credit Mobilier spirit, stands in rather sharp contrast to the German industrial banks which were created for specific industrial purposes.[2] In the German case, the distinction between the bank and the industry became blurred because often the bank was the servant of industry, simply to provide capital at the bidding of the industrial entrepreneurs.[3] On the other hand, sometimes the bank itself was the dominant partner which dictated to the entrepreneurs. Not so the Swiss. When the interests of the banks became highly involved with those of a particular company in an industry, because of the provision of substantial capital sums, a member of the board of directors of the bank also became a member of the board of directors of that particular firm. The joint-stock form of industrial organisation was, therefore, the most useful innovation in this regard. Certainly the possibility of minimising competition through cartelisation, as was more typical in other countries, was not available to the Swiss entrepreneur/banker combination because of the intensity of competition arising from foreign competitors, and this circumstance had the fortunate result of sharpening both skills, that of finance and entrepreneurship.

THE SWISS BANKING MODEL

There is a multiple banking structure in Switzerland which includes cantonal banks, the great banks, Grossbanken, and many specialised banks which provide very much more than do the banking and financial services of the British or North American models. In addition, there are credit unions, regional and savings banks, 'other banks', and foreign banks (categories 1 through 5 according to the classification of the Swiss National Bank) to round out, as it were, what is probably the most varied set of financial facilities available in any country in the world. Keeping in mind the complexity of such a banking system, we can readily appreciate the task of the Swiss banker.

Bankers have the task of evaluating both sides of their balance sheets at the same time; in other words, *two* equilibria. The first is the equilibrium of the supply and demand for deposits which necessarily involves a deposit rate of interest. These are the liabilities of the banks. The second is the equilibrium between the supply of funds made available by depositors and other bank creditors and the demand for these funds on the part of those who would borrow – the investors. These are the banks' assets. Again, there is a rate of interest, a price which equates the supply and demand for these funds as capital. The difference between the two interest rates constitutes the banks' revenues.

This is the essence of financial intermediation. Should bankers make a mistake in their asset evaluation, they must be prepared to provide from their own resources sufficient funds to satisfy their depositors' requirements. On the other hand, should they err in terms of the amount of their own total borrowing requirements (or deposit needs), they will have insufficient funds with which to satisfy those who borrow from the banks. This means a loss of profits.

Consider the task of a banker such as Alfred Escher, the founder of the Kreditanstalt. He likely would have recognised that the demand for borrowed funds was great, that is, the demand for the Credit Mobilier type loans as well as the less risk-prone commercial loans based upon discounting bills of exchange. He may have *hoped* to reach an equilibrium between the supply and demand for capital on the assets side, but that depended upon the amount of funds he could have raised through public subscription.

In terms of the liabilities, he likely knew what his own demand for funds was (based upon how much capital he thought he needed) but he could not have known what he could expect by way of the *supply* of loanable funds which was to be forthcoming from the sale of bank shares. He must have been surprised at the response of the public because the shares of the new bank were actually over-subscribed.

The success of the Kreditanstalt lay in its participation in several areas of banking at once. There was an asset diversification which made possible a spreading of risks as between the long-term, high-risk, railway shares through a whole gamut of Swiss industrial activity to the low-risk short- and medium-term commercial lending. Despite the fact that during the 1860s some 30 per cent of the bank's assets were in unprofitable railway shares, through careful restructuring of its assets (by sharply reducing the number of shares held in textiles and increasing loans to the more viable food and machine industries) the Kreditanstalt was able to survive the depression of the 1870s reasonably well.

Similarly, in liabilities the bank was limited by its constitution to bond issues equal to the value of its shares. This prevented the bank from overextending its liabilities.

This contrasts sharply with the German-Swiss Credit Bank in St Gall (Deutsche-Schweizerische Kreditbank). There was a strong political motive in the formation of this bank, as St Gallen politicians hoped to develop eastern Switzerland as a parallel to the South German economic region. Crucial to this political objective, shared by the south Germans who were becoming ever more suspicious of north German industrialisation efforts, was the construction of an east Alpine railway which would skirt Lake Constance and thereby unite German, Austrian and Swiss commerce. Accordingly, a Credit Mobilier type bank (the German-Swiss Credit Bank) was founded in 1855 in St Gallen with the participation of private banks in Germany as well as in Zürich.

Almost at once, the bank, which appeared to have such a promising beginning, found itself with over half of its share capital tied up in shares of the United Swiss Railways. Because of heavy cost over-runs of the railway, dividend distribution was not possible and the market value of the shares fell sharply. Indeed, the value of the shares held by the bank itself was eventually written down from 5 million francs at the outset to just one hundred thousand. By the time of a second reorganisation of the bank in 1870, total share capital had been reduced from the original 25 million francs to just 3 million, and what began as a Credit Mobilier type bank was reduced to the level of a purely local bank, finally to re-open as the Swiss Union Bank.

It is clear from this that the original founders of the bank in St Gallen (politicians rather than bankers) had conceived of an industrial region which could not exist until railway infrastructure had been provided. Yet, the practical realities of both railway construction and the art of banking had escaped them. The assets demand which they had expected to exist either collapsed or proved to be only an illusion in the first place, and since the bank had not provided for risk dispersion by including other banking activities, which Escher had carefully provided for in the Swiss Credit Bank, there was no means by which assets could be 'propped up' until the railway could prove its worth.

The failure of the bank to maintain profitability of its assets meant the inevitable corresponding collapse on the liabilities side of the demand for bank shares. Eventually, a loss of confidence in the bank forced a process of bank re-organisation at substantially lower levels of balance sheet totals. At the same time, there must have been considerable losses for the investors, for there was no prospect of compensation.

In Basle, the banking and credit situation was quite different. Private bankers in that city had been quite successful in satisfying the credit requirements of trade and commerce as well as investment in Credit Mobilier types of projects. In addition, the Basler Bankverein (the 'old Verein') had also been successful in handling the longer term, large scale investments which the members of the Verein, singly, could not undertake. However, recognising that Basle was losing its important banking status to other centres in eastern Switzerland (Zürich in particular) '...a number of local businessmen, mainly young, have joined together to form such a financial institution (an institution designed to satisfy loan requirements of cantons, railways, etc.) here under the name Basler Handelsbank.'[4]

This bank is particularly interesting in that it, like the Kreditanstalt, began with an oversubscription of shares. At the same time, it was determined not to commit its resources excessively to the railway construction activity (the Swiss Central Railway) but to maintain strong commercial credit outlets. Unfortunately, the recession of 1864 resulted in considerable losses in this region of Switzerland and the Civil War in the United States made investment in lucrative US bonds impossible. With the exception of the years 1870–3, when banking activity increased sharply, the Handelsbank was plagued by a continuous stagnation of business which lasted until the 1890s. Thus, despite the brilliance of the bank's management, which made possible the distribution of annual stock dividends, the bank failed to grow and its share capital had to be reduced through stock redemption.

Clearly, in this case, we have an example of excessive competition brought about partly by the circumstances of history and, in addition, a surfeit of banking facilities in the Basle area. Deposits only trickled into the bank in response to higher deposit rates. On the assets side the demand for loans and investments simply stagnated due to the economic circumstances of the time. Only through a careful and selective structuring of assets was it possible for the interest earnings to exceed the cost of deposits so as to maintain some profit for shareholders.

The Bank in Winterthur, later to become the Schweizerische Bankgesellschaft, was an unusual phenomenon in that it perceived its assets to be already in place. As a result of the completion and the beginnings of goods transport by the first railroads, Winterthur became an important railway junction. This meant that warehousing facilities were of considerable importance for goods in transit; accordingly, the construction of a large warehouse facility was begun by the local commercial society. The entire structure was turned over in 1862 to the newly formed Bank in Winterthur which had been established with a capital of 5 million francs.

For such a bank as this, the times could hardly have been more propitious. The cotton situation, due to the American Civil War, was desperate, with prices rising to considerable heights. Stockpiling of cotton, therefore, using the physical facilities of the warehouse and the financial facilities of the Bank, proved to be ideal circumstances for the Bank which satisfied, through credit, the requirements of Swiss cotton manufacturers. Such stockpiles were useful as a hedge against further price increases. The result was that the Bank was able to double its share value.

With the close of the Civil War and the resumption of American cotton exports, the warehousing assets of the Bank declined markedly. At the same time the Bank, to its credit, was able to diversify its assets into other activities – insurance, mortgages, and the development of other banks both in Winterthur and in Herisau. Other local industries such as the locomotive works and saltworks were financed as well so that by the time of the abandonment of warehousing as an asset, the bank was well on its way to becoming a 'grossbank'.

The decade of the 1860s was a 'Cobden decade' and was characterised by the formation of joint-stock companies all over Europe. Banks were excellent vehicles for limited liability corporations and the Eidgenössische Bank was rather typical of this spirit of optimism. This bank, located in Berne, was to combine all banking functions including note issue. It was capitalised at an extraordinary 60 million francs, though not all the shares offered to the public were taken (only

6 million francs were paid up). Headed by the colourful Jakob Stämpfli, the bank attempted to increase the note issue of Switzerland; indeed, it aspired to become the most important note-issuing bank in the country. This it did by some 2 million francs when an embezzlement of a million francs in its Zürich office caused a massive return of its banknotes.

The issue of banknotes by the Swiss banks must have been seen as a most attractive method for expanding both assets and liabilities for the reason that, as liabilities, they are cost free. The consequence could only be an increase in profit. The 'strategem' works just so long as the Swiss public are willing to accept these notes as a genuine increase in the money supply, but, and this is the main point, the Swiss were a careful people, and the slightest degree of suspicion is sufficient to trigger a wave of distrust in these banknotes.

Turning away from being a bank of note issue, the Eidgeñossische Bank attempted to become a deposit bank after the fashion of English banks. Hitherto, it must be pointed out, Swiss banks used largely their own funds acquired from the sale of shares. Again, to refer to the conservative nature of Swiss psychology at the time, the principle of deposit banking was quite new and confined only to specific areas of the country. When local offices of the Eidgennossische Bank were opened in Zürich, St. Gallen, Geneva, and even Basle in 1873, offering interest rewards for chequing accounts, they were seen as aggressive competitors of local banks and, therefore, not welcome.

In actual fact there was insufficient business activity, or if one wishes to express it in terms of the Gross Domestic Product, the GDP of Switzerland was not sufficiently great to warrant the introduction of another bank with strong competitive ambitions. The nature of the banking service is such that it requires the movement of commerce, generating income as goods change ownership, during which process banking services are rendered. It is then that deposits can also change ownership in the opposite direction as goods, and banking also provides that facility more expeditiously than if cash were used. This means that since the period of the 1870s was not conducive to business expansion, any new bank had to force its way into an already served and relatively static market for its services.

The result was that the Eidgenössische Bank turned from bill discounting to investment banking as its final source for profit. Thus, it concentrated its assets more and more in the securities field as well as in railway loans. By the end of the 1870s, the railways had incurred considerable losses, and the securities and industrial credits had to be largely written off. In a word, the assets side of the balance sheet shrunk disastrously under the circumstances of the time.

THE FINANCIAL STRUCTURE OF THE EARLY SWISS COMMERCIAL BANKS

From the standpoint of our modern perspective, we can easily recognise both the tasks and the problems inherent in the developing Swiss banks during their formative period. Their function at that time was a simple one – that of mobilising capital and applying it to those investment opportunities where the returns will be both sufficiently great and the risk of loss of capital will be minimal. It was a trade-off. The assets must be structured so as to provide the necessary earnings as well as sufficient liquidity. This was, at best, a difficult balancing act because without a stock exchange facility by which investments might be liquidated, the banks could find themselves unwilling owners of physical assets which were difficult to be disposed of.

At the same time, the art of deposit banking had not yet spread to the infant Grossbanken. Deposit banking was still largely the prerogative of the savings banks; hence the potential for maintaining the security of deposits by 're-cycling' (acquiring additional deposits with which to repay depositors who re-claimed their funds) was not available to the banks. All the funds they had at their disposal were those derived from the sale of their capital stock or from bonds which they had issued and sold. What relatively cheap current accounts they did have on deposit could be quickly tied up in investments which, though quite worthy in terms of their economic value, were nonetheless illiquid. This raised the important problem of a reserve and how much reserve would be required against these deposits.

The problem of reserves was exacerbated by the fact that short term lending via bills of exchange or letters of acceptance, which seemed liquid enough at the outset, would evolve into long term illiquid loans as new and longer term bills were further discounted. Ultimately, the borrower was often unable to pay at all and the banks found themselves the unwilling owners of a factory. Such real assets had to be written down in value or even completely written off, making it impossible for the banks to honour their commitments to either their depositors or their investors.

It was to address these problems, the matter of illiquidity of investments, that stock exchanges were developed. An interesting example of precisely the difficulty caused by the lack of a stock exchange was the experience of the Basle Bankverein with the bankrupt Jurabahngesellschaft. Because of the decision of the Federal Assembly to develop the railway system under private and cantonal enterprise, the Bankverein, as well as foreign banks, had not only made loans but had also purchased shares of capital in the company, i.e. there was no other method of financing the railway in the absence of federal funding. In 1860, the old Bankverein, the original syndicate of private banks, had granted a 5 per cent loan on first mortgage to the Jurabahn Company which undertook to complete the necessary tunnel construction for the railway. When it failed to honour its debts to the bank, both the operating company and the Jurabahngesellschaft went into bankruptcy even though the railway itself was completed, and the Bankverein was faced with the difficult, and long term problem of liquidating its assets held as cover for the loan.

A stock exchange, of course, would have greatly assisted the Bankverein in the task of asset liquidation, and it was precisely because of situations such as this that a Bourse a la Criée was finally opened in Basle in 1876.[5] So it was that the interesting decision by the Federal Assembly, to leave the development of railways in the hands of the cantons and the private sector, though of doubtful value at best, had the positive result of encouraging the development of Stock Exchanges for the reason that railway securities and other similar forms of equity could not be readily liquidated without a market price. This decision (to provide an exchange for the liquidation of railway shares) ran counter to the arguments of Swiss liberals who preferred outright state ownership, especially so since arguments for state ownership of railways were already being advanced in Germany.[6]

The banks we are discussing in this section may be referred to as Credit Mobilier banks. We can understand the reason for this title because their own assets were largely structured toward fixed real assets. As such, there is hardly any doubt that the contribution of these banks to the economic development of Switzerland, as well as to the employment of the labour force, must have been considerable. Thus, despite the mistakes and errors in judgement committed by them, their contributions to the economy were great, not the least of these contributions being the establishment of an efficient capital market in the country through the creation of stock exchanges.

The long term result of the new stock exchanges extended far beyond the immediate objective of liquidity. Indeed, it is precisely here that we find that what really began as economic development banks actually evolved into something considerably much broader in scope – commercial banking combined with investment banking and ultimately to become universal banking. Wilthout pause we can now say that the economic development and prosperity of modern Switzerland rests upon the welfare of one of its greatest industries, its Grossbanken.

But the growth of the Grossbanken and the stock exchanges which they developed was not greeted by the mass of the Swiss population with enthusiasm. Again, we have the fundamentally conservative nature of the people expressing itself. The great banks were seen not as welcome additions to the capital market but as monopolists that were bent upon cornering the supply of capital which appeared to be in short supply. The higher interest rates offered by the great banks and the possibility of speculation in the stock exchanges seemed to be attractive to both the native Swiss and foreign suppliers of capital.

This could have been expected. Even in Switzerland, a country with a high savings potential, capital was, because of the great combined demand of the railways and industrial development, the scarce factor of production. This was not true in the Switzerland of the old Confederation when capital for domestic use was in surplus. Then, the Swiss exported capital because the higher rewards obtained in capital markets abroad. Now that the commercial banks had developed a more modern capital market for Switzerland, it was to be expected that other uses for capital, outside the market, could hardly compete, and for good reason, for the building of railways and, later, large scale corporate industry had to take priority.

CANTONAL BANKS

Cantonal banks were quite different from the regional commercial banks because they were more the instruments of government policy than profit-oriented institutions. The Zürich Interest Commission, discussed above, was probably the first of such banks, dating back into the eighteenth century. The Cantonal Bank of Berne was another, though it was established much later, in 1834. This bank, as noted above, was the first of the note-issuing banks of Switzerland.

What is interesting, and unique, in the creation of these banks is the consciousness amongst the Swiss population that the exercise of financial power, along with all the other responsibilities of the cantons, was quite a normal circumstance. This was not just 'socialism' but an awareness of a natural division of powers and responsibilities as between the public and private sectors. What was to be the source of conflict throughout the several revolutionary movements in Europe had been an already established fact to the Swiss.

To appreciate the historical significance of these banks, we must recognise that they were being developed prior to the period of commercial banking which gave rise to the great commercial banks, referred to in the previous section as Grossbanken. They arose because of the peculiar federal nature of the early Confederation which existed prior to 1848. At the time there was a felt need for economic development in the form of infrastructure, transport, regional connections between cantons, public buildings, health, and so on. In terms of developing production or manufacturing industry, the cantonal banks were not at all interested because, in the political philosophy of the day, there was no accommodation for this particular aspect of economic development. Risk or speculation, the hallmark of productive activity, was to be strictly avoided.[7]

So it was that by the time of the 1848 constitution, there really were only two 'concentrations', as it were, in the banking system of the new Confederation. The first was the venerable private banks which already had had a long history. The second was the cantonal banks which provided both mortgage capital for small business enterprises (such as farmers, tradesmen) and the infrastructural investment with specific political objectives. Obviously, in between these two major banking activities (the private and the cantonal banks) there was a vacuum. So it was that there was a growing awareness of a strong need for the commercial banks which had already been developed in England. It was these commercial banks which were to develop, after bankruptcies, amalgamations, etc. into the Grossbanken.

Table 8.1 though by no means perfectly accurate, does give us an approximate quantitative evaluation of all of the Swiss banks at the end of the year 1850.

The focus of banking activities is evident in the values for the various components of the combined balance sheets. Savings deposits are almost the entire prerogative of the savings banks which were by far the most numerous – 150 of a total of 171. In addition, the concentration of investments of these savings accounts lay in the mortgage area, precisely as one might expect given the circumstances of the social and economic structure of Swiss society at the time. Cantonal banks relied heavily upon their own resources (their respective governments and their own bonds) for their funds, with 50 per cent of total liabilities

Table 8.1

	K	B	Leu	L	S	Total
Number of banks	5	3	1	12	150	171
Active (Assets) in million of francs						
Cash	1.2	–	0.3	8.7	2.5	12.7
Foreign exchange	3.9	–	–	6.7		10.6
Credits (loans)	5.6	–	–	10.4	3.6	19.6
Mortgages	11.4	0.6	4.9	0.1	36.4	53.4
Bonds	2.6	–	0.1	–	2.5	5.2
Other	1.3	0.1	0.1	1.0	0.4	2.9
Total	26.0	0.7	5.4	26.9	45.4	104.4
Passive (Liabilities) in millions of francs						
Banknotes	0.5	–	–	7.3	–	7.8
Chequeing accounts	–	–	–	4.2	–	4.2
Current accounts	2.0	–	–	–	2.0	
Savings accounts	4.0	0.2	–	–	42.0	46.2
Bonds	5.5	0.1	4.5	2.0	–	12.1
Own resources	13.0	0.3	0.9	10.0	3.4	27.6
Other	1.0	0.1	–	3.4	–	4.5
Total	26.0	0.7	5.4	26.9	45.4	104.4

K cantonal banks
B agricultural credit banks
L local banks (i.e. commercial banks)
S savings banks
Source: Ritzmann, Franz, *Die Schweizer Banken* (Bern and Stuttgart: Verlag Paul Haupt, 1973), p.46.

deriving from this source. Their assets also were concentrated heavily in mortgages and shorter term loans. Agricultural banks (practically all of the entries under this category consisted of those of the Basellandschaftliche Hypothenbank), yet in their infancy, showed similar investments, though savings accounts for these banks were showing a greater relative importance than in the past.

The regional commercial banks, certainly the most interesting of the classifications, from our point of view, were conspicuous because of their weakness. At the time, only eight banks issued banknotes (one of these was certainly the Kantonalbank von Bern) showing clearly the unreadiness on the part of the Swiss public to accept anything as a medium of exchange except their own familiar coin. This contrasts rather sharply with the fact that just 30 years later, in 1880, there were 36 banks of note issue with a circulation of 93 million francs.[8]

Nevertheless the capacity to issue banknotes to the amount of 7.3 million francs meant that the notes were the second largest source of funding for these banks, the first being their own resources of 10 million francs. The commercial credit activity of these banks was still rather small, just 4.2 million francs, suggesting that business enterprise had not yet reached the point of using commercial banking facilities to the same extent as in England.

POLITICS AND BANKING

Early in the post-1848 history of the Confederation, political parties assumed considerable importance both in the cantons and in the federal government. While Switzerland had escaped the revolutions and conflicts of Europe, it would be quite incorrect to assume that all was peaceful within the structure of the new Confederation.

The Constitution provided for an extraordinary complex of legislative and admistrative bodies consisting of:

1. The federal assembly, made up of two houses, the council of states (Stande Rath) composed of two representatives from each canton
2. The national council (National Rath) consisting of deputies, one for each 20,000 of the population
3. The federal council (Bundesrath) consisting of seven members elected by the federal assembly and
4. A judiciary of eleven members also elected by the federal assembly.

In addition to all of this, the cantons had their own governments which were continuously being revised in the direction of more democracy in the form of the referendum. Laws made by the cantonal legislatures could be subject to either the facultative referendum or the obligatory referendum (which must be submitted to the public for approval). The ultimate result was an inevitable overlapping of powers and responsibilities such that the 1874 revision of the Federal constitution, which provided for similar referenda for the federal government, meant that more rights and privileges of the cantons were surrendered to the federal government. Despite this restructuring of responsibilities, the cantons themselves to this day are still not mere administrative divisions of the country but living political realities in their own right. Local customs and peculiarities are thereby preserved, all within the framework of the Swiss Confederation.

It is not difficult to appreciate, therefore, how political conflicts, both locally and federally, could arise. Efficiency, in a purely political sense, is almost impossible to achieve, and conflicting political parties must appear at both levels of government. As in similar political systems elsewhere, there arose in Switzerland a conservative establishment consisting of inherited wealth, business success, and political influence. What was uniquely Swiss was the long established tradition of combining both politics and business. Powerful, and colourful, individuals, such as Escher and Stämpfli, dominated the political scene at both the cantonal and the federal levels.

The banks became an important part of the perceived established 'system', particularly the regional commercial banks. While we find little historical evidence to support the fact that these commercial banks were actually part of the structure of 'aristocratic dominance', it remains that they were so perceived by opposing political parties because the personalities involved with the banks also played dominant roles in both levels of government. The result was the growth of a network of still more cantonal banks which were designed to assist those classes of people who were unable, for whatever reason, to have their credit requirements satisfied by the commercial banks. The new cantonal banks, therefore, were part of the democratic revolution of the 1860s and 1870s, and as the so called 'democratic parties' gradually gained control of cantonal governments, they set up their own banks guaranteed by their respective cantons.

The Basellandschaftlichen Kantonalbank was an example of just such a bank which was established in 1863 in opposition to the expert advice of Stämpfli.[9] Running counter to the establishment, it found itself in considerable difficulty for the first few years because of the refusal of property owners to patronise it. Since the new canton (Baselland) had as yet no finances of its own, it had to finance its bank with bonds which did not sell very well in the financial markets. After the government was changed, the bank was reorganised with a new bond issue and public confidence in it was realised at last.

In Zürich, the establishment of a cantonal bank likewise met, at first, with opposition. Nevertheless, the Zürcher Kantonalbank did make its appearance in 1870. Like the other cantonal banks, it was required to make credit available in smaller amounts, suitable to small business enterprise, and offer mortgage credit at lower cost to the borrower. In this latter sense, it is difficult to distinguish the cantonal banks from the mortgage banks which were established for this express purpose; indeed, the only distinction we can find between the cantonal banks and the mortgage banks appears to have been that the cantonal banks had a broader scope of operation, to include some commercial banking, than did the mortgage banks.

Other cantons soon followed the lead of Zürich and Baselland to become, in a remarkably short time, major contributors to the credit market of Switzerland. Again, we would stress, they were part of the same democratic movement which developed in the cantons and eventually led to the revision of the Constitution in 1874.

THE DEPRESSED 1870s

The decade of the 1870s, was characterised by a general deflation throughout Europe. On 9 May, 1873, stock prices on the Vienna stock exchange collapsed, and this began a long chain of bankruptcies. There had been an exceptional growth of joint-stock companies in Europe, many of which were formed purely on the basis of speculative paper credit. In the United States, the stock market had already closed on 20 September, 1872 precipitating many bank failures. The consequence of these events was the 'difficult seventies' for Switzerland, with a loss of export markets for watches and clocks; however, railroad building, which had begun afresh, proved to be a source of stability for the Swiss economy. The banks, on the other hand, whence the finance of railways largely originated, did not fare so well. The Bankverein in Basle, newly constituted as a joint-stock company, was in considerable difficulty after just one successful year, 1871. Thereafter, railways were either in bankruptcy or nearly so during the remainder of the decade. This was reflected in the total liabilities/assets of the Bankverein, some 72 per cent of which consisted of 'own resources' (capital and reserves). Deposits were hardly more than 10 per cent of total assets/liabilities. Indeed it was severely questioned by foreign shareholders at the time that the Bankverein should even continue as a bank. Under these adverse economic circumstances, why should cantonal banks find any hope of initial success?

We would suggest that it was precisely these economic circumstances of the time that contributed to both the initial founding of the banks and their growth. The regional commercial banks, quite simply, were in no position to satisfy the credit needs of both mortgages and the small commercial loans required by tradesmen. With their assets tied up in domestic railways on the one hand, and under the adverse economic conditions introduced by the panic of 1873 on the other, the commercial banks were already far too committed in the economic affairs of the world to accommodate the purely local credit requirements of the cantons.

The cantons were not only social and political realities, but were also economic 'realities' with specific commercial and financial requirements. Further, since the art of banking had not yet developed to the point where large banks could establish small branches in local communities, it remained for the cantons themselves to furnish their own. This they did by either providing the necessary capital or guaranteeing bonds which were then sold in the capital market. Indeed, the success of the cantonal banking system can be expressed by the fact that by the decade of the 1880s, the banks and the precursors of cantonal banks accounted for some 700 million francs or one-third of total bank credit at the time.[10]

OTHER BANKS

At the same time that the great Swiss banks were developing the stock exchanges as a means whereby capital investment might remain sufficiently liquid, small businessmen and farmers were themselves turning toward their own devices for an efficient allocation of capital. We recall that the early Swiss businessmen depended upon their own savings to provide the resources for growth and development; this was the consequence of what we might call the 'Protestant ethic'. When the need for capital outgrew the capacity of the individual businessman to provide, as a consequence of the industrial revolution during the 1820s and subsequent decades, it became necessary for the savings of the community to be mobilised as a supplement to these ploughed-back earnings. The result was a rather unique Swiss solution to this problem.

Originally, during the earlier centuries of the old Confederation, farmers in need of capital for expansion were forced to by-pass the ban of the church on usury by a device which amounted to purchasing land in exchange for an annuity, or a Gült. A kind of 'sales agreement', the Gült was a heavy burden for the early Swiss farmer to bear because it was, literally, in perpetuity. In the course of time and with the rise of the Protestant movement, the system gave way to the lien mechanism in which the land itself was the security for a loan – in other words, the mortgage which was confined to land. Urban mortgages, designed to assist in the purchase of buildings, had to await the development of fire insurance during the nineteenth century.

There was another unique feature of the Swiss mortgage market. Mortgage creditors were successful in forcing through the cantonal governments laws permitting foreclosure notices which made the mortgage the equivalent of a short-or medium-term loan. The purpose here was to avoid locking-in the mortgage interest rate for a long period, thereby taking advantage of a fluctuating interest market. Foreclosure meant that a new mortgage at a higher interest rate was possible. Similarly, the creditor could hold a mortgage at a higher mortgage rate (during short or medium periods) when rates in general were falling.

The result of this peculiar characteristic of the Swiss mortgage market meant that mortgages assumed the same feature as a long-term bond. In the case of bonds, rising interest rates collapse capital market values whereas falling rates increase capital values. The same was true for the mortgage. In a word, there existed a risk of falling capital values should expectations for rising interest rates be general, and this meant that the actual interest rate charged for the mortgage must reflect this risk, so it became a higher cost for the farmer to pay than would ordinarily have been the case.

As a defence against this unfortunate circumstance, mortgage banks were established either with government control or as private joint-stock corporations under the influence of government. This highlighted the extraordinary psyche of the Swiss farmer – individualist, to be sure, but quite capable of cooperation with the objective of structuring his own destiny when the need arose. Nevertheless, to have actually formed banks for the purpose of rectifying an obvious shortcoming in the Swiss credit system must have been a unique achievement.

In Zürich canton, a mortgage lending institution already existed in the form of a reconstituted Leubank. This bank, after suffering enormous losses in its foreign investments because of the massive inflation during the French Revolution, was reconstituted into a domestic mortgage bank. The cantonal government ensured the value of its share capital in addition to exercising a measure of supervision over its loans and investments. Other mortgage banks appeared in French-speaking Switzerland during the mid-century – the Neuchatel Caisse Hypothécaire the Caisse Hypothécaire of Fribourg, and the Crédit Foncier of Vaud, to mention a few.

In Basle, the Hypothekenbank in Basel, founded in 1863, was designed to satisfy the need for urban mortgages. In St Gallen and in

Winterthur similar banks were begun. All of these banks, plus the cantonal banks set up for the express purpose of mortgages, actually formed over one-fifth of the entire credit volume of the Swiss banks by the year 1883.[11] It is obvious, therefore, that their success was indicative of a rather considerable demand in the credit market which was not being satisfied by the commercial banks.

The question arises: are these genuine 'banks' in the true sense of the word or are they just agencies designed to channel capital already provided by governments into specific areas? We would argue that such institutions as the mortgage banks were not truly banks in the sense that they equated two equilibria, one on the liabilities side and one on the assets side, to create an equilibrium of equilibria as did the commercial banks. This latter is a much more difficult task because it requires two credit markets, the market for savings *and* the market for loans, to achieve an optimum efficiency in the distribution of scarce capital resources.

On the other hand, the development and the use of mortgage banks did respond to a public awareness, real or imaginary, that the commercial banks were creating a monopoly in credit markets and could exploit this situation to their advantage. Whether or not this is true we shall never know, but there is scarcely any doubt that a social conflict between the great banks and a large section of the Swiss population did develop which has lasted even to the present time.

The agricultural banks of Switzerland do invite comparison with their German counterparts; indeed, it is difficult not to assume some connection, if it be no more than an awareness of the earlier German credit movement. The Raiffeisen and Schultz-Delitsch banks could more accurately be likened to the Credit Union concept in Great Britain and North America rather than the Swiss agricultural bank. German peasants had deposited their meagre savings with Raiffeisen banks (there were no shares) which then loaned them to members of the same community. These 'village societies' were eventually linked by a Central Bank located at Neuwied which Raiffeisen himself had founded in 1876, the shares of which were owned by the village societies.

The substantive difference between the Swiss and German institutions arose from the differing circumstances of land holding. The German peasant worked and lived in a tight feudal structure and the Raiffeisen society was a means by which he could purchase necessary capital and equipment. For security, the peasant had only his existing capital and his small holding. In reality, however, the security for the loans to peasants lay in the fact that they were already well known in their own community, hence their degree of risk could be readily assessed.

Not so the Swiss farmer. In Switzerland there was no oppressive weight of an ancient feudal structure; quite the contrary, the agricultural banks were for the express purpose of lending for the purchase of land by the peasants themselves. At the same time there was little risk in these loans (relatively) because fire could not destroy land in the same way that buildings could become a heap of ashes (hence, without fire insurance, hardly an adequate security for the urban mortgage).

This made it possible for Swiss peasants to influence their government, and since 'government' in this case meant the cantonal governments of the New Confederation, funds could be allocated for the purpose of making credit available. Thus, instead of cooperative efforts amongst peasants in small communities after the Raiffeisen model, institutions created and designed by governments, in response to political influence, were serving the credit needs of farmers. One is almost tempted to recognise an étatism here, but that would be incorrect. Nor would pure socialism be the answer. The state mortgage banks were an effort to restore competition in the credit market, thereby making available to farmers the credit facilities which commercial and manufacturing activities had already enjoyed. There is, therefore, scarcely any difference between the mortgage banks, the cantonal banks, or other similar banks. They act purely as investment channels with capital already provided for them and seek to allocate that capital to its most lucrative or socially beneficial use.

CONCLUSIONS

Swiss banks developed under the influence of a most unique political and economic system. It was the peculiar federal and cantonal system (not merely the governments themselves) that contributed their own measure to the creation of a banking system which could not really be duplicated anywhere in the world.

Consider, as an example, the development of economic infrastructure. Most governments rely on the power of taxation to acquire the necessary wherewithall for the necessary public investment. Cantonal governments, however, preferred to form banks which, though really hardly more than investment houses, became the means through which the necessary capital could be channelled. These banks, once fully developed, were able to expand their lending into other fields such as agricultural mortagages, thereby serving other objectives as well. In other words, whenever the Swiss wished to accomplish something by way of serving the general welfare, they formed a bank for the purpose.

The greater the influence of democracy in the cantons the greater was the tendency to develop these banks. We cannot argue, therefore, that the Swiss were late in developing a 'modern banking system' (whatever that may be). Quite the contrary, while the Swiss had the example of Schultz-Delitsch in Germany or even the Raiffeissen banks, they developed their own unique system of local savings, cantonal, and mortgage banks which became both numerous and universal throughout the country by the mid-nineteenth century.

Between these specialised cantonal banks and the private banks that had existed for centuries in Switzerland, there was a gap. While the private banks had become adept at the art of investing their clients' capital either in Switzerland or abroad, so as to gain the greatest return with the least risk, there was no provision for a banking service which the new joint-stock companies being formed at the time were very much in need of. In addition, there were Swiss family business enterprises that had already grown too large to be sustained from their own earnings. In a word, a new demand for credit, hitherto not recognised, was growing during the middle of the nineteenth century.

Along with this new demand there arose a need for payment services so as to increase the efficiency of day-to-day business activity. In this sense, and only in this sense, can it be argued that modern Swiss banking was late in development. Why was it late? It was late for the simple and obvious reason that Swiss business activity had never experienced a felt need for such banking services until relatively late in the history of banking.

Those banks which did bridge the gap between specialised cantonal banks and the private banks, referred to as 'regional commercial banks', not only served the needs of business enterprise but also became principal contributors of capital for the construction of railways. In this sense, they were Credit Mobilier banks as well.

It is with these banks also that we find the true application of banking principles, that is the acquiring of society's savings through the reward of interest and transforming those savings into capital for lending thereby reaching a higher level of economic efficiency. While there was certainly no conscious act on the part of these banks to increase efficiency in the use of savings, there certainly was an awareness of greater profit. At the same time, they learned by experience the dangers inherent in high risk. Thus, when high returns on investments appeared attractive, the risk of defaults and bankruptcies reduced these high returns to something very much less. The practice of risk-spreading was therefore learned early in the history of these banks, and this meant foregoing an incentive for possible short term profit maximisation in exchange for prudence. Those banks that learned that lesson well evolved into the Grossbanken for which the Swiss are now so famous.

There is scarcely any doubt that the capital-intensive construction of Swiss railways was of paramount importance to the Confederation, both as a strategic transport facility between northern and southern Europe and as a link between cantons. Yet even within the boom of construction itself there were excesses of building which were not economically justified. Nevertheless, as an industrial investment, railway construction certainly moved total capital investment closer to its social optimality than did other forms of investment, such as the purchase of US bonds, which contributed nothing in terms of infrastructure to Switzerland itself.

It is this extraordinary capacity, we would suggest, to recognise that a balance must be struck between investment for profit and investment for social benefit that characterises the history of these banks. At one extreme, bankruptcy may result; therefore, to avoid bankruptcy, prudence in investment is essential. It was as simple as that. This was the empiricism displayed by the successful banks such as the Bankverein and the Schweizerischekreditanstalt which, we suggest, characterises Swiss banking even today. They learned by experience to take advantage of the wider risk dispersion which stems from banking activities which were distributed amongst different activities as well as different types of investments.

This was not understood by the mass of the Swiss population that looked upon these bankers as an elite who dictated the financial control of investment at the expense of the masses. One might sympathise with them because during the difficult years of the nineteenth century, their vision extended hardly further than their immediate town, valley, or canton. And stemming from this myopia there developed a series of specialised banks; such as cantonal banks and mortgage banks, which were among the first of their kind.

Notes

1. In the United States the matter of the free coinage of silver became a political issue which divided the economically influential East from the agrarian West. To the western silver producers, the Federal law of 1873 which discontinued the coinage of silver was a 'crime'. The politics of free silver continued until the end of the century. See Friedman, M, and Schwartz, A., *A Monetary History of the United States, 1867–1960*, NBER, (Princeton University Press, 1963) Chapter 3, p. 113/4.

2. This is the argument of Gerschenkron, that before industrial development could reach the 'take-off' point in Continental countries, the institutions (such as banks) had to be created in order to supply the necessary capital. Only in England was there sufficient capital and institutional capacity to encourage economic development on its own.

3. An interesting observation on this point is worth quoting as follows: 'The existence of so many banking houses and the relative ease with which investment capital could be obtained in industry therefore acted as a dynamic force in so far as it facilitated company foundation and expansion in Germany. But at the same time the way in which this was done sometimes tended to make the companies subsequently more cautious and less competitive in their behaviour. The influence of the banks seems to have been to reduce competition in order to minimise the risks, and they entered willingly into the cartel agreements and other agreements in restraint of competition which characterised German industry after 1880.' Milward, Alan S. and Saul, S. B., *The Development of the Economies of Continental Europe, 1850–1914*, (London: George Allen and Unwin Ltd, 1977,) p. 48.

4. Basler Handelsbank, 'Festschrift zum 50jahrigen Jubilaum 1862–1912', quoted in Bauer, *Swiss Bank Corporation, 1872–1972*, Swiss Bank Corporation, 1972, p. 37.

5. Bauer, *Swiss Bank Corporation*, pp. 39, 65.

6. In Bismarck's letter to the Bundesrat, February, 1879, the argument for state ownership of railways was summarised as follows: 'Among the various forms in which railways have been developed in civilized countries, the system of State railways pure and simple is the only one which is able to fulfil in the most satisfactory manner all the tasks of a national railway policy, by creating uniformity throughout the country and equality for all, and by promoting equally the welfare of all interested in railways. Only in the case of State railways is it possible to utilize to the full and in the most thorough manner the enormous capital invested in railways; only in the case of State railways is it possible to give direct and effective protection to the public interest which is the Government's duty; lastly only in the case of State railways is it possible to establish a simple, cheap, and rational railway tariff, to effectually suppress harmful differentation, and to create a just, diligent, and able administration which is guided solely by considerations of the general good. Therefore the State railway system must be considered as the final development in the evolution of the railway system.' Pollard, S. and Holmes, C., *Documents of European Economic History, Vol. 2* (London: Edward Arnold, 1972)

p. 129. Swiss liberal politicians had advocated the nationalisation of the railways on just such grounds some twenty years prior to the German legislation. Bismarck's argument is convincing; however, in Germany the final results hardly bore out his original concepts. Discriminatory and complex tariffs reflecting the foreign trade policies of the state, charging what the traffic will bear, and profits accrued for the State suggested otherwise. On the other hand, the efficiency of the German railways was the greatest in the world, according to Germans who were proud of their railway system. Clapham, Cambridge University Press, Cambridge, *Economic Development of France and Germany, 1815–1914*, (1961), p. 349.

7.   Bergier, Jean-François, *Wirtschafts Geschichte der Schweiz*, (Zürich: Benziger, Verlag AG, 1990) p. 334. Bergier's summary of the origins and development of the Swiss banking system in this final chapter of his book, though brief, is an excellent introduction to the subject.

8.   Bauer, *Swiss Bank Corporation* p. 73.

9.   Ritzmann, Franz *Die Schverges Banker*, Verlag Paul Paulktang, Bern & Stutgart, 1973, p. 80.

10.   Ibid., p. 81.

11.   Ibid., p. 78.

9 Capitalism at the Turn of the Century

SWISS BANK CONSOLIDATION

The years 1870 to 1890 were characterised by the abandonment of the bi-metallic monetary standard. The resulting deflation was a disaster for the United States, which was in the process of literally 'blundering back to gold' from the greenback standard of the Civil War era.[1]

For Europe the abandonment of the silver standard meant the inevitable collapse of silver prices, which fell with the abundance of silver production from the once 15:1 ratio to gold to as low as 40:1 at the beginning of the twentieth century. Massive domestic inflations would certainly have resulted had there been a return to a bi-metallic standard, as had been advocated by some. This would have been the consequence of both an influx of silver combined with the growing use of chequeing accounts and other money substitutes.

Yet it was the abandonment of the bi-metallic system which not only avoided domestic inflation but also caused precisely the opposite, deflation, as the economies of Europe swung, pendulum-like, to the other extreme. This is why international commodity prices trended downward, suggesting that gold itself was already too scarce a commodity to be used as a basis for currencies, so forcing the debate regarding bi-metallism to continue. There was, however, a marked increase in the rate of economic growth in Europe which resulted not only from the completion of the railway building era but also from technological progress in the electrical and chemical fields. There was also an increase in the standard of living of Europeans, who demanded more of the better things of life.[2]

At the same time that increased trade and commercial developments made improved standards of living possible, there appeared a movement designed to oppose the forward leaps of technological progress. We find this comment from the Eleventh Annual Report of the Basle Chamber of Commerce regarding the circumstances to be most eloquent. It speaks for itself.

... the nations summon up all their intellectual and inventive powers and, at great cost and pains, drive tunnels through the mountain barriers Nature has set between them, but no sooner have they succeeded than, in their delusion, they erect in place of the natural barriers they have successfully overcome artificial tariff walls which prevent them from availing themselves of the benefit which the newly opened country can offer.[3]

No better characterisation of the economic circumstances of the day could be made. The railroad era, which climaxed with the completion of the St Gotthard railway in Switzerland, had been a resounding success during the years when Cobden's ideas were in vogue. Yet already by the end of 1886, state socialist principles and nationalistic tariffs were coming to the fore.

For Switzerland, the end of railroad construction meant that a major impetus for employment ceased. To be sure, the financing of the railroads must be considered as the greatest achievement of the banks during the nineteenth century. Probably the most highly capital-intensive railroad network in the world, it required immense amounts of financing and could only have succeeded with the assistance of the railroad banks, that is, banks formed as intermediaries between the ordinary banks and the railroads. The first of these, the Eisenbahn-bank, was wound up in 1886 after some seven years of service during which it had succeeded in rescuing several railroads that had approached bankruptcy in the 1870s. Additional intermediaries, the Banque Nouvelle des Chemins de fer Suisses, formed for the purpose of the construction of the Simplon tunnel, and, later, the Centralbank fur Eisenbahnen in Luzerne were created for the express purpose of taking over about one-half of the shares of the Centralbahn – a railroad which was in considerable financial difficulty at the time.

The principle underlying the railroad banks was simple enough. Railroad stocks were characterised by considerable illiquidity. Therefore banks which purchased these shares outright severely endangered the value of their assets since the shares were subject to considerable variation in their values on the stock exchanges. A bank created for the purpose of purchasing railroad shares, maintaining its own liquidity responsibilities, can then sell its own shares and bonds to other banks. But why should the shares of the intermediary bank not be subject to the same price variation as the railroad shares? Because the intermediary bank maintained its own measure of liquidity to support the market value of its own shares. In effect, the same probability calculus applied to the banker's bank (since there were many creditor banks) as to the ordinary large bank with its many creditors to whom it was liable.

Despite the creation of these intermediary banks, the banks themselves held a considerable amount of railroad shares in their portfolios. Indeed, it is no exaggeration to argue that the greatest single achievement of these regional 'other' banks was the actual finance of the Swiss railway system. These banks, along with local and cantonal governments, not only purchased shares and bonds as assets for their own accounts but also acted as intermediaries to sell railway shares to foreigners, mainly German, thereby tapping foreign capital. They were particularly helpful in eastern Switzerland, in the canton of Graubunden, where railroads such as the Rhaetischebahn required enormous capital investment in bridges, tunnels, and so on over what must surely be the most forbidding railway territory in the world.

Inexorably, however, the Federal government was moving toward the purchase of railroad shares ultimately to form Swiss Federal Railways. This policy had been forecast as long ago as 1883, when the Federal Parliament passed a new auditing law requiring a uniform, and more practical, method of keeping accounts and balance sheets. It was obvious to astute observers of the day that there was a singular purpose in this – the ultimate purchase of all the railway shares. In order to accomplish this, an accurate evaluation of the shares was required. These expectations were realised when, by the end of the 1880s, the government proceeded to purchase shares in the major railroads. The climax of this policy was reached in 1891. At that time the Federal Council received approval from the Federal Assembly to purchase one-half the shares of the Centralbahn, the other half to be purchased by a bank syndicate. The government's share was to be financed by federal bonds at 3 per cent. In itself, the purchase was not important, but the Council declared its intention to take over *all* shares of the Centralbahn and to ultimately unite all the railroads of Switzerland under federal ownership.

For the Swiss, a nation already famous for its disagreements, quarrels, and long-term grudges amongst the cantons, this was a spark to ignite a conflagration. The old antagonisms, real or imaginary, though long buried, surfaced once more. The quarrel between east and west (that is, at which point, Simplon, St Gotthard, or the Splügen, would the Alps be pierced with a tunnel) appeared again. Since the purchase by the Federal Railways Department of 38,000 shares in the newly formed Jura-Simplonbahn in 1889, this question assumed a much greater significance because it showed a singular preference for the western route as opposed to the east. As a result, when the proposal to purchase all the Swiss railways was put to a referendum on 6 December 1891, it was defeated.

The interesting consequence of the proposal, and its defeat, was to precipitate a massive speculation and collapse of values on the stock exchanges. Values of railway shares had risen in anticipation of government purchases. In addition, German buyers of shares had become more numerous as the Prussian government had begun its process of taking over their own railways 1879. The result was a bullish stock market boom in Switzerland at the same time that in the rest of the world markets were depressed.[4]

But not for long. The rejection of the government's plan by the people in the referendum meant a similar down trend in Swiss markets, precipitated, of course, by the collapse of railway share values. Thus, the Basle Chamber of Commerce could report in the year 1891, 'For most countries, and also for us, the year must be described as one of economic recession, for most lines of business as a lean year, for many a year of loss or even ruin, and only for a few as a good year.'[5]

But more than just a 'lean year', there were many bankruptcies and near bankruptcies. The Schweizerische Unionbank in St Gall had to suspend its dividends for that year, and the Züricher Bankverein also approached its demise but was, fortunately, saved. Four firms which had actually conspired to rig the market in their favour, during the speculative period fuelled by the expectation of government takeover of the railways, were permanently suspended.[6]

But even this was not all, for there were many individual embezzlements, as well as other schemes, to take advantage of the bullish speculative market. These were not only in the world of business enterprise but also in government officialdom. It was these which encouraged demands on the part of the general public for government intervention, and, it should be added, demands that the government take the resonsibility for putting its own house in order. Banks had participated, in the sense that they had made loans against stock market securities and even on the shares of the ruined Kreditbank Winterthur. Finally, even the sound banks, such as the Bankverein and the Schweizersche Kreditbank, which had included large numbers of railway shares in their assets, suffered from the collapse in their values on the stock markets.

THE INEVITABLE FEDERALISATION OF RAILWAYS

As we have shown, railway construction in Switzerland had been entirely the work of the private sector combined with the individual cantons with the banks playing a central role as intermediaries. In this sense we might argue that it was indeed a remarkable achievement. What then was the objective of the Government in its proposed purchase of railways which were not only already built but were also successful in their operation? The answer, we would suggest, lay in the unique political and economic structure of Switzerland and its turbulent history. The conflict between east and west regarding the most opportune location of the transalpine route to the south, with the locational advantage to each region being very great, arose again. To bridge, as it were, these regions of the country with a uniting government railway would seem quite appropriate – a unifying influence. At the same time the natural Swiss abhorrence of foreign control of a strategic transport system, real or imagined, would be laid to rest. With railway rates established by the Government-controlled Centralbahn it would be difficult for foreign-controlled railways (actually railways owned by the private sector, both domestic and foreign) to push up rates in the interest of greater profit.

Appropriate as the argument may have been at the time, the outcome was quite different. Prices of railway shares on the stock exchanges rose considerably, with speculators anticipating the purchase of shares by the Government. Banks, rather unfortunately, proceeded to encourage such speculation by advancing funds for that very purpose. In the Züricher Kantonalbank alone advances against railway shares rose by some 46 per cent from 1889 to 1891.[7] Additionally, there were severe losses in the commercial bill area of lending due entirely to the discounting of finance bills, again for the purpose of speculation on the stock exchanges. Further speculation in Swiss railway shares took place in Germany, where railways were almost all completely nationalised, increasing Swiss prices still further.

All this was occurring at the same time that sharp losses on foreign stock markets such as London were being recorded. This was the time of the difficulties of Baring Bros. of London, and world stock markets were feeling the impact of a general world recession; at the same time the Swiss stock markets (perhaps *because* the sluggish foreign markets had re-directed capital toward the speculative Swiss market) were wallowing in an orgy of bull speculation purely because of the anticipation of railway nationalisation.

When the referendum proved to be against nationalisation, the result was doubly severe precisely because of the world-wide slump in economic activity. The Swiss stock markets entered a strong bearish period which brought down not only railway stocks but those of other industries as well. The Basle Chamber of Commerce reported a 25–48 per cent loss of value on 25 'representative shares'.

As far as the Swiss banks were concerned, the result was disastrous. Market rigging by some banks proved to be their undoing. Other banks with business relations with these banks also suffered. Thus, those banks that had performed the intermediary function so effectively, particularly as they had so successfully bridged the gap between the sector that accepts the risk in the business enterprise, such as railway construction, and the sector that provides the capital but does not want the associated risk, were literally undone in the entire process of speculation. Banking lessons had to be learned, and while it is easy enough for us to look back in surprise at the obvious, we can easily forget that in our own modern age of risk balancing with the aid of derivatives (with modern computer technologies);[8] the handling of risk with the objective of its minimisation had not yet become a science.

To a certain degree, one may assert that the decade which closed the nineteenth century was the end of an epoch in Swiss banking. The 'weaker' banks (however 'weaker' may be defined) disappeared in the crash which followed the orgy of stock speculation. The practice of placing assets with other banks, referred to as interbank deposits, which had grown over the years, brought even the stronger banks into dire straits.[9] Indeed, it would be difficult to find a more expressive description of those years than that of the Basle Chamber of Commerce itself. It stated (with 20/20 hindsight) that the banking crisis could have been predicted with certainty and, having arrived, could be described as necessary for the cleaning up of business life.

> The plethora of new banks, the unnecessary increases of capital solely for purposes of agiotage, (i.e. speculation) the price manipulation and speculation in their own shares by the banks, the abuse of advancing money on securities and the gambling fever it encouraged, the abuse of repledging deposits to obtain funds to keep the swindle going, the scramble for big and sometimes shady business, etc. had created a state of affairs that could not possibly continue without precipitating a crisis.[10]

THE PURCHASE OF RAILWAYS BY THE CONFEDERATION

Swiss banks were able to finance the construction of railroads by means of two banking functions:

1. the intermediation between those who have capital (the savings at their disposal) and those who require it, and
2. the balancing of risks.

The first function is really a mechanical one of transmission, but the second requires as high a degree of risk management (and control) as is possible, and is best described as the adjustment of loans and investments in accordance with liquidity and non-liquidity as discussed in the beginning of this chapter. Those who invest in bank shares may do so with the assurance of a minimum risk to their financial assets as a consequence. Banks, in their turn, must control as much as possible their *own* risk exposure, a matter quite separate from that of mimimising the risk of their creditors, yet closely related. It was through the accomplishment of both these functions that the more successful Swiss banks were able to prosper and grow during the latter part of the nineteenth century.

How was this achievement possible during an age of no computers, bank derivatives, or other devices whereby risk might be managed? The answer to this interesting question lies in the extremely high quality of management; indeed, we have been very much impressed with the early technique of management and control of the more successful Swiss banks. The reason is the fact that the bank managers themselves, before they became managers, were generally successful entrepreneurs in their own right. In addition, they also sat as members of the boards of directors of clients to whom they granted loans or from whom they purchased equity. This also meant that an important requirement for these people, in order to become a manager in the first place, must have been a capacity for prodigious amounts of work, so much so that their modern counterparts must certainly flinch at the amount of energy and time put into their efforts.

Consider, for example, Karl Feer-Heerzog, an engineer and silk ribbon manufacturer in Aarau, who was vice-chairman of the Basler Bankverein in 1872. He had traveled to Paris and proceeded to acquire for his bank, *through his own efforts*, the status of the official Swiss subscription office for the issue of French government loans. This was on the occasion of the huge indemnity which France was forced to pay to Prussia at the close of the Franco-Prussian War. Recognising the 'golden opportunity' available to his bank, Feer-Heerzog was able, at one stroke, to advance both the status and prestige of his bank with the minimum of risk. Not content with this accomplishment, he later became the first chairman of the board of directors of the Gotthard-bahn, undoubtedly the most important single railway in central Europe.

Another example was J.J. Schuster-Burckhardt, a banker of considerable reknown. He was a member of the board of directors for *seventeen* companies both in Switzerland and abroad. Of these seventeen he was chairman of ten. Such men were giants compared to their modern counterparts and could put forth great efforts on behalf of their banks. Most important for our purposes, by their efforts, they were in a position to control their bank's risk exposure, probably the most important single aspect of Swiss banking.

Additionally, from the genius of these early Swiss bankers was developed the models for the industrial and financial development of the Swiss economy – transport, chemicals, textiles, electrical industry, and banks – all within the private sector and with probably a greater degree of economic efficiency than any government planning board could possibly have achieved. Perhaps it was a happy coincidence that the possibility of profit and the economic welfare of the Confederation were equated or, more likely, it would have been the far-sighted bankers' approach to investment with the minimum of risk which itself led to profit maximisation and, at the same time, to the economic growth of an export-oriented economy. We must give these bankers credit, however, for eschewing the shorter term speculative profits which had brought so many of the lesser banks to ruin, preferring the longer term gains for their banks.

By 25 March, 1897, the Confederation had declared its intention to purchase the railways at a calculated value per share which was somewhat lower than the stock market had anticipated. The consequence was a collapse of railway share prices and, since railways were a major investment of the banks, the result was a similar collapse in bank shares. Nevertheless, the time had come for the Confederation to take over the railroads, for the simple reason that the public so desired it. There was a public prejudice, real or imagined, against foreign ownership, in particular because it was felt that it was a 'matter of shame for Switzerland that most of the owners of the main traffic routes should be resident abroad, that their influence should dominate the general meetings, and that foreign capitalists in conjunction with like-minded persons in our own financial circles who are associated with them through various interests and partly dependent on them, should have the destiny of the principal Swiss railways in their hands'.[11] To be sure, there was foreign ownership, some 60 per cent of the Centralbahn was owned by foreigners resident abroad, 54 per cent of the Nordostbahn and 95 per cent of the Gotthardbahn were similarly owned. The result was, when the referendum challenging the legislation was called for, that a two-thirds majority of the voting public (an estimated 78 per cent of eligible voters actually voted) were in favour of nationalisation.

The key position of the Swiss banks in the actual financing of the railway construction must not be forgotten. The banks, acting as intermediaries, sold shares and bonds to investors in foreign markets so as to raise some 1.3 billion (1.3 thousand million) Swiss francs consisting of 440 million of share capital, 792 million of debentures, and 124 million of direct subsidies.

At the time of the finance of the 're-purchase' (or nationalisation), the banks again played a major role since the Confederation could not possibly raise such a substantial sum. Accordingly, in 1901, the banks, acting as underwriters, issued 500 million of 3.5 per cent federal bonds which were readily taken up because the rate of interest, at the time, was high relative to other competing rates in a depressed market. The bonds were sold on the Paris Stock Exchange so that French, English and German capital financed a large part of the purchase by the Confederation, so substituting debt ownership for share ownership. Subsequent sales of federal bonds completed the financing.

The last of the railways to be purchased was the Gotthardbahn in 1913, delayed because of the international complications involved. Here also foreign capital was instrumental, this time not for railway construction but for the finance of the federal purchase. All that really happened, in the last analysis, was that foreigners surrendered their controlling influence (which was actually minimal because of the Swiss government's control measures) in the railways in exchange for fixed-interest bonds. The banks once more had intervened to make this 'swap' possible.

There was yet another interesting factor involved in the process of nationalisation. Swiss railway shares disappeared from the stock exchanges leaving a vacuum to be filled by whatever means possible. This was why American railway shares were introduced into the Swiss exchanges (without great success) so that the Basle Chamber of Commerce could state with some regret in 1905 'that no real substitute has yet been found for our nationalised railway shares, which in earlier years gave rise to such brisk turnovers and to international arbitrage'. This latter point suggests a turnaround in attitude for that conservative body because it was precisely arbitrage (which in order to be profitable requires share price fluctuations), and the profits derived therefrom, which it had earlier deplored. Some idea of the 'de-nuding' of the Swiss exchanges can be had from the decline in all railway share values from 353.63 millions of francs in 1896 to 122.38 millions in 1913.[12]

At the same time that Swiss railway ownership was being transferred via the banks, the last decade of the nineteenth century, with the exception of the early years already discussed, was characterised by considerable industrial growth and economic activity, all requiring the services of banks in the form of additional credit. Public authorities, cantons, and cities all needed funding and this put considerable pressure on existing savings with the inevitable result that interest rates generally rose. Additionally, there was a heavy foreign demand for imports from Switzerland in the form of electrical and engineering equipment, which gave rise to the formation of new corporations, mergers, and stock issues, all requiring the services of banks not only for credit but also for underwriting. Swiss bank loans rose by some 60 per cent throughout the period with mortgages not far behind at 50 per cent.

Before the century was over, however, there was the inevitable cyclical contraction of world export markets. A somewhat mild business recession had begun in the United States in June 1899; this was followed with monetary tightness in the US banks, and a stock market panic in the autumn. While the slight retardation in business growth could hardly have been called a 'recession' in the United States, the effect on Swiss exports was sufficient to demonstrate that Switzerland had become so export oriented that its industry was certain to suffer markedly even though only slight interruptions in economic growth in Europe and America occurred. The Swiss economy had been so completely linked with that of the world that this 'leveraged' impact of world events was the result.

Despite the gathering storm clouds of international politics, the Boer War, the Russo-Japanese War, the 1905 Russian Revolution, and the Moroccan crisis, in the new century Swiss exports grew considerably to reach a peak in the year 1905. Again, however, there was an interruption in the form of the panic of 1907 which began in New York with the failure of the Knickerbocker Trust Co. The panic, though short, was characterised by the suspension of payments by US banks in the fall of 1907 and spring of 1908. The very act of suspension avoided a chain reaction amongst other banks and kept the panic from spreading and growing into a full-fledged recession. Again, however, the effect upon the Swiss economy was enhanced because of the impact on its exports.

It would, however, be quite incorrect to lay too much emphasis upon the rather brief periods of banking panics and the interruption of trade and commerce which they brought about. The entire period from the early 1870s to the outbreak of the first World War was one of the immense capital accumulation. The social structure of the time was such that the labouring classes of Europe were performing their tasks of production not for their own enhancement of consumption, or wealth accumulation for themselves but for their employers' benefit. These employers were, theoretically, free to spend the profits of their enterprise in a welter of conspicuous consumption, but they elected not to so do. They did, in fact, use their great share in the distribution of wealth for the accumulation of fixed capital of various shapes and kinds. Railroads, of course, were one particular form, but there were others: factories of all kinds producing goods in the infinite varieties required by society. The great German Empire during this period had transformed itself from an agrarian system to a massive industrial machine which had become Switzerland's principal trading partner. But not only Switzerland, the entire region of central Europe fell within the German sphere of influence.

For the Swiss, the lessons of German banks were not lost. They were very conscious of the progress made by the industrial banks in the finance of industry; indeed, those policy-making staff members of the Schweizerische Bankverein became convinced that the efforts of the banks abroad to meet the heavy capital requirements of new industrial enterprise must be met by Swiss banks themselves. In order to avoid being 'crushed' by the competition, Switzerland would simply have to follow the lead of these great banks. There was, thus, a kind of 'nationalism' in the sense that the banks saw themselves as being in the forefront not only of Swiss economic independence but also of Swiss prosperity.

But what about the home market and its credit needs? Here the already well-established cantonal banks were supplying the credit requirements of small business enterprises so that as the larger banks extended their activities throughout the country, they moved slowly and cautiously into all areas of the country to supplement the cantonal banks rather than to engage in head-on competition.

But more important for the Grossbanken was the foreign sector. The Schweizerische Bankverein, under the leadership of its extraordinary chairman, Schuster-Burckhardt, opened the first branch of a Swiss bank in London in 1898. For this purpose additional capital was required, which was quickly secured to the amount of 5 million francs, so that by the first of July the branch was opened for business at 40 Threadneedle Street.

The phenomenal success of this venture into the foreign sector was the indicator for the future for Swiss banks. The home market was already reasonably well accommodated with banking services, so much so that to expand throughout this market required some careful research into the potential for a credit niche before risks could be undertaken. The foreign market, on the other hand, particularly in the financial capitals of London and New York, offered a much broader base for financial services. Not only were they already well-developed centres for commerce and finance, but the future growth of these cities was assured.

We thus find that the foundations of the modern Swiss banks (the Grossbanken, of course) as international banks were being laid during the turn-of-the-century period just preceding the first World War. We note that the international branches were not just 'industrial banks' per se but were much broader. To be sure, industrial credit was available to those foreigners who could satisfy the requirements, but most important were the discounting of first class bills, stock exchange orders, and foreign exchange operations as well as acceptance credits for commercial activities. These were important because greater profits were to be had in these areas rather than in purely industrial lending. Stock underwriting was another activity which proved highly successful.

All of these banking functions required an intimate knowledge of the conditions surrounding foreign commerce and finance. It meant that staff personnel were required to develop a fluent knowledge of languages other than their own and to understand the peculiar differences which distinguish one country's commerce from another. Customers ranging from Moscow to Copenhagen and Stockholm and from Milan and Trieste to New York and Havana, with businesses which involved underwriting, loans for an Egyptian irrigation system, a US railroad bonded loan, and acceptance trade credits: these were all included in the Swiss bank's accounts.

This suggests that the 'new' career of the Swiss banks, the entrance into the foreign field, was, though a logical extension of centuries of foreign banking, a market-oriented activity. We would again suggest that this contrasts sharply with the German banks which centred their activities on the development of purely German industry. Whereas the

German banks concentrated on domestic industrial development, including industrial cartels, the Swiss banks included both foreign and domestic industrial development as just one of their market-oriented assets structures. This broader approach to banking proved to be the Swiss characteristic then and for the future.

It is not difficult to appreciate that Swiss bankers had undertaken a much more difficult task than their German counterparts. German industrial cartels would ensure the security of the banks' loans and investments. Loans to industry in freely competitive markets, on the other hand, entailed a considerably greater risk for the Swiss banks. In addition, the complexity of banking activity grew with its extension into the foreign field. Foreign exchange rates, different customs and procedures, and the appropriate assessment of risk inforeign countries were just a few of the many and complex obstacles to be overcome.

To be more specific, the banks had not only to structure their loans and investments in such a way as to protect their liquidity but also to divide their assets into both foreign and domestic, at the same time providing sufficient liquidity in both cases: all the while, it may be added, realising profits on their activities because shareholders' must have their rewards as well. In response to such a degree of complexity, the Swiss banks developed their own operating standards and formulae, so that they eventually became, as we shall argue in subsequent chapters, a world-class banking system second to none.

We can hardly over-emphasise the importance of these banking standards. While we have argued that banks engage in a deposit 'manufacturing process' involving raw material which is transformed into forms of credit suitable to potential borrowers, the analogy can easily be over-strained. Since the 'raw material' is entirely borrowed from individuals, in the form of stocks, bonds, and deposits, a responsibility for honouring these obligations is entailed which is quite different from that of an industrial manufacturer. Banking skills, therefore, are not only much more complex but also occupy a strategic position in an economy. The liquidity of those who lend to the banks depends upon the skill of the bankers, and in turn, the maintenance of liquidity on the part of the bank lenders is vital for the entire economy. Thus the strategic position of bankers in the economies of western Europe, particularly in Switzerland, was becoming ever more apparent during the years from the turn of the century to 1914.

At the same time that the banks and the banking function were assuming a growing importance in the economy, there appeared a shortage of outlets for investments (or assets) relative to the available supply of deposits ('raw material'). This became obvious with the negotiations for the construction of the Simplon tunnel. Here was an opportunity for banks to provide financial capital to a project of some considerable value both in terms of profit to themselves as well as the political advantages which would accrue to western Switzerland. Three banks, the Schweizerischer Bankverein, the Schweizerischer Kreditbank, and the Union Financiére agreed to a joint financing of the Simplon. The rivalry for this business was so intense at the time that the three banks clashed with a coalition of cantonal banks which was successful in capturing the 1898 Jura–Simplon loan for themselves. From this experience the famous Swiss banking cartel grew, which ultimately, by 1914, included the Eidgenössische Bank, and the Kantonal Bank von Berne with a small participation of the private bank, A.G. Speyr. The coalition of cantonal banks, the Verband Schweizerische Kantonalbanken, was also included in the cartel agreement so that whenever securities were issued by public authorities, they were parcelled out as between the banking cartel and the Verband in accordance with the pre-arranged agreement.

Was the banking cartel damaging to healthy competition amongst the Swiss banks such that investors were deprived of returns which could have been greater? Apparently not. It would appear that when the cartel sold securities to the public, thereby acting as intermediaries, it actually tended to reduce the sale for purely speculative reasons, selling only for genuine investment purposes. On the other hand, when the cartel members purchased the securities for their own account (not as intermediaries) the financial capital obtained therefrom was spread over a wider distribution of banks. The banks themselves were still in competition in the sense that the proceeds of the sales had to be competitive as between banks. What the cartel agreements did accomplish was an equitable distribution of investments among banks which had more credit available than could be completely utilised. In other words, there was a surplus of bank capital in the years preceding World War I relative to the outlets. This stands in sharp contrast with circumstances today.

THE NATIONAL BANK OF SWITZERLAND

Unlike the Bank of France and the German Reichsbank, the central bank of Switzerland was not designed to control the money supply or complete a financial system. In France, the central bank was created as the result of an inherent inability to control the money supply as witness. In this sense, the Bank of France an essential link in the system of payments. Similarly, the Reichsbank was founded for the express purpose of controlling the issue of notes, in which some 33 banks were participating, within the German empire. This objective was successfully achieved until the disaster of hyperinflation during the early 1920s.

The Swiss National Bank stands out in sharp contrast. The Swiss monetary and banking system was 'up and running' well before the appearance of a central bank. With 36 banks of issue, there was sufficient discipline and control that a surplus of banknotes was not at all the problem. In fact, we can only really suggest that the National Bank added a necessary further centralising influence which the Swiss constitution itself had failed to complete. It complemented the constitution by its institutional existence. Thus, if the French and German central banks were necessary as a check to the issue of notes, the Swiss National Bank was also important to the development of a nation.

To be sure, the Swiss themselves, being Swiss, were by no means aware of this aspect of a central bank. Article 39 of the Constitution, revised as of 1891, provided for the exclusive right to issue bank notes to be vested with the Federal government. In order to implement this particular provision, enabling legislation was required to provide for a central bank. This was challenged by the electorate and the consequence was a referendum which was defeated. The arguments against the State bank were fourfold:

1. There would be 'confusion' between the central bank credit and the credit of the cantonal banks.
2. There would be excessive political influence brought to bear upon the bank by political authorities.
3. There would be an insufficient contact between the central bank and the actual business community in Switzerland.
4. There was a risk that central bank funds might be confiscated in time of war.

The first of these arguments suggests a distaste on the part of the Swiss community for the *modus operandi* of the Bank of France which did, in fact, lend to the private sector as well as the banks. In Switzerland, such 'confusion' would have to mean an excessive amount of credit, because all credit is bank credit and cannot be distinguished as to its origin.

The second argument was real in the sense that Swiss businessmen preferred not to have government interference, a fact made quite clear by Swiss history. Since the gold standard prevailed and there was no equivalent of modern monetary policy, this concern was certainly genuine. To ameliorate the concern suggested in the third argument, many branch offices of the central bank would have to be opened throughout the many cantons so as to maintain a liaison between the bank and all areas of the country.

The fourth argument is, at first sight, nonsensical since no central bank has any funds to confiscate. On the other hand, there is the possibility that the State bank could *create* domestic funds for use in wartime. This was proven during World War I when belligerent powers used their banking systems for precisely that purpose. It is unlikely, however, that this was understood by the Swiss public (or any other public) at that early period.

What does emerge from all these concerns is that a Schweizerischer Bundesbank would have been an interloper in an already established and thriving business community. While the four arguments could probably have been answered by an explanation of what particular form and structure the central bank would take, the fact of the matter is that they were not.

The issue resurfaced in 1899 when the Federal Council proposed that a central bank would be established with the participation of the private sector under the supervision of the government. This also failed because of the (now well-known) absurd dispute as to where the bank would be located – in Berne or in Zürich.[13] Finally, the Draft Bill for the central bank was presented in June 1904, providing that the bank would be semi-public with its headquarters in Berne and the board of managers in Zürich. The Bill was not challenged (that is, there was no referendum), and the Swiss National Bank came into existence with a General Meeting on 22 August 1906. It opened for business on 20 June 1907.

In actual fact, the formation of this Bank was overdue. Already the practice of re-discounting bills of exchange by the Bank of France and the Reichsbank had become quite common. In order to settle the daily balances of the banks in France and Germany with their respective central banks, short bills were being used. In this way necessary amounts of cash (that is, gold coins and paper notes) were being supplied to the banks by their central banks, 'paid for', as it were, with short bills. When such bills became longer, the short bills being exhausted, there was an indication that cash was becoming in short supply within the economies. This was a signal for the banks (both the central bank and the other banks) to tighten up their lending practices.

In terms of international payments and exchange rates, the bill method was also important because financial capital flowed to where it could receive the best treatment: the highest interest rate with the most likely possibility of security and confidence. At the same time, the practice of borrowing for the purpose of settling daily indebtedness between nations had become quite common; this was a substitute for settling balances in gold. Again the bill of exchange was the instrument for this purpose and the central banks were the important agencies. Since the foreign evaluation of the Swiss franc was in Paris, where Swiss overseas transactions were settled, it was becoming ever more obvious that without a central bank it was not possible to exert any control over the value of the Swiss franc by means of the discount rate for Swiss short bills of exchange. This contrasted rather sharply with the practice of the well-established central banks which were able to influence the daily fluctuations in the values of their currencies. The urgent need for a central bank to accomplish precisely this function underlay the legislation establishing the Swiss National Bank.

The other rationale for the central bank was the note issue itself. Considering that there were 36 note-issuing banks in the entire Confederation, one might, at first sight, conclude that there was a plethora of money in circulation. Such was not the case. Competition, the geography of the country, and inter-regional rivalry meant that many banks could successfully issue notes without excessively increasing the amount of circulation medium relative to the amount of goods and services to be purchased. When the national banknotes became the only notes in circulation at the close of the transition period (mid-1910), their value amounted to 254.8 million francs which was about 20 million *more* than the banknotes of all the note issuing banks at the beginning of the transition period (mid-1907). Considering that there was a considerable amount of metallic currency in circulation as well, the pre-National Bank note issue could hardly be referred to as excessive.

What did result from the switch to national banknotes was the loss to note-issuing banks of some very important funds for lending purposes. In 1906, banknotes had amounted to 8.37 per cent of the balance sheets of cantonal banks and 6.42 per cent of balance sheets of other banks.[14] But the interesting feature of these banknotes, which was seen as 'dangerous' by contemporaries, was how the notes came into circulation in the first place. The cantonal banks had been taxed not on the amount of notes issued but on the privilege of note issue – a fixed cost. This meant that banknotes were continuously pressed upon commerce rather than commerce drawing banknotes as they were required. Furthermore, the theoretically 'unsavoury' practice of the accommodation bill, a bill accepted by a bank which had little to do with commercial transactions, was becoming so common that '...only a minority of (bills) had any reference to transactions in goods'.[15] At any rate, the use of the accommodation bill ceased with the new National Bank since the bank would only discount valid trade bills.

In actual fact, an important source of funds for smaller Swiss banks was removed. These banks had discounted finance (accommodation bills) and re-discounted them with larger banks. Such bills were actually long-term loans because, as short-term accommodation bills, they were never repaid but were simply rolled over to become *de facto* long-term loans. The removal of this privilege by the National Bank plus the monopoly of the note issue meant that the Swiss monetary system had changed forever. The National Bank assumed the powers of a modern central bank which meant that control of the money supply, by way of the monopoly of the note issue, become its sole responsibility. Furthermore, since the note issue was universal throughout the Confederation, individual regional banks lost much of their independence, so that a single, unified banking system began to develop. In effect, the new central bank completed the task which the Constitution had started, that of the unification of Switzerland.

CONCLUSION

The period from the end of the nineteenth century until the outbreak of World War I was probably the most outstanding in terms of economic development the world had ever seen. Certainly it was a triumph of capitalism. It was a triumph in the sense that banks and other financial institutions learned how to transform financial capital into industrial capital in a manner hitherto undreamed of. In terms of Keynesian economics (yet to be written), savings were being transformed into investment at a rate never exceeded before or since. It mattered little which took place first, the savings or the investment; the fact was that much of the financial capital was being created by European banking systems through monetary expansion, then the savings necessary to accompany the investment were accomplished *after* the investment by means of a massive unequal distribution of income.

The Swiss banks, noted simply as 'other' banks in 1850 (see table 8.1, chapter 8) grew by means of expanding their own capital and investments, through consolidation, and by absorption of other smaller, weaker banks to become the powerful Grossbanken which we know today. Most important, their expansion was largely outward, that is, outside their own country, for after the railway construction era had come to an end, the investment opportunities within the country were insufficient to permit substantive expansion. Cantonal banks were already too well entrenched within Switzerland to make further domestic competition worth while. This, combined with an extraordinary capacity for long hours of hard work and an ability to recognise those investments which have possibilities for growth as opposed to those which do not and the ability to successfully balance risk against profit, made it possible for the Swiss banks to grow and prosper. Unlike their German counterparts which identified nascent industry, then proceeded not only to invest but to become part of the industry (so much so as to develop industrial cartels), the Swiss banks both participated in the directorships of industry and also developed stock exchanges. Along with these exchanges they developed their own stock and bond underwriting services. This meant that their overall financial activities were much broader than their German counterparts.

Certainly the Swiss bankers of the day recognised the importance of their participation in the great burst of capital investment which was so characteristic of that time. The opening of foreign branches, ie banks which operate independently of the main office in Switzerland but with the capital backing of the main office, suggests that they were very conscious of the direction of world affairs, hence where their own future lay. In this, their capacity to adapt to the conditions and circumstances of the host country and its unique financial structure proved to be their strongest asset.

In sum, Swiss banks emerged from this capitalistic 'transitory period' as full-fledged world banks. The banking system had evolved, through experience, by the elimination of its weaker members through the continuous dynamics of the business cycle, and, finally, through the complete restructuring of the monetary system itself with the institution of the Swiss National Bank.

The potential danger of the accommodation bills disappeared as the 'new monetary order' asserted itself. Most important, the introduction of the new banknotes brought into being a new technique of monetary control, in effect ensuring that monetary expansion need not exceed the rate of increase of goods and services, a tragedy visited upon many countries of central Europe following the holocaust of the 1914–18 War.

Notes

1. The Bland-Allison Act of 1878 re-instated the silver dollar as legal tender, but it neglected to provide for the free coinage of silver. It did, however, provide for the issue of silver certificates as the equivalent of government purchases of silver to the amount of 2–4 million dollars per month, but that was all. Had the US retained the bi-metallic system, the flood of silver from the Comstock Lode would certainly have driven gold out of circulation and the 'great deflation' in the United States would not have taken place. We can speculate further in the sense that Europe would also likely have checked its movement toward the gold standard; the Latin Union could have continued on its silver standard; and money and banking history would probably have to be re-written!

2. See Clapham, J.H., *Economic Development of France and Germany 1815–1914* (Cambridge University Press, 1961) p. 382.

3. Eleventh Annual Report of the Chamber of Commerce to the Basle Association of Commerce and Industry on the year 1886, pp. 5–15.

4. The Baring Bros. catastrophe in London and the heavy losses suffered by European investments in the Argentine were the principal factors in this bearish trend in the world markets.

5. Sixteenth Annual Report of the Basle Chamber of Commerce, pp 11–16.

6. These were the Allgemeine Kreditbank in Basle, the Basler Check und Wechselsank, the Berner BodenKreditanstalt, and the Kreditbank Winterthur. Bauer, *Swiss Bank Corporation*, 1872–1892, Swiss Bank Corporation 1972, p. 85.

7. Bauer, Hans, *Swiss Bank Corporation, 1872–1892*, p. 83.

8. Portfolio swaps, options, captions, futures: the list of devices to minimise or overcome risks of the kind that turn-of-the-century banks faced seems endless.

9. Even the Basler Bankverein, probably, along with the Kreditanstalt, the strongest of the Swiss banks, suffered a decline in its share value from 862 francs to 563 francs because of a reduction in its dividends caused by losses in its securities accounts.

10. Sixteenth Annual Report of the Chamber of Commerce to the Basle Association of Commerce and Industry, 1891, pp 11–16.

11. A quotation from a document of 247 pages issued by the Federal Council on 25 March 1897. Bauer, *Swiss Bank Corporation*, p. 122.

12. Bauer, *Swiss Bank Corporation*, p. 128.

13. Adolf Joehr, in his book *Die Schweizerisch Notenbanken*, argues with some evidence that the location objection was a subterfuge. The real reason was that cantonal finance authorities had hoped to stifle potential competition from a central bank in the matter of the right of note issue. Certainly this is a more rational argument.

14. Bauer, *Swiss Bank Corporation*, p. 131.
15. From this source is taken the following rather ambiguous quote: 'Often bills were accepted which had been manifestly made out by speculators for the purpose of creating funds, and there were also a great number of bills securing advances, over the deposition of which the lending bank arranged to be vested in writing with unconditional powers in order that it might use the cover of these bills for other transactions. The result was a note circulation which lacked flexibility.' Apparently banks were developing the practice of stating precisely for what purposes their notes could be used and that they could not be returned to the bank in exchange for gold. This meant that note cover, in terms of metal, became unnecessary such that an expansion of the 'money supply' could become infinite. Statistics do not bear out that such a practice had become sufficiently universal to become dangerous. *Schweizerische National-bank*, Memorial, 1907–1957, Zürich, 1957, p. 169.

Part 3
The Tragedy of the
Twentieth Century

10 The End of an Era

The titles we have chosen for this part and this chapter must appear trite or even 'over-dramatic' to those of the current generation. However, the year 1914, and the ensuing holocaust of war, did indeed mark the end of an entire political and economic system in the European world as empires crumbled and the map of Europe was re-drawn. Not so many, however, might realise that the monetary and banking systems of that world which had, by the year 1914, reached a peak of efficiency were to collapse into confusion and chaos. It is in this context that these titles are appropriate.

It is rare in world history that the evolution of an institution is actually so abruptly halted. With apologies to the paleontologist, one might use a parallel borrowed from that science – the natural catastrophe of an earth-asteroidal collision which ended the age of dinosaurs. This would truly be analogous to the impact of the 1914–18 war on the monetary and banking systems of Europe. All were wiped out, purely and simply, except one: that of the Swiss. The Swiss survived, to build upon their past experience, and to evolve still further, within the structure of the changed world circumstances, into one of the world's most efficient banking systems, while other countries' banks and banking networks had to begin anew with only memories of past experiences as guides. This was no easy task, and the resulting confusion, including both the post-war inflations and the great depression which was to follow, was truly monumental.

The genius of the Swiss bankers lay in their capacity to take advantage of this new environment. This is important because not only did they emerge from the war virtually intact (though as we shall show they suffered considerably from losses of foreign investment as a result of that war) but they knew from their immense background of experience how to take advantage of changed circumstances. This is not to suggest that they gained at the expense of the less fortunate, rather that they were able to exploit their position as an island of security in a sea of monetary confusion. They did so by injecting the stability of their own banking system into the massive and uncertain instability which was so characteristic of the post-war era. In this sense, Swiss banks, to a great degree, contributed to the return to normalcy which ultimately followed.

THE INDUSTRIAL AND FINANCIAL WORLD BEFORE 1914

During the fateful years preceding the war, Swiss banks became very conscious of the fact that they were lagging behind their European counterparts in terms of mobilisation of the savings of the public for investment purposes. Accordingly, the practice of establishing 'agencies' in smaller Swiss towns to collect in-payments and pay out-payments on behalf of the parent bank was developed. In this way, it was possible for deposit collection and payment to became much more universal than before. This was an extremely important step because, though the banks did not realise it at the time, the bank deposit was becoming an increasingly important part of the money supply. The first agency of the *Bankverein* of this type was established in Rorschach in 1907, and since it proved to be successful it was followed by many others elsewhere.

Establishing contact with the general population in this way meant that the banks, which had hitherto largely depended upon their own resources, would now be using borrowed funds, the lenders being the general public. In the case of the *Bankverein*, according to balance sheet data which we are fortunate in having for those years, deposits grew from a mere 31.9 million francs in 1901 to 182.4 million francs in 1913.[1]

At the same time, it became necessary to considerably increase the ratio of the balance sheet total to 'own resources' (capital and reserves), at the same time that balance sheet totals rose. In 1901, the *Bankverein's* total of balance sheet total amounted to 146 million francs. Capital and reserves (own resources) were 51.2 million, which yields a ratio of total assets to capital plus reserves of 2.85. By 1913, this ratio had grown to 5.4, the consequence of the use of 'other people's money' (deposits) for purposes of lending which required significantly higher reserves. The same phenomenon of deposit growth was recorded for all the major banks of Switzerland as is apparent from the liquidity ratios in Table 10.1.

The interesting point is that the growth of deposits of these major banks was not at the expense of other banks in Switzerland. Of the 306 banks in the entire country in 1913, there was a total of capital and reserves (or own resources) amounting to 1,790 million francs. The balance sheet total for all these banks was 10,300 million francs, which gives a ratio of 5.75 of own resources to the balance sheet total Thus the ratio of 5.75 was remarkably similar to (actually slightly above) that of the major banks.

Table 10.1   Liquidity ratios in Swiss banks, 1913 (in millions of francs)

	Capital & reserves	Balance sheet total	Ratio of assets to capital & reserves
Schweiz. Bankverein	109.8	588.2	5.4
Schweiz.Kreditbank	100.0	538.8	5.4
Schweiz. Volksbank	79.5	501.0	6.3
A.G. Leu	45.2	245.5	5.4
Eligenossische Bank	44.5	244.2	5.5
Union Bank	36.0	206.1	4.5
Basler Handelsbank	47.0	162.8	3.5

Source: Bauer, H., *Swiss Bank Corporation, 1872–1972*, p. 195.

This growth of deposits can be partially but by no means entirely attributed to the removal of the right of note issue. Something else of considerable importance was taking place in Switzerland just as in other countries of Europe, an expansion of deposits using a smaller amount, about 20 per cent, of cash. Further, this deposit expansion was taking place by an increase in the amount of loans and advances such that loans were actually *creating* new deposits. The process of deposit expansion would not be by means of payment by cheque, as was typical of the British system (this method had not taken root either in France or in Switzerland), but rather a deposit in a bank would be honoured by the bank with the payment of cash at sight. In this way, a given amount of cash could be used as a means of transferring the ownership of bank liabilities roughly five times greater.

It will be clear that for such a system to operate successfully, very many banks, bank branches, and agencies must be well distributed throughout the entire country so that not only would the banking habit on the part of the public be encouraged but also banking facilities would be available to everyone, and, indeed, so they became. Should there be any discrepancies in the inflow and outflow of cash amongst banks (the above example assumes an exact equality between inflow and outflow) these would be settled through interbank deposits.

The 'banking habit' must be so well established that the public will prefer (or at least be willing) to immediately return its cash to the bank of its choice upon receiving it for discharge of an obligation. There must be little or no hoarding of paper currency. Furthermore, there must be an advantage in using the bank's liabilities instead of cash. Paper earns no interest; whereas sight deposits are just as good as paper and merely require a visit to the nearest banking facility. For the Swiss public after the turn of the century, this was a change from the practice of their forebears who preferred to hoard their own metallic currency, i.e. metal is truly 'hoardable' while paper is not.

The increase in deposits noted above for the Confederation must certainly have been accompanied by a corresponding increase in loan assets. There is, to be sure, no other reasonable method by which bank deposits *can* be increased to such a great extent. We can identify this increase in loans using the historical material of the *Bankverein* which, as the largest of the Swiss banks at the time, must also have been typical of all the major banks in terms of its behaviour. Thus, during the same period noted above when deposits rose from 31.9 million francs in 1901 to 182.4 million (or 5.7 times) by 1913, loans and advances rose from 64 million francs in 1901 to 289.2 million in 1913, about 4.5 times.

The relationship is close.[2] The fact that loans and advances increased by more in absolute terms (225 million france against 150.5 million francs for deposits) is due to the increased availability of types of funds other than deposits, that is, own funds such as capital and reserves, bonds, and 'other' liabilities which were also used for lending.

The marked increase in loans and advances experienced by Swiss banks were by no means at the expense of other more traditional forms of credit. Bills of exchange increased from just 28 million francs in 1901 to 130.2 million in 1913, reflecting the greater commercial activity which was typical of the time. Loans to stock markets also increased from 12.5 million francs in 1901 to about 60 million in 1913.

These numbers, while interesting enough for the purpose of indicating growth, do not reflect the tremendous expansion in the activities of the *Bankverein* nor the nature of this expansion. Indeed, we can say without reservation that the period just preceding World War I was a truly expansive period for Swiss banking. The broadening of activities well beyond the function of pure banking is precisely what is so important. In qualitative terms, the banks were structuring themselves to assume that shape which would be their characteristic for many decades into the future.

Yet, at the same time, the bankers failed to recognise the holocaust of World War I which was to come. In this they shared the same unawareness of what the future would bring with many Swiss businessmen and politicians. They took up foreign positions which, in retrospect, seems to us very strange. Again, using the *Bankverein* as a case in point, this bank took 25 per cent of shares in *Banque Internationale de Bruxelles* and provided a member of its own board to be the vice-chairman. In the case of a French bank, *Banque Suisses et Francaises* (Paris), a controlling interest was actually secured.

But the most curious areas of expansion were in the Austro-Hungarian empire despite the rumours, the Balkan troubles, and so on, which suggested that banks and bankers should maintain a defensive position and retain or even increase their liquid assets. New connections were formed with *E. Weinberger & Cie* of Vienna before the turn of the century when Weinberger acted as the agent for the *Bankverein*. Later, in 1912, the *Bankverein* picked up a 25 per cent participation in *k.k. priv. Bank-und Wechselstube*, and then they exchanged seats on their respective boards. In addition, as late as July 1914, the *Bankverein* took up 5.8 million francs of a 5 per cent bond loan of the *Ungarische Hypothekenbank in Budapest*. These and other participations and underwriting syndicates suggest the high degree of credit which the states, cities, and enterprises of the Austro-Hungarian empire enjoyed prior to the war. It also suggests the inability of the Swiss bankers to appreciate the catastrophic nature of the coming years; indeed, who *could* have done so?

Without a doubt, had the bankers foreseen, or even had the slightest suspicion of, the future they would have made more than just half-hearted attempts at expanding into the New York credit market, certainly a much more secure area of banking activity. In retrospect, one can hardly imagine portfolios of assets more fraught with risk than the foreign investments in the Austro-Hungarian Empire, the Balkans, and Central Europe in general. Nevertheless, we can begin to appreciate the nature of the great activity which underlay the huge increase in balance sheet values. The importance of the banking industry to the country had already reached major proportions by the year 1913, particularly in the area of foreign investment. It was estimated by Grossmann and Sombart, two of the most prominent economic historians of the day, that on a per capita basis Switzerland had capital investments abroad amounting to 1,575 francs as compared with just 1,075 francs for France, 445 francs for Germany, and 1,981 francs for Great Britain. With a population of 3.7 million in 1910 and no colonial empire such as the other powers possessed, such a large amount of foreign investment relative to the size of the country is not only a remarkable achievement but an important mainstay for the economy.

INDUSTRIAL ACTIVITIES

In the development of Swiss industry, Swiss banks had shown their Saint-Simonian influence. Though not so completely integrated with industry as their German counterparts, they nevertheless did directly contribute in some measure to the economic growth of Switzerland. We emphasise 'in some measure' because, unlike their German counterparts, the Swiss banks' direct participation in Swiss industry had mixed results. So the question remains, why ought the banks to have persevered in what were so obviously non- profitable ventures? The answer is they became 'captive' to the industry itself. It was the failures of direct industrial participation which shifted the direction of Swiss banking activities toward financial participation in the form of underwriting of both shares and bonded indebtedness.

In chemicals, the success of CIBA was balanced by the failure of the chemical works of Brugg (*Chemische Fabrik* A.G.). By 1910, the German chemical industry was proving to be entirely too competitive for the Brugg plant to be successful. The only real opportunity for chemical production lay in the field of dyestuffs which were suited to the large Swiss textile industry. Transport costs from the more distant German producers were sufficiently great to ensure the success of the *Basler Chemische Fabrik* which specialised in dye production. Any other attempt to compete with German producers, especially those products which were finer, hence smaller in bulk, would be difficult because the cost of transport would be relatively small.

More unfortunate in their consequences were banks' investments in the embroidery industry. The French attempt at tariff protection for their domestic production had resulted in a tariff war with Switzerland in the decade of the 1890s. Upon the expiry of the Commercial Treaty with Switzerland (31 January 1892), the French government applied its 'minimum tariff' to Swiss imports which was, in effect, a prohibitive tariff. The result was a serious decline in Swiss exports to France. Among the industries seriously affected was embroidery, of which exports to France declined by 50 per cent.[3] Even though the tariff war had ended by 1895, it had a disastrous impact upon the embroidery industry, because by the time the banks became involved the 'industry had built up too much credit, its profits were excessively reinvested in new plant, and large overseas stocks had been accumulated', so said the *Bankverein* Committee in Basle. In other words, the industry had expanded well beyond the capacity of its markets, which were already shrinking. Indeed, any profitability as far as the bank was concerned actually depended upon the loans to that industry because there was no other source of income for the head office of the industry in St Gall. The Bank had become a 'captive' of the industry quite against the will of its main office in Basle.

Another astonishing industrial concept which, in retrospect, is difficult to understand was the amalgamation of several granite businesses on both sides of the St. Gotthard into one, the *Aktiengesellschaft Schweizerische Granitwerke*. In this case, a syndicate of banks had issued many of the shares of the new company; unfortunately, all that was ever produced, according to the Annual Report of the *Bankverein* for 1904, was loss. Eventually, by 1913, the firm had uncovered liabilities of 1.63 million francs and was, consequently, on the point of bankruptcy. Once more the problem here was excessive foreign (Italian) competition.

The metals industry had somewhat greater success. According to the last census prior to the first World War, there was an increase in numbers of employees to 166,960, about 20 per cent, by 1910. Textile employment, on the other hand, grew by only 8.5 per cent, to 177,875. Thus the growth potential was clearly in the metals and electrical machinery area, a fact which Swiss banks were quick to realise. *Aktiengesellschaft Maschinenfabriken Escher, Wyss & Cie*, an engineering company, issued shares in 1896 that were placed by three banks, the *Bankverein, Credit Suisse*, and the *Eidgenossische Bank*. Still, all was not well and after some re-organisation and financial restructuring, shares in the firm were sold to the German company, *Felten und Guillaume-Lahmeyer*. The entire episode demonstrated quite clearly that small Swiss engineering firms did indeed have to compete with large, well-established German firms and that economies of scale were not so easily attained in small concerns in this industry. Nevertheless, the banks felt that the maintenance of a Swiss character was important and by 1909, with the assistance of additional credit, *Escher, Wyss* had restored its reputation as a builder of turbines.

It is the persistence of the banks in standing behind their metalworking industry which is significant. This was most evident in the development of electrical engineering which during the pre-war period was still in its infancy. Power stations, transmission equipment, and electrical distribution companies were financed by the banks (via their subsidiary companies discussed above), many of which were in France, Italy, and Austria-Hungary. These, in turn, purchased their equipment from Swiss industries, thereby achieving a re-cycling effect of the original bank credit back to the originating Swiss bank. In order to achieve this, Swiss equipment had to be not only of the highest quality but to have a reputation for that quality.

A major step forward in the electrical engineering industry was taken by the formation of a combine in 1910 between the *Elektrizität sgesellshaft Alioth* in Munchenstein and *Brown, Boveri & Co.* in Baden. The *Bankverein* assisted this operation with the declared policy object-ive of uniting Swiss companies within the industry with a common purpose. But here, the location of the companies was not in Switzer-land, but outside the country, closer both to sources of raw material, a capable labour force, and to markets. Thus we note, for the first time in modern history, the tendency for Swiss companies to establish themselves abroad and, at the same time, maintain their control within their own country.

We should, of course, not ignore the unfortunate attempt at the manufacture of Swiss automobiles by the Martini company at St Blaise. The banks assisted in the financing of this effort along with a French group, Clement Bayard, which supplied not only some capital but also technical expertise. While the quality of product was high, the Martini went the way of many auto manufactures that could not compete against the scale economies of the great corporations of Europe and America, though it managed to produce cars from 1897 to 1934.

These examples, selected from the documents of the largest of the commercial banks, serve to highlight the lending activities of these banks and the nature of the credit problems which they faced and, in some instances, managed to overcome. The list is not at all exhaustive; there were other examples, such as small regional railroads, which were still being financed by the banks, and which required a careful exam-ination as to their credit-worthiness.

Thus, while the activity of foreign investment was progressing very well, ironically enough to be completely ruined by the Great War, domestically, the banking industry was undergoing considerable restructuring during the turbulent years of 1910–1914. In 1913 there were 306 banks in the country. In 1906, on the other hand, there were 331, suggesting that some 25 banking establishments disappeared in the seven-year period. The Federal Department of Economic Affairs estimated that, including bank mergers, some 60 banking establish-ments had been struck off the register.

In addition, there were two banking crises of some considerable importance during the period 1910–1914 which were significant because of their permanent impact upon the entire Swiss banking system. The first was in the Canton of Thurgau. In this canton, in 1912, the Thurgauische Hypothekenbank, founded in 1852, had engaged rather heavily in land speculation. In addition it had tied up its funds in long-term mortgages both within the country and abroad, in Frankfurt, Cologne, and Berlin, in response to the higher rates of interest there. The result was a very low degree of liquidity. It was the lack of liquidity which proved to be the bank's undoing and resulted in the depositors' lack of confidence in banks in general. This lack of confidence even spread to the savings banks of the canton. In this case, a banking consortium had to be formed to supply the liquidity which depositors required and to save the savings banks. In the case of the Hypothekenbank, large amounts of assets were simply written off as permanently lost. A solution to the crisis was found in a takeover by the Schweizerische Bodenkredit-Anstalt in Zürich after considerable re-organisation and sacrifice on the part of the shareholders.

In Ticino, a second banking crisis arose in January 1914 which was even worse. Here two banks failed, the Credito Ticinese and the Banca Cantonale Ticinese, and later, a third bank, Banca Popolare Ticinese followed its predecessors into bankruptcy. Depositors suffered a loss of some 40 million francs–25 million in Italy and 17 million in Ticino – as a consequence. After some lengthy negotiations involving petty jealousies and rivalries, a banking consortium was again formed to assist in the founding of a new bank, *Banca del Ticino*, to restore the banking and monetary system of the canton. Eventually, in 1915, the Banca del Ticino was converted into a new cantonal bank, Banca dello Stato del Cantone Ticino.

As to the causes of the Ticino crisis, just about every banking error in the book was cited. There was a lack of spreading of risks, insufficient liquidity (and its counterpart, excessively illiquid assets), not enough share and reserve funds, and, even more interesting, nepotism involving both the selection of staff and the granting of loans. As to the entire period 1910–1914, after-the-fact studies of the banking crises pointed out the lack of competitiveness, speculation, unsound business policies, and inadequate supervision as additions to the above list of banking errors.

A few banking statistics can also shed light on the situation. In 1913, the major banks had a ratio of 44 per cent of quick assets to client's deposits; whereas for local and medium-sized banks the ratio was 31 per cent. Profitability (gross profit relative to capital), on the other hand, was 16.12 per cent for major banks and 13.79 per cent for the local and medium-sized banks.[4]

In sum, we can suggest that at the same time that the Swiss banking system was achieving remarkable results in the foreign sector, with investments per capita second only to Great Britain, it was 'shaking out' many weaknesses in the domestic sector which were characteristic of any banking system which grows too fast. This self-cleansing was not just a matter of eliminating the imprudent banking practices; it was rather a constructive learning and consolidation process which eventually resulted in a high degree of security for depositors, on the one hand, and banking efficiency on the other. We can say that each Swiss bank emerged from the experience as part of one of the more mature banking system in the world. Certainly, as we shall see, the system survived remarkably well the catastrophe which was to ensue.

THE GREAT WAR

With investments outside the country totaling some 6.3 billion francs amongst some 40 countries throughout the world, there is scarcely any question that, even being neutral, Switzerland could only lose heavily as a consequence of the war.[5] Actually, the year 1914 did mark the end of an era of capitalistic expansion which was, and still is, unprecedented. Investments had crossed boundaries, commercial activity had thrived, and economic growth reached a level that was inconceivable at mid-nineteenth century.[6] In a real sense the dream of Richard Cobden, that economic relations by means of free trade would become so strong amongst nations that political differences and wars would cease for the simple reason that the economic loss would be insupportable, was brought to an end by the war.

The Swiss, with some 3.7 million people in 1913, were to a large extent dependent upon the resources of the world outside their country, for they had few natural endowments within their borders. Their real wealth consisted entirely of their own ability to import commodities of lower value and export goods of correspondingly higher value, such value being added by their own manufacturing and processing. In the last year of peace, the Swiss imported about 2 billion francs worth of commodities and exported 1.3 billion, a deficit in the balance of trade of some 700 million. This deficit was made up by the flow of income from investments abroad both in terms of loans, credits, and direct investments. Already they had learned to 'leap customs barriers' (an earlier version of the modern Japanese technique) and to establish

Swiss firms in other countries. The income from such direct investment alone amounted to close to 200 million francs.

Unfortunately we do not have figures as to the inflow of interest and other income from investments, but it must have been considerable, enough to more than account for deficit in the balance of trade. After all, Switzerland was the oldest of the capital-exporting areas north of the Alps, and, as such, had developed a reputation for banking and capital intermediation second to none in Europe. It is easy to understand, therefore, how and why Switzerland had so much to lose from the storm which followed in 1914.[7]

Julius Landmann, professor of Political Economy at the University of Basle, had asserted that except in the case of the joint-stock banks, liquidity was not equal to even modest demands let alone the extremes of wartime conditions, since the cover available to meet the claims of all creditors out of assets was not as yet adequate to discharge total liabilities at all times.[8] At the same time that liquidity was inadequate, there was an enormous concentration of demand for liquidity because of the mobilisation of a quarter of a million men. The cash was required to meet the personal needs of the soldiers as well as their families, who suffered the loss of their breadwinners.[9]

But this did not comprise all of the demands made upon banks' liquidity. The general public, in a kind of panic during the initial stages of the crisis, demanded its own cash, and to avoid an excessive drain of metallic currency, the newly formed National Bank was exempted by the Federal Council from redeeming its banknotes in gold or silver. Smaller banknotes, 5 and 20 francs, were issued to satisfy the public's need for cash payments, and, in addition, to protect the banks from an excessive drain of liquidity, the National Bank issued a circular letter on the second of August authorising payments of only 200 francs from deposit accounts and 50 francs from savings accounts. Finally, the Federal Council suspended the collection of commercial bills of exchange. This suspension lasted until the end of September, and meant that the entire country's financial system had effectively ceased to exist.[10]

The difficulties faced by Switzerland and its banking system during the early days of the war can readily be appreciated. Bills of exchange formed an important part of the assets of banks. For the *Bankverein*, the bank for which we have detailed accounts, they totalled 100.2 million francs, about 20 per cent of all assets. We may be certain that this proportion was approximately the same for all of the other commercial banks.

It will be recalled that bills of exchange were essentially 'two-way' transactions; they involved payments from debtors to creditors within two countries through bank intermediation. Thus, an exporter within Switzerland was paid by an importer within Switzerland and the only actual gold payments between countries were to settle differences between what were essentially 'internal' transactions. Banks, by discounting bills, paid the exporter and thereby accumulated paper bills which were purchased by importers to be sent to the country of origin (the exporting country) for collection when due. The system worked with remarkable efficiency just so long as the bank's trading partners were able to keep their own internal payments working as well. And that was the difficulty during wartime. With the belligerents reducing their exports to practically nothing, Swiss importers could no longer pay Swiss exporters. The result was an accumulation of bills by Swiss banks as they discounted the exporters' bills. So it is that we see the amount of bills in the Bankverein's assets rising from 100.2 million francs in 1914 to 222.9 million by 1918. In 1919, the amount of bills reached a high point at 359 million francs.

In order to accommodate customers who wished to discount their bills, bank deposits were required. This is why the wide distribution of deposits in many countries proved to be a handicap during wartime. In such emergencies, governments always freeze foreign deposits so as to use them for purchasing essential imports. As a result, it was difficult, if not impossible, to recall these deposits, hence the dilemma faced by the banks, a shortage of foreign deposits to finance assets which were not only large but growing.

After the immediate problems of liquidity shortages had passed and the shock of war declarations had been overcome, the real economic difficulties of a neutral nation entirely dependent upon imports of raw or semi-finished materials had to be faced. Indeed, the degree of the difficulties involved can be seen from the rapid decline of imports into Switzerland which fell from 7.9 million tons in 1913 to 5.9 million tons in both 1915 and 1916 and just 4.2 million tons in 1917 and 3.5 million tons in 1918. These restricted imports were only made possible by the establishment of appropriate government agencies which had the means at their disposal to ensure that imports from the Central Powers and the Allies would not be re-exported to their respective enemies.[11]

With mobilisation of manpower, labour shortages existed, and, at the same time, meant that the substitution of domestic production for imported food and raw material products was essential. Most important for the banks, some kind of normalcy had to be restored with long-term deposits returning to the banks to finance this increased domestic production. This was finally accomplished by raising interest rates on longer term deposits until a flow of cash returned to the banks – the same cash that had been withdrawn during the initial panic period.

The costs of mobilisation were covered with federal government bond issues which bore interest rates of 4 to 5 per cent. By 1918 there were nine issues with a total of 830 millions of francs.[12] In addition, a food loan was raised in the US to an amount of $15 million with a further $20 million after the war. Further foreign funding in the form of foreign currency was provided through the banking system itself by means of loans from foreign banking groups so as to increase the foreign reserves of the National Bank. The Swiss franc equivalent of these loans was provided by a government special body, the Schweizerische Finanzgesellschaft, so that importers were able to finance on credit their imports of necessary foodstuffs by borrowing from this agency. Foreign exporters were paid in their own currency from the equivalent of the foreign loans.

Through such ingenious financial devices, the Swiss were able to keep food shortages to the minimum. Indeed, federal subsidies amounting to some 400 million francs were used to restrain any price increases. Nevertheless prices did rise for the consumer as total demand inevitably exceeded the available total supply. Food prices rose by some 123 per cent over the war years while prices of items of common daily consumption rose by 104 per cent. Wholesale prices increased by 200 per cent.

Seen within the context of the great inflations of Europe, such price increases must appear trifling, and indeed they were. Nevertheless, the Swiss were neutral and the question remains, why need prices have risen at all? This highlights the interesting question which has vexed economists for generations. Which came first, an increase in prices which requires an increased money supply to accommodate the higher prices, or an increased money supply which caused the higher prices? To be sure, there must have been some price impact because of the money dis-hoarding process as funds were released from households which had reacted by hoarding cash during the early weeks of the war. In addition, there were government and railway treasury bills which the National Bank had taken up and which were redeemed. Further, there was an influx into Switzerland of metallic currency to take advantage of the better exchange rate of the Swiss franc as foreign currencies' rates fell well below par values. Nevertheless, despite these relatively minor incidents, it must be acknowledged that a huge excess of aggregate demand over aggregate supply existed under wartime austerity and shortages of labour and raw materials must have been the principal driving force underlying the higher cost of living.

In other words, the first cause mattered little since it became a chicken/egg situation almost at once with the task of separating the monetary cause and effect not only impossible but fruitless. What is significant is the fact that the Swiss people never lost confidence in the value of their currency during the war period. Had they done so, velocity of circulation would have risen and the hyperinflations characteristic of many continental countries would have spread to Switzerland itself. Nevertheless, wages did lag behind prices and there was considerable privation amongst poorer families who suffered more, relatively, than those with higher incomes. On them, the burden of mobilisation and shortages fell particularly hard; indeed, when the war finally ended, a general strike ensued during the month of November which lasted for several days, a consequence of the economic, political, and social circumstances of the time. It was followed by the great influenza epidemic which swept Europe and claimed some 25,000 lives.

As far as other banking activities were concerned, the stock exchanges, for all practical purposes, were closed until mid-1916. A massive influx of Swiss securities occurred during 1915 as foreign holders took advantage of the declining exchange rate of their own currencies to enjoy a profit. This was exacerbated by government propaganda in Germany which discouraged the holding of foreign securities with the result that there was a considerable capital outflow (of Swiss francs) to the respective countries.[13]

It will be obvious to readers with a reasonable familiarity with the history of Europe during and after the war that Switzerland and the Swiss people endured very much less in terms of hardship than the painful privation and suffering in the rest of the continent. Of that there is not the slightest doubt. Indeed, we might add that the contribution of Switzerland and the Swiss Red Cross during those tragic years did much toward ameliorating to some degree the horrors which Europe inflicted upon itself. Even though a paragraph saluting these people for their efforts is quite out of context in a work of this kind, we nevertheless do include it as a reminder to readers that we are always conscious of the fact that life does not necessarily consist of banks, bankers, and finance alone.

AFTERMATH, THE COST

So the Swiss as a nation and people emerged from the war virtually unscathed, especially when compared to their fellow Europeans. Nevertheless some interesting developments in banking technique should not be overlooked. We recall that a collapse in the demand for deposits (notably foreign deposits) occurred due to the onset of the war. A partial substitution for this lost deposit demand could be made by substituting domestic demand for foreign demand. This would result from the expansion of domestic production as a substitute for lost imports and would require a run-down of cash reserves as bank lending increased. The liabilities counterpart of this increased lending was the rise in cheque accounts and other deposits.

Had the banks not increased their deposit rates, there would have been a risk of greater inflation especially if the public had demanded its short-term deposits in the form of cash: paper, actually, since the National Bank was issuing paper in the form of 5 to 20 franc notes instead of metal. Without such rate increases, there could have been an increase in velocity of circulation with a consequence of hyperinflation such as had occurred in other European countries.

But not all banks were able to increase domestic lending in the manner described; indeed, some were absolutely ruined by the loss of foreign loans, particularly those whose assets were confined to German mortgages. The great German inflation had simply wiped out these assets. The A. G. Leu & Co. of Zürich was an excellent example of precisely this situation. This bank, the oldest in Switzerland, had originated from the Zürich Zinscommission (Interest Commission) founded in 1755. It had enjoyed a reputation which was quite justified over the centuries; however, at the end of 1920, it found itself with write-offs of 35.8 million francs, 31.4 million of which were due to the consequences of the German inflation.

It should be pointed out here that the mortgage contracts with German clients had had a gold clause which required re-payment in gold marks or their equivalent. It would appear that such contracts were quite safe. However, the government of Imperial Germany suspended these clauses in September 1914, and they were never re-instated. The consequence was that the mortgages became entirely worthless. Against these write-offs the bank had only 20 million francs of 'own resources'; 12.5 million in reserves with the balance from its own capital shares. Obviously the situation was hopeless and required substantial restructuring of asset values.

The shares of this bank were reduced in value by 50 per cent , from 500 to 250 francs, and were designated as ordinary (common) shares. In addition 20 million francs worth of preference shares of 500 francs par value were issued, but only 9 million were actually purchased in the market. The balance remained with the banking syndicate formed to come to the rescue of the Leubank and which had hoped, originally, to place all the shares in the market. By holding these, the syndicate gained some considerable influence over the entire re-structuring process of the bank.

We have no estimates of the total value of assets lost by Swiss banks and finance companies as well as in portfolios held by individuals. In foreign securities held by the banks alone the Swiss Bankers Association estimated that the decline in value was from 8,000 million francs to 2,500 million francs.[14] Other financial assets denominated in foreign currencies, such as credit balances in foreign banks, insurance policies, credit balances in foreign banks owned by companies, and even industrial firms with balances tied up in claims to physical stocks of inventory suffered considerably as well. In fact, *any* financial claim denominated in foreign currency constituted a loss of capital as the value of the foreign currencies collapsed. This was the inevitable result of the circumstance of being a hard-currency country which had long-established relations with its larger and more powerful neighbours; as the values of foreign currencies declined the value of those assets denominated in those foreign currencies declined as well.

Another interesting aspect of the difficulties involved in a hard-currency country was the matter of 'currency dumping'. In this case, foreigners, such as French and German nationals who had lost confidence in the value of their own currency, secretly shifted cash or deposits into a Swiss bank account, generally with a private bank or other financial institution. Having the value of their assets thus protected, these individuals had effectively hedged against any further declines, actual or expected, in the value of their own currency. The Swiss banks which ultimately held these foreign currency claims against the foreign institutions must have been subject to a continued loss of their asset value as inflation in these countries proceeded apace.[15]

In view of the extraordinary position in which Switzerland found itself following the war, we are entitled to ask the questions: who actually lost wealth? who really paid the price? Obviously shareholders of *Leubank* and other similar institutions lost considerably from the write-down of their assets. Those banks that, unfortunately, held financial assets denominated in foreign currencies were also losers. Those banks in particular that had funded projects in Czarist Russia lost 100 per cent of their investments in that country.

But not so obvious were the losers in the case of those commercial banks that had increased their loans and deposits during the war, thereby increasing total demand along with the money necessary to finance that greater demand. In this case, the only result was that the banks had merely shifted the burden of asset loss to those less fortunate Swiss whose incomes failed to keep pace with rising prices. These unfortunates were these at the 'bottom line' who pressed in 1918, in the form of a general strike, for social and economic reform.

AFTERMATH – PROSPERITY AND DEPRESSION

One result of the War, for good or ill, was the transfer of the 'centre of financial gravity' from London to New York. This had far-reaching consequences, for it was the newly organised Federal Reserve System which dictated economic and financial circumstances throughout Europe. Yet, as all the evidence then and subsequently has shown, the decisions of the Federal Reserve Board were not taken with Europe in mind; quite the contrary, the United States was very much the insular nation quite unaware of its influence world wide. Certainly the Board's actions had a profound effect upon the Swiss.

Immediately after the cessation of hostilities, there ensured, amongst the belligerents, an inflation of some considerable magnitude. The great inflations of Europe are well known. But in the United States, wholesale prices had risen by 1920 to nearly one and one-half times from their level in 1915. From the end of the war until 1920, the rise in the general price level was about 30 per cent . What is interesting is that most of the price increase occurred in the US during peacetime, before 1917 when the US entered the war. After 1917, there was little change in prices.

This phenomenon, a static inflation rate during the war and a sharp increase in prices after cessation of hostilities, has been fairly typical in modern times and has little rational explanation aside from price control by governments. It has been suggested that the withdrawal of cash from the banking systems during wartime restricts the expansion of credit, and the return of that cash after the war permits a credit expansion to such an extent that this, combined with a pent-up demand for new peace-time production, results in a sharp inflation.[16] Whatever the cause, the result is clear – a post-war inflation.

For Switzerland, this meant massive increases in imports from those Continental countries with depreciating currencies. So long as the exchange rate *vis-à-vis* the Swiss franc moved downward more rapidly than the domestic price levels in those countries increased, imports were relatively cheap to the Swiss. On the other hand, Swiss exports were extremely expensive to other countries whose currencies were declining in value. The result, of course, was inevitable. In 1920, the surplus of imports over exports reached the extraordinary level of 1,000 million francs with exports being just 22.8 per cent of imports.

But, fortunately for Swiss manufacturing industries, this circumstance was short-lived. In the United States, where decisions taken by the Federal Reserve Board were destined to impact sharply upon the economies of Europe, the question of the paramountcy of the Treasury versus the Federal Reserve was a matter of keen debate. Benjamin Strong, Governor of the Federal Reserve Bank of New York, had been determined for some time to wrest from the Treasury the necessary independence for discharging his duties *vis-à-vis* the American economy. Thus, the Federal Reserve discount rate was to be raised to check the inflationary trend during the immediate post-war period. However, to do so would mean greater borrowing costs as the Federal debt required continuous funding, and since the price of Federal bonds moved inversely with interest, more bonds were required to be sold. Additionally, higher interest rates meant a greater servicing cost for this larger quantity of bonds.[17]

Ultimately, Mr Strong's arguments prevailed. But, and this is the principal point, just as he himself had already expressed his misgivings as to its appropriateness at such a late date for raising the discount rate, the Federal Reserve did raise the discount rate rapidly and sharply in January 1920 to the unprecedented level of 7 per cent. Mr Strong, unfortunately, was absent when this occurred, due to ill health. The result, as occurred again later in 1929, was a reinforcement of an economic downtrend which was already in progress.

For Europe, especially Switzerland, the results were devastating. The adjustment to a new Europe with a new system of states with many more tariff barriers was already proving to be difficult enough, but it was the actual shortage of capital with consequent heavy demands on the Swiss capital market that proved to be more than the markets could sustain. The consequence was that interest rates on long-term railway bonds rose to 7.4 per cent . Thus, while Europe was turning to the US capital market for its investment requirements and finding high interest and tight money from that source, the Swiss themselves were finding their own sources of capital inadequate. Perhaps for the first time in modern history, the unity of a world-wide capital market was finally being felt by Swiss and Europeans alike. Furthermore, the conditions in this world-wide market were being dictated by the Americans who were the principal source of supply of credit, a circumstance which was to prevail for decades into the future.

There was another ground-breaking development in the capital market of 1921. For the first time, Switzerland and Europe found that there was an insufficient supply of capital in the sense that all demands upon the supply could not be met at the same time. This was manifest in the collapse of industrial shares during this first post-war depression (the more modern word 'recession' had not yet come into vogue) when capital shifted out of equity, selling shares for whatever price could be had. The excess of selling on the market resulted in falling prices.

At the same time that there was a shift out of shares, there was a corresponding movement of capital into public bonds causing an increase in their price, or what is the inverse of the price, a fall in the yield. When the yield on such bonds declined to such a level that further purchases of bonds were not worth while, the extra capital, rather than moving back into shares, simply added to additional market liquidity. This was made more evident because the practice of issuing new bonds by public authorities to cover the cost of public works had not yet developed sufficiently to absorb this excess of liquidity. Public authorities were still dependent upon the banks for their additional funding requirements when taxation was insufficient.

There was considerable unemployment in Switzerland, peaking at nearly 100,000 in 1922, as the export industries suffered from the effects of the post-war depression. Prices fell (including the cost of living) as imports became cheaper to purchase, but unemployment, which affected over a third of all industrial workers, meant considerable hardship as incomes fell faster than prices. The hotel industry, of course, had suffered enormously during the war years and found itself in dire straits during this depression period. Even public authorities, such as the cities of Zürich and the Canton of Basle City, were forced to borrow from the banks.

Nevertheless, despite the dismal showing of the Swiss economy, there was still optimism despite the fact that the Treaty of Versailles itself gave no reason for this optimism; indeed, the clauses embodied in this treaty were as backward-looking as the new customs barriers erected by the new states that were created. It was only the League of Nations which inspired the hope that

> ... the system of law and order announced by the League of Nations and resting upon treaties of arbitration will replace the earlier system of mutually opposed alliances which almost invariably lead to war. If the present endeavours to settle differences amicably and by a process of arbitration gain acceptance and are converted into practice, we shall have taken a large and important step toward a real and lasting peace which alone can make the economic and financial reconstruction of our continent possible.[18]

CONCLUSION

In retrospect, the time period of the late nineteenth century and early twentieth century, which reached its conclusion in 1914, can be seen as the most extraordinary span of years in the history of the modern capitalist world. During that time, the foundations of future development were laid in the sense that banking systems had made a most important discovery – it is possible, and profitable, to mobilise the savings of the community by borrowing from the community. This they could do by creating a market for savings, on the one hand, and a market for lending on the other. These two markets can be brought into an equilibrium through the intermediation of the banks; hence serving the economic function of channeling savings into investment. In doing so, the funds thus borrowed from the public are made available to those in the community who can put them to the greatest use. In the Swiss case, those savings 'in the community' were often outside of Switzerland.

To the extent that such loans were made within Switzerland, an increase in the number and amount of deposits occurred, ie a monetary expansion took place as long as we accept the modern definition of deposits as money. This monetary expansion was accompanied by an increase in output of goods and services during the latter half of the nineteenth century, the rate of increase of which has never been equalled since. This was the single most important characteristic of that pre-war era.

It was brought to an end in 1914. All the progress that had been made in banking across frontiers, the low tariffs, and, most important from our point of view, the monetary systems based upon gold had collapsed during the war and post-war years. The Swiss banks suffered enormous losses as their investments abroad had to be written off. The great inflations literally wiped out the value of investments that were denominated in those currencies because the 'gold clauses' were ignored by countries suffering both from hyperinflation and deprivation of lands, the result of an anachronistic peace treaty.

Seen from purely a Swiss banking point of view, the period prior to 1914 was one of expansion in two directions. The banks learned, firstly, to engage in the finance of industry rather than to develop a partnership. Secondly, Swiss banks engaged in the creation of industries outside the borders of the Confederation. While the practice of foreign lending *per se* was not at all new to Swiss banking, the establishment of industry, whether by consortium with other banks or through their own efforts, was new. Though disastrous from the standpoint of the 1914–18 catastrophe which followed, it was the beginning of the truly Swiss nature of banking which has been so characteristic of banks to the present time.

Why did the banks venture into foreign lands to incur risks which, though not foreseen, proved so disastrous? The answer is simple enough; just as in the early half of the nineteenth century, there was too much capital in Switzerland for domestic investment only. The Cantonal banks had already taken much of the small business and agricultural lending as their own prerogative. Once railroad building had been, for all practical purposes, completed, the commercial banks, or Grossbanken, found that investment rewards as interest and dividends were greater abroad and therefore worth the risk. In doing so, they established a pattern of Swiss banking which was not only unique but extremely important for the Swiss economy, as we hope to show in ensuing chapters.

Notes

1. We ought to point out here that there was an initial jump in deposits from 2.6 million in 1895 to 28 million in 1896, which was the result of three amalgamations with (1) the Zurcher Bankverein, (2) the *Schweizerische Unionbank*, and (3) the *Basler Depositenbank*. As a consequence of these mergers, the new Bankverein became firmly established as one of Switzerland's great banks.
2. The correlation coefficient between the two series is 0.944 for a simple fit and 0.96 for a logarithmic fit.

3. *Reports on Tariff Wars between Certain European States*, British Parliamentary Papers, 1904, XCV, pp. 782–5.
4. Bauer, op. cit., p. 198. *Swiss Bank Corporation, 1872–1972* Swiss Bank Corporation, Basle, 1972, p. 198.
5. Estimates made by E. Grossmann and W. Sombart, both economic historians of considerable repute.
6. J.R. von Salis described this period in glowing terms: 'Never before had the world witnessed a comparable efflorescence of its natural forces, never had the earth's population multiplied at such a rate, never had the planet's riches been exploited so extensively and systematically nor the barriers dividing peoples and continents from one another dismantled so radically.' *Weltgeschichte der Neuesten Zeit*. vol. 3.
7. Some historians, particularly Werner Sombart, had argued that 'Capital, i.e. high finance, rules the world and makes our statesmen dance like puppets on a string.' Behrendt, a Swiss historian, disputed this: 'The World War was not decided upon in the offices of banks but in the salons of a few courts and the officers' messes of certain general staffs. Inferiors to these powers, even the plutocracy had to submit to war.' Behrendt, Richard, *Die Schweiz und der Imperialismus*, pp. 87.
8. Landmann, 'Geldmarkt und Bankpolitik', published in *Zeitschrift fur Schweizerische Statistik und Volkswirtschaft, 1914*, p. 291. The exception he made for joint-stock banks meant that a reserve of capital could be used for meeting depositors' demands. Other banks, such as cantonal banks and private banks, did not have such a reserve.
9. While it may seem callous to our modern, welfare-oriented minds, the Federal Government did not provide for the needs of the families of soldiers or the soldiers' civilian requirements even though compulsory universal conscription was the practice. One can readily imagine the hardship suffered by the poorer soldiers and their families.
10. Actually, velocity of circulation of commercial funds collapsed to zero since bills could not be collected. The Bankverein did collect what foreign deposits it could (some 20–25 million francs) after they were released by foreign governments, so as to increase its foreign resources. It did so at considerable loss because the exchange rates of these currencies had already collapsed. Indeed, the very strength of the Swiss banking system, which had placed much of its assets in a broad distribution of countries, proved in this instance to be a weakness because so many of these assets (consisting of foreign deposits in foreign banks) were now uncollectable.
11. *The Schweizerische Treuhandstelle beim Politischen Department* supervised the imports from the Central Powers. Importing companies were required to post certain sums as guarantees with their banks which were responsible to the government import department. The Société Suisse de Surveillance Economique served as the surveillance agency for goods imported from the Allies.
12. The total cost of mobilisation was 1,190 million francs but a quarter of this amount was not paid for until the fiscal years 1919–21, after the conclusion of hostilities.

13.   An interesting sidelight regarding the difficulties of the London branch of the *Swiss Bankverein* deserves at least a footnote because it points out the unfortunate hysteria which accompanied the war. In October 1914, an article appeared in the *Financial News* which pointed out that 'Swiss banks are said to be under German influence' (the *Bankverein* was the only Swiss bank in London) and that through their machinations, they had brought about the closure of the London Stock Exchange. Despite the fact that the report could easily be proven as false, it spread rapidly as a rumour until the Swiss Federal President Hoffmann wrote as follows to the Chairman of the Board of the *Bankverein:* 'I venture to send you enclosed a cutting taken from the *Secolo* (a Swiss newspaper) of the 3rd/4th ins. in which it is laid to the charge of the Swiss banks in general that the disorder created in London on the outbreak of the war and leading to the closing of the Stock Exchange and to the run on the Bank of England was caused by a manoeuvre of German financiers who were supported in this by some Swiss banks. It is hardly likely that anyone will wish or be able to pass over this item from the *Financial News* in silence if, as I have no hesitation in assuming, the accusation is without foundation. I was thinking of asking Mr. Carlin to approach the *Financial News* and, on presenting them with specific denials from the major Swiss banks, to induce them to correct this item. However, I should not wish to proceed in this matter without first informing you, and I should be grateful for your opinion.'

    Again, in its edition of 15 August 1918, the *Morning Post* alleged that the Schweizerischer Bankverein was a German bank and, in fact, a branch of the Deutsche Bank in Berlin. This accusation was, of course, stoutly denied by the management of the London branch. Nevertheless, the damage and *potential* damage to confidence in the bank was obvious. It became clear to the Basle Board of Directors that a translation problem from German into both English and French existed. After some lengthy deliberations, a letter dated 31 March 1917 was circulated changing the name of the bank to Société de Banque Suisse (French), Societa di Banca Svizzera (Italian) and Swiss Bank Corporation (English).

14   Eighth Annual Report (1919–20), p. 22, Orel Füssli Verlag, 1920, p. 22

15   Fehrenbach has an interesting account of the 'traveling Swiss banker' who managed to pick up considerable sums in securities and gold illegally since the export of capital and gold was prohibited by the French government. The implication from this is that Switzerland actually prospered at the expense of France and other countries. To be sure, *some* Swiss must have benefited, but we find it difficult to accept that the nation as a whole enjoyed such prosperity. He cites the instance of one, Ernst Guizot, an employee of the now default Basler Handelsbank, who traveled in France anonymously, and was able to collect securities, gold, and other monetary assets from frightened French people who were anxious to hedge their assets against expected falling values of the French franc. Fehrenbach seems to ignore the fact that every hedge requires a counter-position (there is no free lunch) and if the French gain from locking in the value of their assets in Swiss francs, the Swiss banks must

lose precisely the same amount in terms of foreign exchange. Still, it makes interesting reading! (J. R. Fehrenbach, *The Swiss Banks*, Chapter 3, 'The Plain Brown Envelope', (McGraw-Hill, 1966) p. 36.

16.   Friedman and Schwartz, *A Monetary History of the United States*, (VBER, Princeton University Press, 1963) Princeton, NJ, p. 219.

17.   The question of paramountcy of the government or the central bank is neither unique to the US nor was it characteristic of that period only. It resurfaced after World War II in the US and in Great Britain. Certainly the Continental countries have also experienced the same problem with the exception, we might add, of Switzerland.

18.   Annual Report of the Swiss Bank Corporation, 1926. This was written after the Treaty of Locarno and the admission of Germany into the League in 1926. Subsequent events, of course, proved that such optimism was, as yet, misplaced.

11 Reconstruction

INTRODUCTION

The years following the 1922 post-war depression were characterised by a re-building of the monetary and banking systems of Europe on a quite different foundation than had been seen in the past. Stability returned to Germany with the introduction of the Rentenmark (one Rentenmark = 1 billon paper marks), and in the autumn of 1923 the budget had finally been balanced. Similarly, the currencies of Austria and Hungary had been stabilised.

During this period it had proven impossible to maintain the currency relationships of the Latin Monetary Union which, as a consequence, was officially abandoned in 1926. The former members, France, Belgium, and Italy, managed to stabilise their currencies at levels very much less than formerly.[1] At the Genoa conference in 1922, the gold circulating standard was replaced by a 'gold bullion' standard (or gold exchange standard) which meant that central banks could hold as foreign reserve either gold or foreign exchange that was suitable as a substitute for gold.

In Switzerland, the return to a peacetime situation from a war footing meant that a surplus of labour and a shortage of suitable employment existed. Accordingly it was decided to proceed with the electrification of the railways, a massive undertaking involving heavy capital expenditure. Four electrification loans totalling 630 million francs were floated on the capital market, and later a fifth loan of 175 million in 1925. At interest rates of between 4 per cent and 6 per cent these constituted a heavy drain on the public finance. These massive capital expenditures required considerable production from the domestic civil and electrical engineering industries and meant that unemployment fell markedly, from about 100,000 in 1922 to only 10,000 in the years 1924–5.

For a country so highly dependent upon imports as Switzerland, it was absolutely essential that either old export markets be re-built or new ones be developed. There was no choice, yet the task was made more difficult by the universal growth of protectionism. 'Extreme nationalism is rife in almost every quarter, and, as its main weapon, uses protective tariff barriers whose effect is often tantamount to an embargo on imports.' Further, 'The most disquieting feature is the way in which the sound economic development of Europe is being misdirected and jeopardized for a long time to come.'[2] These were thought-provoking, if not ominous-sounding, words from Switzerland's largest bank; only the passage of time was necessary to prove their accuracy.

For Swiss banks, it was equally essential that they regain their former positions as exporters of capital.[3] This they began, for the first time in post-war years, in 1922 with a loan to the city of Amsterdam for 10 million florins and another to the Paris-Lyon railroad for 50 million French francs, both at 6 per cent interest. The interesting feature here is that both loans were in foreign exchange, not Swiss francs, and recalls the very early business of Swiss banks – that of the simple exchange of one currency for another according to its gold content. The significance of the foreign exchange loan was that its repayment was in foreign currency, thence to be exchanged into the currency of the lender, Swiss francs or otherwise. The risk of a devaluation of the foreign currency was therefore borne by the Swiss banks, such risk to be compensated, presumably, by a correspondingly higher interest rate on the loan.

It was this export of capital which prompted much debate amongst the Swiss politicians. Why export capital when so much investment was required domestically? This argument implied a confusion, in the minds of those who advanced it, between 'capital' and simply money. The resolution of this confusion was both interesting and significant from the standpoint of a small country which had already been engaged in the business of capital export for centuries, so much so that the economy of Switzerland had become completely inter-related with the economies of the rest of the world. The banks had both raised capital abroad and invested capital abroad when such investment yielded a greater return (concomitant with exchange risks) than domestic investment. To increase the return on domestic investment, thereby to compete with foreign investment, would certainly have required tariffs for the protection of Swiss industry which, in turn, would lower the standard of living of the Swiss public.

There was another advantage in lending capital abroad. Often the same foreign loans were accompanied by additional export orders for Swiss industry, particularly the engineering and electrical industries, thereby generating employment in those industries. Here, once more, the integration of the Swiss economy with other countries was brought home with even greater force than before the war.

A NEW STRUCTURE OF WORLD BANKING

Not only was there an integration of the economy of Switzerland with the world economy but the Swiss banking system was also becoming part of a world banking system. From a world monetary structure based upon gold as an international currency, there had been an important, and not so subtle, change marked by a shift in the centre of the world's financial system from London to New York. This meant moving from a gold standard to a *de facto* dollar standard. In this sense, therefore, the history of Swiss banking takes on an entirely different context because just as the world's banking system adjusted to changing circumstances, so did that of the Swiss.

Seen in the broadest context of history, this world currency upheaval can be recognised as a necessary adjustment to a new world system of trade and payments – a system which was long in preparation and development. Indeed, this 'new system' did not completely arrive until well after the end of World War II. To put it simply, the former gold standard, which the dollar standard replaced, was becoming inadequate for the finance of the massive flows of payments which were forthcoming.[4] Even were the price of gold to increase so as to create some currency flexibility, it would still be highly unlikely that gold, with its extremely low elasticity of supply, could have met the enormous future requirements for an international currency.

Yet the substitution of the dollar for gold as an international reserve meant that the European countries that had hitherto relied upon gold for international transactions would henceforth use dollars instead. This required that the United States must continuously maintain a deficit in its balance of payments in order that Europe could acquire the dollars needed for its international reserves.

There was another, perhaps more important, issue than just the international payments involved which was to become even more pressing after World War II. The amount of currency in circulation in European countries had been determined by the amount of monetary gold held by the central banks of these countries. The relatively simple act of selling surplus gold from the coffers of banks (such gold having been acquired on behalf of their clients who exported more than was imported) in exchange for additional amounts of their own currency meant that there was a direct relationship between gold and the domestic currency as determined by the price level of gold in terms of that currency. Using dollars as a substitute for gold meant that the amount of a nation's currency in circulation depended upon the amount of dollars it had in its central bank, which in turn depended upon the monetary policies which happened to be followed by the US government and were in effect at the time.

This situation was certainly intolerable. Why should European countries agree to a US dollar standard instead of some other international standard? The answer lies in the fact that it was the best that could be done at the time, given the circumstances. There simply was no alternative.

On the other hand, the astonishing degree of naiveté and even the fundamental misunderstanding of the basic principles of international payments on the part of the Americans during the decade of the 1920s staggers even our modern imagination. To be sure, one has the benefit of hindsight, but the conflicting policy measures that were developed during this period could only be attributed to the fact that one agency of the US government must have been unaware of what another agency was attempting to accomplish. Such was the nature of that democracy, with its checks and balances as an accepted part of the system of government, that mutually conflicting measures could be adopted by Congress, for example, the Smoot-Hawley tariff making it impossible to earn dollars through exports to the US, on the one hand, and a continued insistence upon payment of war debt on the other. Yet, even within these self-evident contradictions, the world monetary system was still undergoing change.

Meantime, what was the position of Switzerland and the Swiss banks in this 'new' international financial system? To the Swiss, the post-war era was a period of adjustment to the new circumstances of more tariff barriers and a spirit of nationalism amongst the new states. Since the country imported more commodities, in terms of either tonnage or value, than it exported, there was always the inevitable balance of trade deficit. Yet export industries were important to the economy as sources of employment. The engineering, clock and watch industries, metals and chemicals showed considerable growth during the 1920s while the more traditional textiles, food manufacturing and embroidery declined in importance. These latter export industries were subject to the growing protectionist sentiments of European countries, a continuous source of concern to economic thinkers of the day.[5]

Switzerland, just as any other democratic nation which might have been in similar circumstances, had to undergo the stress of soul-searching in the process of becoming a modern capital-exporting nation to supplement its export of goods. It was not easy for the population of the nation to understand the significance of capital export, especially under the circumstance that capital itself appeared to be in relatively short supply within the country. This process of Sturm und Drang (to borrow the well-known German phrase) emerged on the occasion of the raising of the French railway loan (mentioned above) which, along with a loan to the city of Amsterdam, carried an interest rate of 6 per cent. At the same time, in the year 1922 a Swiss Federal Railways loan had been easily negotiated on the domestic capital market at 4.5 per cent – a difference of one and one-half percentage points, indicating the greater profitability of foreign investment.

This situation also caused some concern in the Department of Finance and was the subject of some discussion with the banks. Tax revenue was lost to Switzerland because the coupon tax required by all bonds issued on behalf of domestic borrowers was effectively avoided by the banks through the sale of foreign bonds to Swiss investors. This matter of a loss of revenue to the Swiss Federal Government, through the sale of foreign bonds, was to be a recurring irritant to both banks and the Department of Finance.

The argument in favour of the 'export of capital' showed a remarkable degree of sophistication. Obviously, the higher interest rate on foreign bonds, combined with coupon tax avoidance, underlay the motives of banks. Profit maximisation was their true objective. But no substantive argument could be made on these grounds alone. It was necessary to show that it was better for Switzerland *as a nation* that such export of capital take place.

It was Julius Landmann, a most distinguished professor of political economy at the University of Basle, who presented the case that in order for capital to be fully utilised at home, domestic interest rates must be competitive with foreign rates. But, to reach this objective, the profits of domestic industry must be greater. Further, to achieve greater domestic profits, domestic prices must also be raised, and this would certainly, for Switzerland, involve the restriction of foreign competition by means of protective tariffs on manufactured imports. In other words, Switzerland would become precisely the same as other nations in Europe that sought, through tariffs, the increased development of their own domestic industry through the restriction of foreign competition.

But Switzerland could not afford to be in such a position. Recognising the realities of the Swiss balance of payments situation, Landmann argued that restricting competing imports for the purpose of raising prices must also mean a corresponding restriction of exports because this would mean that Swiss exports would no longer be competitive in world markets. Being a small country, highly dependent upon its export industries, Switzerland's productivity, its national income, and, ultimately, its standard of living must therefore suffer as a consequence. Scarcely a better argument for free trade could have been presented even today and this at a time when the sentiment of the major powers was very much opposed to the concept.

But the argument did not stop there. In the Federal Council, a representative stated the following:

> If we raise difficulties about the export of capital, we shall make it harder to sell our own goods abroad. The results of capital export cannot economically take any other form but the export of goods ... But it seems to the Federal Council that individual transactions with countries abroad are better judged by the exporters, banking experts and private investors than by state officials, in other words those who ultimately have to bear the risk and therefore, in their own closest interests and after many a hard lesson taught by experience, will exercise the necessary caution.[6]

This is an expression of what was an extraordinary understanding not only of the position of Swiss banking in the world but also the important economic contribution of banks to the nation as a whole. It expresses a philosophy which was both uniquely Swiss and the result of an inheritance from centuries past. It also recognised that capital export meant a corresponding purchase of Swiss capital goods by those countries to whom the capital was exported, a recognition of the economic inter-relationships of the countries of Europe. In hindsight, we might express some regret that all the world did not arrive at similar conclusions long ago.

As far as the business activity of the Swiss banks was concerned, the era of the 1920s was one of considerable change and adjustment to the new conditions. The commercial bill of exchange was being supplanted by direct cash payments in commercial activity, and this meant a great deal of necessary foreign exchange trading. But it was precisely during this period that dealing in foreign exchange markets, a traditional Swiss bank activity, carried the greatest risks. Arbitrage, a typical 'normal' activity in foreign exchange markets, advanced to the next stage, that of pure speculation as to the future values of foreign exchange, a process to be discouraged by the commercial banks.

On the other hand, the situation in Europe, regarding national currencies and their determination outside the normal free market structure, encouraged the practice of 'suitcase banking', particularly amongst the private banks. New nations called into existence by the Treaty of Versailles as well as old nations determined to follow a new spirit of nationalism (founded upon the development of self-sufficiency bordering upon autarky) used their currencies as devices suitable for the achievement of their objectives. This was not the free market system of currency evaluation so characteristic of the pre-War gold standard. Under such conditions, those capitalists accustomed to the pre-War system looked to Switzerland as a 'haven' for the security of their earnings; after all, the world had been changed forever by the brutality of war, but Switzerland had not. It was still on the gold standard.[7] Enormous amounts of foreign deposits flowed, therefore, into Swiss banks purely to escape the political and economic uncertainties of the new regime.

Using the balance sheet statistics of the Swiss Bank Corporation, the largest (at the time) of the 'big' banks, we can identify the changes in deposits which reflect the influx of foreign deposits during this period (Figure 11.1).

In the years following 1920, the effects of the sharp recession of 1920–1 can be clearly recognised as a collapse in deposit totals to almost 600 million francs. After 1924, however, the steep climb to 1,155 million francs in 1930 was due almost entirely to the inflow of foreign funds which were seeking an escape from the uncertainties of a strange and different economic environment.

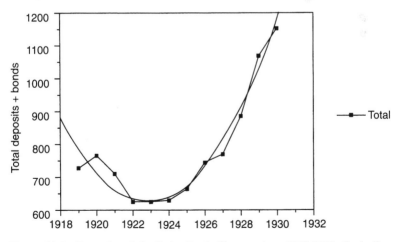

Figure 11.1 Deposits of the Swiss Bank Corporation, 1919-1930, (including medium-term Bonds) in millions of francs

This influx of foreign capital into the Swiss banking system had the effect of strengthening the unique intermediary and underwriting function of the banks. We find, thus, that foreign capital coming into Switzerland via the banks would be re-invested by the banks via the growing capital market. The Swiss capital market had been for some time a means by which the public authorities could finance their deficits, but when these same authorities found themselves in surplus funds, they channelled these funds into bonds and shares through the market, thereby adding considerable liquidity to the domestic market. This additional liquidity made it possible for the capital market to become international in the sense that foreign bonds and shares could be quoted and sold both to banks and investors alike.

The growing importance of foreign securities is suggested by the statistics. Between 1922 and 1929, about 912 million francs of foreign loans were negotiated through the Swiss market. These consisted of mostly German state loans and loans to German industry bearing high interest rates. But, and this is the main point, fully two-thirds of this (678 millions) were placed by the banks in the three years between 1926 and 1929.[8]

In addition to their purely underwriting service, banks made loans and participations directly to foreign customers. According to Kellenberger, total net capital exports both in this form and through the capital market amounted to 2,100 million francs between 1923 and 1929.[9] A rather substantial sum for a country of such small size, yet it was growing rapidly in terms of financial influence. It was this growth which was sharply curtailed by the massive depression of the 1930s.

THE COLLAPSE

It is no exaggeration to say that no one, except the most prescient few, foresaw the collapse which was to come. With the advantage of some of the exhaustive research into the causes and events which led up to the great crash of 1929, we can now recognise that during the period of the 1920s a fundamental maladjustment in the world's financial system was developing and even gathering momentum as the decade wore on. A massive disequilibrium in terms of liquidity which, to us at this vantage point, seems so obvious, was the inevitable result.

Rather like a vacuum cleaner, the United States, the great creditor nation, was continuously sucking in both the world's gold and the world's liquid assets. This it could easily do in view of its increasing demand for money which in turn was the natural result of its ever-growing national income. Since it was still on a gold standard, albeit one that did not meet the *standards* of a pre-war international gold standard, the largest part of the supply of the world's monetary gold ultimately became the property of the United States.

This forced European countries onto a gold exchange standard using dollars as a substitute for gold. With this new gold-exchange (or dollar) standard, the world entered into a quite different system of exchange rate determination. Old foreign exchange markets, bounded as they had been by gold shipping points, along with the stable currencies of the past had been completely destroyed by the war. With the new system, foreign exchange markets bore little or no relation to the economic realities of a country but responded entirely to the market forces of supply and demand however they might be determined. There was no opportunity, in other words, to arrive at an economically correct exchange rate such as that which had required centuries to develop under the pre-1914 gold standard.

THE SWISS SITUATION

It is interesting to observe that while the Great Depression had its beginnings in the United States, hardly 8 per cent of the national income of that country was exported (or imported). This was not true in Europe, where exports and imports were not only a much larger share of the economies of the countries but were also vital to their continued economic well being. The devaluation of the pound, for example, which made imports expensive to the British, had a serious impact upon European exporters who were dependent upon British markets. Switzerland was a prime example. Exports had achieved a level averaging about 2 billion francs (21 per cent of a national income of 9.5 billion francs) during the 1920s but fell to just 801 million francs (10.7 per cent of the national income) in 1932. Imports also declined from 2.7 billion to 1.7 billion francs during the same period. Watches and clocks suffered disastrously from the US tariff system while earnings from manufactured goods declined considerably.

It was impossible for such a contraction in economic activity (paced by declining exports) not to have a serious impact on the numbers of unemployed. But the impact was, at first, dampened by a continuation of building works and a decline in the cost of living by some 20 per cent, at the same time that earned incomes fell by only 12 per cent, hence an increase in real incomes. This maintained purchasing power and staved off unemployment until 1934 when building construction dropped off sharply. After that year, the numbers of unemployed rose to 100,000, to become a major economic and social problem.

The difficulty lay not only the collapse of export markets as foreign economies succumbed more and more to the Depression but also the fact that the Swiss franc became overvalued as foreign currencies (the pound, then the dollar) devalued. Exports became relatively expensive in those markets while imports became inexpensive. Cheaper imports helped to lower the domestic cost of living for the Swiss; nevertheless, the deficit in the balance of trade considerably widened and the Swiss authorities felt it absolutely necessary to impose import quotas along with a device whereby imports were linked to exports.

Most important, as far as the banks were concerned, compensation and clearing agreements were arranged with many countries which 'locked' Swiss trade bi-laterally with its trading partners. Such arrangements had a detrimental effect upon the banks which function best in a free, unobstructed, multilateral trading environment. The complications which are necessarily involved in these arrangements made banking transactions that much more difficult.

Additional measures included export subsidies and risk guarantees which the Government was able to implement. Such measures tended to increase the amount of state intervention in the economy, hardly pleasing to some conservatives, but since there was no opportunity for 'new deal' type measures involving state contracts (the Federal Council had expressed the view that Switzerland was already well supplied with economic infrastructure) there was little else that could have been done to encourage employment.

Once more, the root cause of the difficulty, as in France, had been an overvalued currency; but in the Swiss case, the franc had *not* been arbitrarily pegged under the conditions of the gold-exchange standard. The rest of the world, engulfed in the 1914–18 war, had literally destroyed its monetary system, the gold standard, but not Switzerland. The Swiss franc remained aloof, the only single currency of the western world untouched by the disaster of war. Meantime, as we have already argued, the rest of the currencies emerged from their crises of inflation with arbitrarily assigned foreign exchange values quite unrelated to the realities of their economies.

As in France, the Federal Departments of Finance and Economic Affairs attempted to advocate a strong dose of deflation as a remedy to the difficulty. This would lower the costs of production of exports to make them more competitive in a world of devalued currencies. They had originally hoped to reduce costs by about 20 per cent in this way so that exports could enjoy some of the world trade revival which occurred between 1934 and 1936.

Unfortunately, however, Switzerland did not participate in this trade revival. So the result was inevitable. The Federal Council decided (under the constitutional powers granted to it in 1931) to reduce the gold content of the franc by about 30 per cent – an obvious alternative to the stern measures of deflation. The announcement of devaluation occurred at the same time, 26 September 1936, as the French devaluation, the Council having had advance notice of the French action.[10]

The result was swift. Gold, which had been leaving the country in anticipation of devaluation, flowed back into Switzerland along with a considerable amount of short-term funds. The National Bank increased its gold holdings by more than a billion francs and interest rates on loans declined to below 4 per cent, precisely what the depressed Swiss economy required.

BANKING IN THE DEPRESSION

During the post-war years, the great Swiss banks had established themselves as permanent members of an international banking system. Their practice of being debtors to the international community by accepting its deposits, then re-lending those deposits to become creditors of that same international community had become commonplace. The skills involved were well beyond those of ordinary domestic banks, because placing deposits in secure, relatively risk-free loans required an intimate knowledge of not only the business climate but the political circumstances within each individual country as well. The major Swiss banks had simply outgrown their purely domestic banking responsibilities to become themselves major contributors to the Swiss economy.

This was no mean accomplishment. Banking in most countries at that time justified its existence by increasing the economic efficiency of the domestic economic system. National income growth rates of the magnitudes experienced in such countries as the United States, Germany, or other countries of western Europe would have been quite impossible without both the efficient transmission of payments and the provision of credit facilities to industries which required them. In Switzerland, on the other hand, banking had well exceeded its domestic contribution to become an industry genuinely contributing to the Swiss national income in its own right, in terms of payments for its services to the international community. This was no small achievement, which banks in most other countries did not attain until well after World War II.

One can appreciate, therefore, the severe blow to the Swiss banks dealt them by the German government in the bank moratorium and foreign exchange restrictions in 1931. These restrictions were successively tightened until they became so complete that by 1934 no foreign exchange transactions at all were permitted by the Nazi government.

What had happened in Germany to implement these restrictions was the creation of a Conversion Fund administered by the Reichsbank. This Fund was set up for the purpose of collecting the interest and amortisation payments with which German debtors were obligated. Debtors of Swiss banks discharged their debts as normally, not to the banks but to the Conversion Fund. Occasionally, the Reichsbank did transfer some of these funds into foreign currency when the foreign reserves were sufficiently large. In addition, the Golddiskontbank, a subsidiary of the Reichsbank, was authorised to buy the credits (those obligations of the debtors to the creditors) at one-half of their face value. The balance, the other half of the face value, was used to subsidise exports from Germany.

The purchases by the Golddiskontbank were then sold as 'scripts' in the market and could be used by foreign importers to *pay* for German exports! Thus, instead of remitting debt payments to creditors in the currency of the creditors, as would have been the normal method of payment under a multilateral trading system, the Conversion Fund made it necessary for the creditors, in effect, to take their payments in German goods. What it really amounted to was that German exports were being used to pay for German imports directly. If the market for scripts was sufficiently 'bullish', the original creditor might receive more than just the value of one-half of the loan in German goods. Furthermore, to add an incentive to the foreign creditor (now an importer), the greater the demand for German goods the greater was the value of the scripts and the more would the exporter receive as payment; hence it was to the advantage of foreign importers, to the extent that they were engaged in both the export and import business, to encourage buyers in their own country to become consumers of German products. The entire scheme, the brainchild of Hjalmar Schacht, the president of the Reichsbank, rested upon the capacity of an authoritarian regime to implement it, and so it did with remarkable success.[11]

For the Swiss banks the effect was disastrous. The Swiss Government, because of the importance of Switzerland to the Germans (notably tourism), was successful in negotiating a clearing agreement with Nazi Germany. In this way, the interest payments on foreign debts were, at the least, collected. (Swiss hoteliers effectively paid the interest payments to Swiss creditor banks from the proceeds of their German guests!) But still the banks were not free of their difficulties. Since the Government had obligated export proceeds to the use of payment for necessary imports, not for creditors, the banks were not able to collect their capital payments at all – the best they could hope for was the interest.

It takes little imagination to conceive of the magnitude of the disaster which befell the Swiss banking industry at the time. We recall that Swiss industry itself was struggling to maintain its export markets especially under the burden of an over-valued franc. This meant that industrial credit requirements simply collapsed, meaning that the business slowdown had a leveraged effect upon the banking business itself. In the face of this unfortunate situation, the eight major banks formed a self-help syndicate for the purpose of granting credit against securities that were not eligible for discount at the National Bank. Another bank syndicate was formed to support purchases on the stock exchanges of Swiss stocks, some 10 million francs for this purpose. These are examples of the surprising tendency amongst Swiss bankers to 'rally round' each other during times of emergency.

A still further action taken by the Government at that time was a Federal Loan Agency[12] with a capital of 100 million francs to assist banks in difficulty. All this was not enough to save the Schweizerische Diskontbank in Geneva which, after some stringent efforts at rescue by the canton, the cantonal banks, and the Confederation, was liquidated in 1935. In total, 35 banks in Switzerland suffered the same fate (according to the Federal Banking Commission) during this fateful period.[13]

Banking, by its very nature, is not directly concerned with the production of goods and services but with the 'production' of credit. The means by which such credit transfers ownership is money, and therein lies the banks' contribution to economic welfare. So when 34 countries which were Switzerland's trading partners operate exchange controls involving one-third of all the Swiss foreign transactions, hence requiring the use of clearing agreements to carry out, the traditional function of banks is no longer required. Banks are excluded from a large part of the very business activity for which they are, by their nature, best equipped. Very much more than a mere devaluation of the

Swiss franc is required for banks to recover from the disastrous consequences of the depression.

One might ask: why use the banking industry at all? why not work entirely with bi-lateral clearing arrangements? A detailed answer to such a question is really not appropriate here except to point out that barter, which bi-lateral trade really means, does not make the best possible use of a nation's resources. It does not permit 'shopping around' to get the best deal in terms of both sales and purchases. This is certainly true in international trade just as in domestic trade.

Another obvious fact presents itself. As has been noted already Swiss banks had achieved such a pre-eminence in their international status that their international banking function was contributing to the national income of Switzerland with the significance of a major industry. To reduce the effectiveness of that major industry must also impact sharply upon the standard of living of the Swiss people themselves in the form of a lower national income. This is the inevitable consequence of the collapse in multi-national trade and commerce for which the depression and the policies of successive devaluation of currencies were responsible.

The exreme nature of the banking situation can be easily recognised from a few figures. Total 'borrowed funds'[14] declined from 15.8 billion francs in 1930, to just 14.8 billions in 1934. Since the major banks (grossbanken) had become the principal borrowers from foreign sources, they suffered the most with a decline in their borrowed funds from 6.6 billions to just 3.0 billions, about 55 per cent.

A better perspective can be gained from Figure 11.2, which shows the impact of the depression, in terms of borrowed funds, upon the Swiss Bank Corporation alone. The peak year for the deposits occurred in 1930, at almost 1.2 billion francs. Thereafter the decline set in to reach a low point of 700 million. 'Other liabilities' (short term drafts and acceptances) also fell to reach a low point of just 41 million francs from a peak of 247 million in 1929. At the same time that these events were transpiring, the banks 'own funds' (capital and reserves) remained fairly constant. These were serious circumstances indeed. Yet the Swiss Bank Corporation and the Credit Suisse were the only two of the ten major banks that survived the depression intact, without financial reorganisation of any kind.

Just about the only circumstance that occurred during that sad era that can be considered as truly favourable to Swiss banking was the Federal Banking Law. We can only speculate that this most important piece of legislation was conceived at least in part if not in entirety, as a

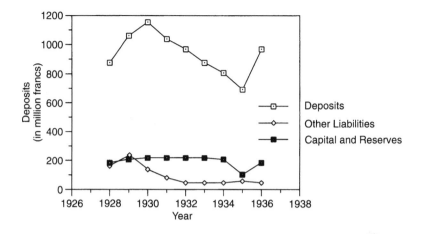

Figure 11.2 Swiss Bank Corporation Liabilities

consequence of the depression. We can do so because it contained measures specifically designed to both prevent the banking problems of the time and to assist those banks that do find themselves in difficulties.

At the same time that the Law provided for the increased security of banks' depositors, there were provisions for economically necessary loans at reasonable costs as well as an improvement in providing information to the National Bank. These are interesting provisions, in that greater security for banks' depositors must have meant an increase in the degree of bank regulation and supervision, yet, at the same time, the Law stressed the counterview that over-regulation would be inimical to the efficient and economical operation of the banking system. A compromise between the two objectives was, therefore, essential.

There was a world-wide banking philosophy that excessive regulation was not conducive to efficiency which was gaining ground at this time, and the Swiss Federal Banking Law reflected this. In the United States, as early as 1894, the Secretary of the Treasury had stated in his Annual Report:

Every prudently managed bank, if left free to conduct its deposit and discount business in the manner most advantageous to its own interests and the interests of its patrons, will undoubedly keep on hand a reasonable reserve to meet not only all the ordinary demands upon it, but to provide for such emergencies as are liable to occur in the community where it is located; but it ought not to be prohibited by law from using such reserve for the only purposes it was designed to accomplish . . . To provide for a reserve which can be utilized even at a time of the greatest stringency and distrust without incurring the penalties of forfeiture, affords a most striking illustration of the impolicy of legislative interference with the natural laws of trade and finance.[15]

This interesting statement, by a member of the US President's cabinet, recognises a principle of primary importance in banking. Bankers must be sufficiently free to conduct their own affairs without the constraint of excessive government regulation. Furthermore, the 'legal reserve' of each bank must be available to it during times of emergency to be used when necessary. The reserve must not be 'locked up' within the confines of the regulating authority.

Later, the Federal Reserve System was devised to provide for an untouchable legal reserve and an *excess* reserve which could be expanded or contracted by the Federal Reserve System when the need arose. But this is quite different from the 1894 approach which was incorporated by the Swiss into their Banking Law as part of its own banking philosophy. It was believed that an excessively stringent regulatory mechanism must cause an increase in bank interest rates and couldnot be a substitute for honesty and prudence in the administration of affairs. An excessive control of banks, in other words, can very quickly become counter-productive. This is, perhaps, the most interesting and lasting feature of the Federal Banking Law.

Broadly there were four areas of bank regulation:

1. There was to be compulsory auditing of the accounts of the banks by independent auditors under the supervision of the Federal Banking Commission (a new body brought into existence by the Law).
2. The approval of the National Bank for all foreign loans in excess of 10 million francs was required.
3. There were strict requirements as to the banks' liquidity and the amounts of the banks' own funds to be committed to liquid assets. These were for the protection of the banks' creditors and constituted the single departure from the 'liberal philosophy' of banking which was the characteristic of the time. These liquidity requirements were designed to encourage depositors through a lessening of the risk and became the hallmark of Swiss banks from that time forward.

4. There were provisions for a grace period for banks to meet their liabilities with some payment deferment. These were designed to assist banks that were temporarily in difficulties but were not expected to completely collapse. Some banks, as might have been anticipated, did feel the necessity to take advantage of the grace periods almost immediately.

Lastly, we can hardly overlook in the Federal Banking Law the famous deposit secrecy requirements which have been so admired, on the one hand, and so misunderstood on the other. Unless the Swiss criminal code has been violated, there is absolutely no access to or information regarding the deposits for which Swiss banks are liable. As might have been anticipated, it has been just this secrecy requirement and its strict enforcement which has been subject to popular suspicion over the years, so making Swiss banking synonymous with suspicious 'money laundering' and the like, which the Swiss banks have done so much to dispel.

It would be difficult to exaggerate the effects of the Great Depression on the Swiss banks. Already, by the decade of the 1930s the banks had achieved the status of international banks with assets distributed amongst many countries. Almost without saying, the minimum requirement for such international investment is the free exchange of currencies in accordance with market values. All this meant that during periods of economic growth, such as the 1920s, asset expansion brought greater earnings to the banks to such an extent that they became a major industry in the country with substantial contributions to the Swiss national income. Expansion, to banks, meant that the banks' creditors, on the liabilities side of the balance sheet, tended to increase, thereby supplying the banks with additional funds for investment purposes. These funds, combined with the usual entrepreneural spirit of bankers, drives their assets to seek the best return, hence producing more economic growth.

The depression, on the other hand, meant that these same assets, which were the investments of the banks, became blocked with newly-imposed foreign exchange controls. Germany, in 1931, introduced its bank moratorium and followed this with restrictions on foreign exchange transactions. By June 1934, the Hitler government had imposed complete control of foreign exchange transfers with only the clearing agreements remaining as a method by which interest payments on Swiss investments might be made.

Simultaneously with these adverse developments in foreign exchange transactions, the Swiss economy itself began to feel the effects not only of the depression but also the consequence of an over-valued Swiss franc. Exports suffered so that the credit requirements of exporters dwindled or were reduced in value. This meant that a declining commercial business of the banks pressed further on their assets, already shrinking from the adverse effects of their losses in the foreign sector. Finally, the stock exchanges, an important source of banking revenue, suffered a collapse in price due to the share liquidation and withdrawal of funds by foreign sources.

But these were by no means all of the problems with which the banks were faced. Swiss banks had long established themselves as Saint-Simonian banks and had participated widely in industry. As the export industries suffered from loss of markets, so did the banks with which they were associated.

Since banks are dealers in credit (they 'manufacture' credit packaged in a form suitable for borrowers from the raw materials supplied by their own creditors), as their assets decline for any reason, they must likewise reduce or otherwise restructure their liabilities, and do so in a manner that will inflict the least harm to their creditors. The drastic reduction in assets suffered by the Swiss banks meant that liabilities had to be similarly reduced. An excellent example of this was A. G. Leu & Co., a well known bank for which the Swiss Bank Corporation had already assumed some considerable responsibility through a large purchase of its shares in 1921. The bank had reduced its capital from 50 to 40 millions of francs in 1934. But that was not all. Matters grew even worse when there was an increased withdrawal of funds in 1935 and some assets had to be sold at decreased market value to honour these withdrawals. It was then that Leubank requested that its grace period, as provided by the new Banking Law, be granted. In the end, a massive restructuring of liabilities had to take place. Depositors suffered a loss of value to a level of 65 per cent of the original, 15 per cent of which was converted into preference shares entitling them to special claims on future profits. These were drastic measures considering that the liabilities of the banks both domestic and foreign are assets to the public.[16]

Throughout the entire period, the Swiss banks had to assume a position of higher-than-normal liquidity. This was necessary to accommodate the demands of their depositors who wished to withdraw their deposits in the form of coin. This was true not only of domestic depositors but foreign as well, so that a drain of gold took place from the National Bank which was so severe that the Swiss Bank Corporation itself had to come to its aid with loans from its own gold reserve. But cash earns no interest and the Swiss banks found themselves with reduced earning potential as a consequence.

CONCLUSIONS

The period following World War I was characterised by a turbulence which was ultimately to mark a watershed in the world's financial history. It was a period which witnessed the demise of the gold standard, and its replacement by a dollar standard. It was a period also which saw a change in the world's financial system with a movement of the financial capital of the world from London to New York. It meant that Wall Street and the movement of stock prices in that market became the signals for movements in other equity markets. Last but not least, the United States, even though international trade was a relatively small portion of its national income, became the world leader in commerce and finance with its currency assuming the dominant role.

This was inevitable. The enormous real growth in the US Gross Domestic Product, with its huge output of goods and services at the same time that European production was severely hampered by tragic hyperinflation, gave it a dominance both in the European export market and as a source of demand for European imports. Most important, for our purposes, was the fact that the Federal Reserve Board in Washington became the source of a monetary policy, based purely on domestic considerations, which would affect either favourably or unfavourably the fortunes of Europe.

Swiss banks showed, throughout this entire period, an extraordinary adaptability to the new circumstances. As a nation, the Swiss had emerged from the war virtually intact with their monetary system based upon gold and their banks ready and willing to accept foreign currency deposits. Thus, as hyperinflation and political uncertainty threatened the value of assets throughout Europe, the Swiss banks became a welcome haven as a means whereby asset values could be assured. The banks, to put it simply, benefited from the risk and uncertainty which prevailed in other countries. In doing so, they were able to expand their liabilities and corresponding investments in foreign countries for the rather obvious reason that the Swiss economy alone could not possibly absorb the surplus. In a real sense, Swiss banks had become truly international banks with foreign assets becoming more important than domestic assets.

One may readily appreciate, therefore, the impact upon Switzerland of the depression as it spread from Wall Street to Europe. The heavy indebtedness of Europeans to American investors combined with the absolute refusal of Americans to accept imports from Europe, thereby to enable them to acquire the wherewithall to pay those debts, meant that only through payments in gold could obligations be discharged. At the same time, the new gold-exchange standard required that some exchange rate amongst currencies be established, and since gold had ceased to serve that most useful function, some other means of assignment of exchange rates *vis-à-vis* the dollar had to be devised. Eventually, overvaluation, in the case of France and the gold bloc, and undervaluation in the case of sterling was the result.

The Wall Street crash in 1929 had its inevitable consequences. A massive deflation throughout Europe and the corresponding loss of purchasing power affected all countries. But perhaps the most important of all was the tendency of nations to 'implode' into an autarky through the imposition of high protective tariffs, foreign exchange restriction and exchange control. The great lessons of history, the Cobden treaties of the nineteenth century, were ignored.

It was this collapse of international commerce which certainly had the greatest impact on the Swiss banks. The domestic market for capital and credit had long since ceased to be great enough to absorb the funds which were coming into the Swiss banking system from abroad. The result was a direct connection between the banks and the economy of Switzerland and its neighbours. Whether it wished it or not, Switzerland was directly influenced by the *domestic* well-being of other countries through both its exports and its investments.

Notes

1. For the Belgian franc, one new franc equaled one-seventh of the old unit, France, one-fifth, and Italy, 28 per cent of the former lira.
2. Annual Reports of the Swiss Bank Corporation, 1925 and 26.
3. We might remind readers once more of the implied connotation of the word 'capital'. As used here, it is, in the first place, the savings of the Swiss public, who prefer savings accounts with their banks. In the second place, and more subtle, it is the process of underwriting securities, both foreign and domestic, which Swiss banks perform for their customers. They acquire these securities, then re-sell them to final investors at a profit. Such activities are exports of capital when the security is foreign

in origin. Technically, when the final investor is foreign, the capital is re-exported via the Swiss banks which act as intermediaries.

4. Similarly the 'new system', i.e. the gold exchange standard (or dollar standard) was to give way to the modern system of global finance which we know today.

5. '... Extreme nationalism is rife in almost every quarter and, as its main weapon, uses protective tariff barriers whose effect is often tantamount to an embargo on imports. The most disquieting feature is the way in which the sound economic development of Europe is being misdirected and jeopardized for a long time to come.' Annual Report of the Swiss Bank Corporation, 1925.

6. Quoted in Bauer, *Swiss Bank Corporation, 1872–1971*, p. 244. Swiss Bank Corporation, Basle, 1972, p.244.

7. Readers are referred again to a delightful chapter in T. R. Fehrenbach's book entitled 'The Plain Brown Envelope' for a discussion of the new structure of the European economy and the Swiss 'island of stability' in a stormy sea. Fehrenbach, T. R., *The Swiss Banks* (New York: McGraw-Hill, 1966).

8. Statistics from the National Bank quoted in Bauer, *Swiss Bank Corporation*, p. 244.

9. Kellenberger, E., *Kapitalexport und Zahlungsbilanz, Vol. I*, p. 245 and p. 307. Pollard and Holmes, Edward Arnold, London, 1972, p. 307.

10. It is curious that the Swiss National Bank had opposed the currency measures taken by the Federal Council. The opposition appeared to be based on a matter of prestige. After all, the franc since 1850 had been a metallic currency (silver at that time) and the rejection of the gold clauses in foreign contracts by debtor countries in the past had been a reason for the severest censure. Now, Switzerland was placed in a similar situation! We find the almost 'quaint' attachment of national pride to a currency (with historical hindsight, of course) to be an oddity reminiscent of the nineteenth century, a misplaced sense of values considering the supreme importance of a return to full employment and prosperity.

11. Schacht, Hjalmar, *My First Seventy-Six Years*, pp. 316–18, re-printed in Polland and Holmes, Document of Economic History, Edward Arnold, London 1972. p. 484–5.

12. Eidgenössische Darlehenskasse.

13. The period for which these figures were taken extends beyond the pre-war depression era into wartime. The Federal Banking Commission's report, the source of the figures, applied to the years 1935–42. Thus we cannot attribute all the bankruptcies to the Depression alone; nevertheless, the Depression years contributed considerably to the difficulties of these banks. Bauer, Hans, *Swiss Bank Corporation*, p. 264.

14. Swiss banks refer to 'borrowed funds' as funds on the liabilities side of their balance sheets which are not 'own funds', that is deposits, bonds, acceptances, and so on. Own funds are capital and reserves. It is these borrowed funds which had grown considerably since the turn of the century and of later years from foreign sources.

15. The Annual Report of the Secretary of the Treasury, 1894, p. lxxx. Footnote 44, Friedman and Schwartz, NBER, Princeton University Press, Princeton, NJ, 1963, p. 117.
16. This does not apply to the cantonal banks which continued their activities during the depression almost unabated. Indeed, in some cases they actually benefited from the loss of business by commercial banks as customers transferred to the cantonal banks.

12 The Tragedy of War and the Dawn of a New Era

INTRODUCTION

Most Swiss bankers must have been well aware of the coming catastrophe of World War II. With preparations for the coming war being laid down long in advance of the outbreak of hostilities, it was just a matter of when, not if. Since the historical relationship between Germany and Switzerland had always been strong, and the objectives of Hitler were so well publicised, it must have been obvious to everyone, especially bankers, that war was inevitable. This contrasted sharply with World War I which took Switzerland, and all the world for that matter, completely by surprise. It was next to impossible, save for seers and fortune tellers, to foresee the events of August 1914. By contrast, the invasion of Poland in 1939 could hardly have been anything but expected.

To the Swiss, geographic proximity with the League of Nations headquarters meant that they had a favoured position as the observers of events, and could easily recognise the impotence of that body in world affairs. The claims of Imperial Japan in Asia, the African conquests by Fascist Italy, and the ambitions of Hitler's National Socialism in Germany were well beyond the capacity of that international forum to cope. Carl J. Burckhardt, the well known Swiss historian, expressed it neatly and succinctly: '... in the Western World, events on the political scene still obeyed a more subtle rhythm ... and (in sharp contrast with) an officialese riddled with legal terminology which was heard from the front benches of parliaments and particularly in the League of Nations and alternated with declarations expressed in extreme generalities'.[1]

There was little that Switzerland could do but prepare itself for the worst to come. As early as 1936, a defence loan was floated with great success, suggesting that the public also was well aware of future events. Accordingly, the nation began the preparations for its own defence with its own military preparations and the establishment of the basic outlines of a war economy in the event that war should come. Probably more important, the process of stockpiling of raw materials and foodstuffs had begun.

THE CATASTROPHE

It is not easy to identify with precision the causes of a disaster of such magnitude as World War II. We might even start with the Hawley-Smoot tariff which made imports into the United States impossible. This was the signal for more 'beggar thy neighbour' tariff policies which spread from country to country, breaking down the spirit of cooperation and 'togetherness' which had grown and developed during the decade of the 1920s. The result was a collapse into an autarky which encouraged a spirit of economic independence, precisely the antithesis of economic cooperation. No longer was it possible for importers in various countries to seek the best bargains amongst competing exporters. The falling exchange rates of their own currencies *vis-à-vis* those of neighbouring countries made such imports impossibly expensive. Only domestic sources of supply could be economically feasible.

Such economic nationalism forces an inward-looking attitude amongst populations as they seek the necessary means of subsistence from within their own borders. But the nations of Europe were, and still are, not completely self-sustaining. As early as the decade of the 1920s, population growth amongst industrial nations had already outrun the domestic capacity to produce food. Similarly, European agricultural nations required industrial products to sustain their living standards. To forego trade, therefore, meant that it was essential that some national resources be allocated to alternative domestic production, even though such production was uneconomic.

For Germany, in which there were some 6 or 7 million unemployed, it was a question of creating both jobs and additional food sources, the latter being the more urgent because when workers were given jobs their food consumption rose to higher qualities of food. Under such circumstances, the rise of National Socialism and with it the tragedy of a single man, der Führer, is understandable. To the Germans it appeared that only an authoritarian régime could cope with the difficulties facing Germany at the time, and the fact that such a régime happened to led by a charismatic maniac was an unfortunate circumstance both for Germany and the world. Clearly, for Hitler, *drang nach Osten* was the only solution. If insufficient resources for food production existed in Germany, additional sources must be found, and these lay in the countries of eastern Europe. What had formerly been available through the normal channels of international trade had to be secured in the form of bi-lateral agreements: the closest substitute for absent domestic resources, yet by no means the 'international trade' with which the world had already become familiar.

The Conversion Funds discussed in the preceding chapter were a form of just this type of 'bi-lateralism'. Underscoring these funds lay the ominous requirements of the German armament industry. One can easily speculate upon the economic circumstances had there been no re-armament, that is, had Germany not embarked upon the tragic road to war under the banner of National Socialism. More export industries could have been developed which would have certainly increased export earnings in competition with other exporters in other nations, thereby earning the necessary foreign exchange to pay for more imports of essential foodstuffs. The necessity for the Conversion Funds would have disappeared, and Europe could have looked forward to another period of prosperity similar to that of the pre-1914 era. But such was not to be.

As Germany devoted an increasing amount of its resources to armament, it became necessary not only to increase the necessary imports of raw material but also to pay for these imports in Reichsmarks, because foreign exchange was in desperately short supply. To accomplish this, the Reichsbank developed a new financial instrument, the Mefo bills, instead of resorting to a direct expansion of the money supply which would certainly have been inflationary.[2]

It would be difficult to find a better statement of the fundamental principles of autarky, as conceived by the German Reich, than that of a secret memorandum from Hitler himself, dated August 1936. In this memo he stated clearly the objectives of his government by outlining a four-year plan with the achievement of total self-sufficiency as its ultimate goal. Synthetic rubber production was to be speeded up regardless of cost, because even though tyres made of such rubber were more expensive than those made of natural rubber, it was better to use the synthetic rubber than to devote scarce foreign exchange to imports of natural rubber.

Another example taken from this memo was the necessity for stockpiling of ammunition which required the current use of essential imported raw material rather than stockpiling the raw material itself for the future manufacture of the ammunition during wartime. A still further example was the necessity to step up production of steel from poorer-quality German ores as opposed to higher-quality Swedish ores. These examples serve to illustrate the overwhelming drive for self-sufficiency which the German state was seeking at the time.

Why the necessity for self-sufficiency? Because Hitler had stated in that same memo two additional objectives of his four year plan:

1. The German army must be ready to fight in four years time.
2. The German economy must be capable of waging war in four years time.

Though admittedly secret, the memo was absolute and unequivocal not only in terms of intent but also in time. For the Swiss, and the Swiss banks, there had never been the slightest doubt of the intention of the German government. Their close relationship with the Germans, both geographically and culturally, made it inevitable that whatever occurred or was even discussed in Germany was immediately reflected in Switzerland. The success of the federal defence loan of 1936 (*Schützet die Heimat!* said the posters) was certainly indicative both of the popular understanding on the part of the Swiss public of the intentions of their neighbour as well as the sentiment of the day. The mystery of the years immediately preceding the war was the fact that the people of other countries, such as the French and the British, could have possibly misunderstood or even hoped for 'peace in our time'.

When war did come, the Swiss had one great advantage over the belligerent powers – their neutrality. To be sure, their armaments and the mobilisation of their soldiers was complete enough, but their war material did not suffer the destruction (bombs and ammunition explode, tanks and guns are destroyed, and so on) that was undergone by the belligerents. The total cost of defence, up to 1945, amounted to 8.4 billion francs, a relatively small sum when compared with that of the participating nations. Further, and more important, inflation was avoided because the primary source of funds to meet this expense was new taxes – a war profits tax, a turnover tax, a luxury tax, and a withholding tax. A 'defence levy', amounting to a capital tax, was also imposed twice during the period.

But there was more to Switzerland's wartime expenditures than purely defence. Other government departments also were forced to increase their spending in order to compensate for lost imports. Hydro-electric power, in particular, had to be further developed as foreign coal imports gradually disappeared. Another cost was the compensation for Swiss exporters who had exported to Germany and Italy under the clearing agreements. (These were to be paid for by the Federal Republic of Germany and the Italian government after the war, but only partial payments were ever realised.) The net result was that of a total expenditure increase under all heads of government of 12.1 billion francs, of which 6.3 billion francs was financed by an increase in the consolidated debt of the Confederation from 2.3 billion to 8.7 billion francs, an increase of 378 per cent. The balance of 5.8 billion francs was financed through increased taxation.

Banks were the principal creditors of the Government. In fact, their investments in federal securities amounted to over one-half their balance sheet totals. Additionally, their cash reserves were placed in treasury bonds with 2 to 4 years maturity, thereby forming a second line of liquid assets. While it might be argued that such investments in federal securities were substitutes for vanished commercial investment prospects, especially with the introduction of new clearing agreements as the German armies swept across Europe, the banks' real contribution to the finance of the Swiss defence effort lay in the lost profits and increased cost of accounting involved in the operation of these new clearing agreements.

In addition, the US blocking of European balances in June of 1940 was another serious blow to Swiss banks. Financial accounts could not be transferred, and a source of funding for Swiss imports was blocked at a time when the country needed them most. Nevertheless, we cannot argue that Switzerland suffered, in financial terms, to the same degree as the belligerents. Inflation was kept down by price controls (which meant that before any price increase could take place, official approval was required) and by the rationing of scarce commodities (doubtless in some cases with some actual benefits to the public health). While some prices had to increase because of the increase in import costs, the total rise in the cost of living was kept to as low as 51 per cent above the pre-war level precisely because of these price controls and the avoidance on the part of the banking system of increases in the money supply. Demand pressures on a restricted supply of goods and services were to a great extent successfully kept in check by these methods.

A POSSIBLE ERROR IN JUDGEMENT?

Recently, some fifty years after the close of the War, considerable concern as to the wartime function of the Swiss banks has come to light. The subject of the matter is two-fold:

1. The existence and legitimate ownership of Jewish refugee deposits accepted by Swiss banks following the proclamation of the Banking Law in 1935 and

2. The acceptance by banks of Nazi gold looted both from occupied countries and from victims of the holocaust.

Claims have been put forward, principally by Israel Singer and Edgar Bronfman of the World Jewish Congress. Additionally, Senator D'Amato, Chairman of the Senate Banking, Housing and Urban Affairs Committee, is currently (1996) holding hearings on the matter. While it is hardly appropriate for us to comment in detail on this subject, it may be worthwhile to include some observations in the hope that what readers have found in the somewhat sensational press reports may be considered more objectively.

In 1934 the German government forbade the export of capital from Germany. This prohibition did not stop the Swiss banks from acquiring a considerable amount of Jewish refugee funds at considerable risk to themselves. The introduction of the Banking Law in 1935 was particularly important in this regard, for there was absolutely no possible means by which these refugee deposits could be disclosed to the Nazis. We must point out, however, that the Banking Law was not created solely for the purpose of acquiring these funds, though Swiss politicians may have had something like that in mind when it was passed by the National Assembly. Indeed, the Law did much more than enact bank secrecy into law; it also provided for a supervisory Banking Commission to enforce all the measures in the law, among other important and much needed innovations in Swiss banking. Nevertheless, it could not have come at a more propitious time as far as the Jewish refugee funds were concerned. Now, some fifty years after the event, most of the accounts are dormant.

In the matter of these dormant accounts, there appears to be some confusion. According to Alan Cowell of the *New York Times*, 'Swiss banks are not legally obliged to keep records of dormant accounts for more than 10 years.'[3] Julius Baer, on the other hand, in his testimony before the D'Amato Committee, asserts without equivocation as follows:

The Chairman (Sen. D'Amato) '... if there is an account that is a dormant account that's been dormant for 50 years, those assets are not folded at some point in time into the bank? Are they carried by the bank?'
Mr. Baer. 'Absolutely. No way, it just goes on.'
The Chairman. 'But they are carried by the bank.'
Mr. Baer. 'If I may say, we may not be talking only about money. We may also be talking about securities, where you have anyway the

deposit law. And there is absolutely no way in which anybody can take that.'[4]

The real difficulty, then, is that of identifying the current owners of these dormant accounts. In the case of Jewish refugee funds deposited in Swiss banks, who are the present survivors of the holocaust or their legitimate heirs?

In the matter of looted gold, a 1985 report by Robert Vogler of the Swiss National Bank suggests that the National Bank was 'politically insensitive in the performance of its duties and even displayed a naive gullibility in its dealings with the Reichsbank'.[5] The reason for the comment appears to be that the National Bank had continued to purchase gold from the Reichsbank on the assurance of the Reichsbank that the gold had not been stolen. Furthermore, as the War drew to its end, two top officials of the National Bank actually engaged in some considerable argument on the matter (as recorded in an exchange of memos), accusing each other of knowing the source of the gold.

It is simple enough for us, with hindsight, to offer judgemental criticism of not only the National Bank but also the other Swiss banks which were instrumental in the Nazi gold transactions during that stressful period. It may be useful, however, to offer a hypothesis which is, we suggest, the most logical circumstance of Switzerland at the time.

After the fall of France, the Swiss were completely surrounded by Axis powers. While the Swiss army, recruited from its citizenry, was indeed a force to be reckoned with, it must have appeared highly unlikely to Swiss bankers that an Axis invasion could have been repelled without enormous losses as far as the nation was concerned. Excluding the invasion possibility, merely an Axis blockade of raw material could inflict considerable hardship on the Swiss people. The bankers, however, possessed an 'insurance policy' which could guarantee the security of the nation. So long as Nazi gold had an outlet (essentially for 'laundering'), the advantage of Swiss neutrality to the Germans outweighed the disadvantage of potential German losses to be incurred from a Wehrmacht invasion, or so it must have appeared to the Swiss bankers.

Our 'hypothesis', then, is this. A Swiss law firm (probably a Nazi sympathiser) would have received a shipment of gold ingots, duly stamped by the Reichsbank, smuggled in via diplomatic pouch, shipped through third countries, or otherwise transferred from Germany to the addressee. The law firm placed this gold with a Swiss Bank and received a corresponding deposit in its name with that Swiss bank. The Swiss bank, in its turn, had little actual use for the gold and exchanged it at the Swiss National Bank for treasury bonds. The National Bank then processed the ingots, ultimately to bear its own name.

Having no industrial raw material of its own, Switzerland must import virtually everything, save the food products which it can produce on its own farms. That was true during the war just as it is today. In wartime, however, the only form of foreign exchange acceptable in payment for commodity shipments was gold. (We may recall that the United States had blocked European dollar assets on 14 June 1940, so that the use of dollars for financial transactions other than trade with the US was prohibited.) The gold, now bearing the stamp of the Swiss National Bank, would have been sent to whatever country was willing to accept it in exchange for raw material. The gold would then be owned by a third country and impossible to identify. Indeed, after a half century, it is likely to have been completely disseminated through many countries to become part of the world's money supply. We can be certain of one fact, if our hypothesis is even approximately correct: there is no gold hidden in the Swiss Alps today, nor was it likely that all such gold was simply hidden in Swiss bank vaults at the end of the war, as has been implied by the British Foreign Office.[6]

What does remain, however, are the liabilities of the Swiss banks to the original depositors, whoever they may be. Unfortunately, the 'third parties', Reichsbank officials or German importers who might have paid for wartime imports via Switzerland with Nazi gold, are also dead, and their Swiss bank accounts are now most certainly dormant.

In view of the enormous publicity concerning these unfortunate times, most of it detrimental to the Swiss, it is natural that the Swiss banks themselves, in the form of the Swiss Bankers Association, should reply in some form. As one might expect, there is very much of a defensive tone in the press releases of this association. In his presidential address Dr Georg Krayer made reference to the Research Bureau for unclaimed assets (dormant accounts) which is managed by the Ombudsman and which is currently engaged in the long process of identifying the owners. We quote from Dr. Krayer's speech as follows:

... we are going along a winding, difficult and not very spectacular road. For some time yet, we are going to endure criticism and reproaches and receive advice. Nevertheless, this is the only possible way to go. We must not therefore anticipate the results before knowing them in detail. It then remains to be hoped that all the banks' adversaries, who, in fact, condemn Switzerland, and the detractors of Switzerland, who want to harm the banks, all the while holding themselves to be better than the banks, pay close attention when the research is finished. I also hope that the question is clearly posed – better than in certain reports and commentaries – about in what cases gold transactions fifty years ago were carried out between central banks. We must be told when it is a question of commercial relations and it must be made precise when business relations have been established between banks and their customers. The polemics of the last few weeks have created total confusion.[7]

It would be difficult to find a better description of this 'total confusion', along with its ultimate resolution, than this.

Regarding the 'attacks', so called, of the World Jewish Congress, the SBA was rather more forthright. In the Press Release in February 1996, when the matter of Jewish accounts was initially raised, the representative of the SBA, Jean-Paul Chapuis, was quoted as saying:

Let us think about it: The question of the assets of the victims of the Nazi regime understandably still creates consternation even today, especially in Israeli circles. For this reason we follow even further all aspects connected with accounts and deposits which were opened before 1945, and we are in constant contact with the Swiss Israeli community council as well as with the representatives of the Jewish World Congress. This cooperation is very valuable for us. It will help us to dispel miscellaneous doubts and to decide what should be done with the assets which, even after the research, cannot be classified according to the guidelines of the SBA. What we demonstrate to you today, especially the figures from our research, changes nothing in the continuation of this dialogue. It is important to me to stress this.[8]

The position of the SBA appears to be quite clear. The results of the research are to be checked by an independent auditing firm and the legitimate owners of the accounts (the successors of the Nazi victims) will receive the amounts which are due. Those accounts which originated in the Jewish clients of the banks and have not been assigned to claimants will accrue to the authorities that represent them. As an additional comment, in the same press release the SBA regrets the use by the press of exaggerated 'amounts in billions' as inappropriate and merely arousing false expectations.

On the matter of the Swiss government's investigation of the 'recent economic history' of the country and the fate of Jewish assets, the SBA gives its whole-hearted support. Furthermore, both the SBA and the Jewish organisations agree that the Swiss government should look into the matter of Nazi loot which may have been excluded from 'statutory recording'. However, the SBA prefers that further investigation into Jewish bank accounts remains the prerogative of the bank Ombudsman rather than merely duplicating such service at the governmental level.[9]

So what are we to make of these 'replies' by the Swiss Bankers Association to the numerous attacks in the press, both within Switzerland and outside? They are, of course, quite reasonable on the surface. Yet we are certainly aware that any research into the many refugee accounts must require years; meantime some, certainly, of the Jewish survivors of the holocaust will have died. The charge, therefore, of such careful and protracted investigation as mere 'stalling' will likely be made by detractors of the Swiss banks.

Before concluding that the banks have truly been 'stalling', we should consider the nature of the task facing the Ombudsman as well as the investigating committee of eminent persons. The period of history just preceding the outbreak of World War II was an extremely difficult one for the Swiss banks and for the Confederation. The franc had been devalued in 1936, making Swiss exports more competitive in world markets. In addition a return flow of capital into Switzerland had begun in response to the cheaper franc. There were, however, circumstances over which the Swiss had no control or influence which made conditions very difficult for the banking industry.

In 1931 the German government had imposed a moratorium on foreign exchange transactions and this was extended in 1934 to become a moratorium on all capital transfers. By means of a clearing agreement with Germany, Switzerland was able to acquire only its interest payments on capital invested in Germany. More important, it meant that the banks could no longer freely dispose of their German assets. This, combined with the effects of the depression within Switzerland, meant that the major banks lost heavily in terms of balance sheet totals; only two major banks, Credit Suisse and the Swiss Bank Corporation, survived both the depression and the war without financial reorganisation.

From the banks' point of view the situation was disastrous. The German moratorium on capital made it impossible for all but the most surreptitious of capital transfers to take place. Small private banks, sometimes referred to as 'suitcase banks', undoubtedly were able to arrange for just such assets to be transferred, illegally, out of the country and away from Nazi jurisdiction. We can be sure, however, that many of these recipients of Jewish assets (to become bank deposit liabilities) were reinvested as assets outside of Switzerland, there being little outlet for such capital within the country at the time. It was precisely these foreign bank assets which, literally, disappeared both under wartime conditions and in the circumstances immediately following the war, particularly in Communist countries – hence bankruptcies were inevitable.

When a bank (any bank) becomes 'bankrupt', the disappearance of assets means that liabilities correspondingly must disappear. Inevitably, some of these liabilities must be deposits, unless, as happens today in many countries, insurance for such deposits exists. But this was not the case during wartime and pre-war Switzerland; there was no insurance for depositors. Thus, Jewish refugee funds, though being guaranteed safety from the Nazi government, *could not be protected from the risks of bankruptcies that all depositors must share.* A fund, however, created by the Swiss banks (perhaps from hidden reserves), from which outstanding Jewish claims may be paid as an interim measure, would indeed contribute to a restoration of international confidence in the Swiss banking system and likely ease the plight of holocaust victims still living.

On the other hand, depositors are actually creditors of the banks. This means that the banks, facing bankruptcy or financial re-construction, and in the absence of Jewish creditors, could have simply paid off their domestic creditors through liquidating whatever assets they possessed, leaving Jewish accounts still outstanding. This is the 'other side of the coin' and presents the case of the World Jewish Congress. Their argument is that such deposit accounts amount to a total of something like 8 billion US dollars. In other words, and the italics again are ours, *there would likely have been very many more Swiss bankruptcies had there been no absentee Jewish creditors.*

There is a myth extant to the effect that Switzerland and its banks profited greatly from wartime neutrality. Such was by no means the case. The only excess profits earned during those years were the usual ones of speculators who gained from rising prices of raw materials which grew ever scarcer as the war progressed. Banks lost heavily from the disappearance of their foreign investments, at the same time being responsible for any interest payments on their liabilities. To be sure, the Swiss people did not lose so much as the combatants themselves, and their citizen army remained intact and unscathed; it is quite wrong, however, to believe that great profits were derived from Jewish or other refugee deposits alone, even though it may well be true that Swiss banks 'profited' at the expense of Jewish refugee funds by suffering less in terms of losses than would otherwise have been the case.

The task of the Ombudsman, a half-century later, is clearly enormous. Where, and in what state, are the dormant deposit accounts of refugee funds amongst banks many of which may have disappeared years ago? Indeed, a further question may be asked – who is responsible, if indeed there is *any* responsibility, for the deposit accounts of banks long bankrupt? Or, we may add further, what was the fate of deposit accounts of banks which had been 'financially re-organised' because of wartime losses? The task of researchers, Dr Krayer's 'long, difficult, and winding road', will likely be even longer and more difficult than he suggests.

Eventually, the Swiss government itself must become involved in an investigation of wartime banking activity. This follows from the fact that any negotiations between Switzerland and other countries regarding Jewish assets must have been conducted at the higher diplomatic level. Additionally, the entire economic history of the time can only be objectively re-evaluated by the government itself, and this will certainly be welcomed by the banks. After all, it is the government's agency, the Banking Commission, which supervised banking activities then and continues to supervise them now.

The participation by the Swiss government has recently been brought out by the D'Amato Committee in the form of a disclosure of some secret correspondence between the Polish and Swiss governments regarding the Swiss-Polish Commercial Treaty of 25 June 1949. In this correspondence it was provided that secret assets, 'secret' as per the Swiss Banking Law, of Polish citizens should be transferred to the Swiss National Bank to the credit of the Polish central bank. This arrangement was typical of the 'clearing agreements' which had been so successful in pre-war Swiss experience. Polish citizens would be paid, assuming that they wished to withdraw their Swiss bank accounts, in Polish currency. Swiss citizens, mostly banks, who had investments in Poland would receive the value of their investments in Swiss francs from the Swiss National Bank. Final differences in the value of these accounts would be settled by means of a monetary transfer between the two central banks.[10]

Unfortunately, it was not known just how such a commercial agreement would be carried out nor was it known just how much, in terms of francs, had been actually transferred to the SNB by Swiss banks and insurance companies. The correspondence was never completed nor did the Polish central bank carry out its side of the agreement. For this reason the Swiss Bankers Association wholeheartedly agrees that a complete analysis and description of the events of that time must be made; not, the SBA insists, in the manner of bits and pieces publicised in the press which beclouds, rather than clarifies, the entire issue.

The SBA further notes in a press release that all documents still in existence in its archives, along with all documents from assurance companies, the government, and the National Bank, will be placed at the disposal of the Department of External Affairs to further the investigation. In this way, the SBA hopes that an accounting for all deposits will be made public as soon as possible.[10]

While we cannot subscribe to an apparent pronouncement of guilt in the court of public opinion without an appropriate hearing from the Swiss banks, we must agree with the conclusions of the D'Amato Committee regarding the alleged lack of cooperation on the part of certain Swiss banks with those unfortunate individuals who have already sought to reclaim their assets. This, if true (and far too many individual cases have been reported to conclude otherwise), is completely reprehensible. We would expect immediate restitution in these cases and sincerely hope, and believe, as suggested by Dr. Julius Baer (in his testimony before the D'Amato Committee), that this will indeed follow.

We would beg, however, that readers consider this entire topic to which we refer as an 'error in judgement' in its larger sense. After all, banking as an industry *per se* is amoral. This does not exclude bankers from the responsibility of humanitarianism to the same degree as government officials or any other industry which considers itself to be socially responsible. Nevertheless, it is quite conceivable in terms of banking theory that unclaimed deposits (that is, the Jewish accounts) could still be continuously recorded under the liabilities column of the banks' balance sheets (those banks still extant) year after year. This would give the Swiss banks a secure, non-liquid, and continuous source of funding for assets. It would be profitable for the simple reason that interest would not have been paid to deposit owners, merely accrued through the years. In this sense, the Swiss banks are vulnerable to criticism on humanitarian grounds; indeed, such criticism could result in a possible loss of confidence as far as foreign depositors are concerned.[11]

Another question to which we have as yet no definitive answer remains. Could the Ombudsman not have undertaken a more thorough investigation into dormant accounts several decades ago? Immediately following World War II, banks were asked by the government to surrender the accounts of Nazi victims; this yielded about 16 million francs which were handed over to Jewish groups. Again, in 1962, any lawyers, accountants, banks, and so on who may have held war refugee accounts were asked by the government to register such accounts with the government. This brought in another 9.5 million francs. Beyond these government requests, the Ombudsman could not begin work until applications had been received from account claimants; many of these did not appear until the end of the cold war. According to the Ombudsman, who continues attempts to locate dormant accounts, '$1.28 million of accounts have been found this year'.[12] The search is an on-going one derived from requests from individual account holders or their heirs.

Finally, an 'independent committee of eminent persons' consisting of ten members (five appointed by the Swiss Bankers Association and five by the World Jewish Congress) and chaired by Mr Paul Volcker has been appointed for the purpose of supervising a group of subcommittees that will further scrutinise bank accounts. This means, obviously, that the Swiss secrecy clause of the Banking Law must be temporarily set aside by the Legislative Assembly. The five Swiss members that have been selected comprise a list of the most prominent people in their field in Switzerland.[13] We hope that a still further identification of refugee accounts, as well as a clarification of the role of Swiss banks and the government itself during the war, may result from the efforts of this committee.

As a matter of further interest, the Resolution passed by the Federal Assembly (13 December 1996) now completes the legal basis for the investigation into both Jewish assets and the conduct of Swiss authorities regarding Nazi gold during the war. Broad in scope, it makes possible a total investigation into the history of the time involving the banks, Parliament, administration, bank supervisors, and banks of issue, as well as other financial sectors in the economy. The essential components of the Resolution are as follows:

1. Guidelines for the Swiss Bankers Association regarding secret documents, deposits and safety deposit boxes.
2. The 'starting point' for the search for secret assets in Swiss banks by the Ombudsman.
3. The federal resolution regarding the historic and legal review of the fate of assets accumulated in Switzerland as a result of Nazi power (referred to above).

4. The 'starting point' for similar investigation by the organisation of private life insurers, currently in preparation.
5. A memorandum of understanding between the SBA and Jewish organisations regarding the work stemming from the independent committee of eminent persons.[14]

It would be difficult to conceive of a more comprehensive statement of intent than these five components of the Resolution. Will they be carried out? It will be entirely the responsibility of the committee of eminent persons to see to it that they are. More to the point, the attention of the world is focused on Switzerland so that both the fate of Jewish deposits and the activities of the Swiss banks in wartime must be finally exposed, once and for all. Additionally, the question of the violation of Swiss wartime neutrality laws, for example, must be answered. Certainly, threats of sanctions and boycott measures on the part of the Jewish organisation against Swiss banks must be counter-productive at this stage of the investigation.

In a larger sense, we cannot avoid concluding that any alleged wartime 'guilt' as far as the banks and the government are concerned must be shared by many others. After all, who *was* responsible for the horrors committed by the nations at war in those fateful years? Decisions were taken by belligerents and neutrals alike which must be now sorely regretted, especially by subsequent generations. (The practice of accepting Nazi gold by the Swiss National Bank, we would suggest, is likely to be one of these.) What is to be gained from dredging the past and reviewing decisions made by predecessors, now deceased? With this query we leave a somewhat painful topic to return to the main thread of our argument. We hope, however, that this brief discussion may contribute in a small measure to a more objective understanding of this unfortunate historical period.

THE US DOLLAR AND ITS FUNCTION IN THE POST-WAR WORLD

With the end of hostilities, the acute shortage of the means of payment for reconstruction, which was felt in all countries, meant that the ascendancy of the US dollar to the level of a world reserve currency was inevitable. Already the world had experience with the gold-exchange standard between the wars, and it only remained for the US dollar itself to resume the position it had occupied before. The

Marshall Plan and the formation of the Organisation for European Economic Co-operation (OEEC) laid the foundations for a new post-war world. By 1950, the European Payments Union (EPU) had been established to facilitate trade and payments amongst its members in accordance with the principles laid down in the OEEC. Switzerland became a member of the OEEC though it did not (the only member country which did not) apply for Marshall Aid.

The role of the Swiss in the reconstruction of Europe must not be minimised. Indeed, relative to its size, its contribution was considerable. The Federal Council noted, in 1948, that donations for relief work and foreign currency credits via the banks amounted to some 2.5 billion francs or 532 francs per capita of population.[15] Nevertheless, the Swiss franc was in no position to serve alongside the US dollar as a reserve currency, for the obvious reason that the Swiss economy was entirely too small to support the demands which would inevitably have been made upon it.

The already heavy demands made upon the Swiss economy and the shortage of foreign exchange had resulted in the development of 'swing credits', that is, a mutual granting of credits for trade and payments purposes. These were not at all the same as the pre-war clearing agreements, which had tied imports to the amount of exports, but actually helped to liberalise payments amongst countries. It meant, in the final analysis, that Swiss banks were making loans (granting credits) to a large number of countries for the purpose of financing 'start-up' projects where they were needed. The qualifications for such loans were not in terms of sound business criteria, as is ordinarily the case, but their developmental 'multiplier effect'. They amounted to nearly 1 billion francs by the year 1950. At the same time, the Swiss participation in the EPU meant that a quota of $250 million was required of it.

In a real sense, the years following World War II constituted an economic miracle while, at the same time, being a triumph for economic cooperation. The General Agreement on Tariffs and Trade was signed in Geneva in 1947. The United Nations Charter was dated 26 June 1945, and included the United States which had retired into isolationism and trade protection in the years following World War I. The US also provided the headquarters for the International Bank and the International Monetary Fund in the capital, Washington DC. It was as if the United States had learned well its lesson from history, determined never to repeat the disaster of World War II.

But economic miracles require, just as do other economic growth phenomena, some financing, and at the same time an expansion of the means of payment. While this is the responsibility, generally, of the world's banking systems, banking systems alone cannot accomplish the task. There have been ample examples in the past of banks which have expanded credit without a sufficient foundation of sound money, and the results, in most cases, have been disastrous inflations. 'Sound money' in the Swiss case, was a monetary base which consisted of:

1. a foreign currency reserve,
2. an open market portfolio,
3. a reserve component, and
4. a 'refinancing component' which meant rescription bonds.[16]

In the Swiss case only the first, foreign currency reserve, was significant as far as size was concerned during the early post-war years; of the others, the reserve component, though relatively small, proved to be of even greater importance.

It is the foreign currency reserve which concerns us at this point. During the years of currency restrictions following the war, there was only one currency, the US dollar, which could be used as a true foreign currency reserve. In a genuine sense the world was on a dollar standard. But this meant that dollar claims against the United States must be available to the central banks of the world either through trade surpluses to the US or by credit extended either by the US government or from private sources.

It was during this post-war period that a new development, it is no exaggeration to say a 'revolutionary change', occurred in the the world's payments system which was to affect Europe (particularly Switzerland) forever. It goes almost without saying that a nation's money supply consists of claims against its own production of goods and services – its Gross Domestic Product. Dollars consist of just such claims when they are owned by Americans. However, when Americans, through the medium of the US banking system, make loans to non-Americans, the dollars perform a 'double duty' in the sense that the dollars loaned are claims against the US GDP, in the first place, and claims against the United States *now owned by foreign borrowers* in the second. They become 'Euro-dollars' at the same time that they are truly domestic dollars; however, they are not necessarily being used for spending as domestic dollars but are available for circulation as currency outside the United States. As such, they perform all the functions of money – a store of value, transfers for deficits in balances of payments similar to gold, and so on.

SWITZERLAND'S BANKS

The impact of the dollar expansion in the United States at the same time that there was an accrual of 'bank' savings deposits (so as to make Euro-dollars possible) was soon to be felt in Switzerland.

Figure 12.1 tells the story.

During the early post-war years, indeed, well into the 1960s, it was gold in the Swiss National Bank which was the significant variable. This was the result of establishing (or 'pegging') a fixed exchange rate for the Swiss franc (4.3730 francs per $1.00). Clearly, with gold at $35 per ounce, this established the price of gold at SF 153 per ounce. The National Bank, under the regime of the fixed rate of exchange, purchased and sold gold and foreign exchange whenever the exchange rate showed any tendency to move beyond the fixed parity. Thus, whenever the franc rose in value on the market, this meant that the demand for the franc (or supply of foreign exchange and/or gold) was excessive. The National Bank purchased the extra supply of gold and/or foreign exchange, thereby curbing the excessive demand and checking the tendency of the franc to rise in value. Conversely, the National Bank sold gold and/or foreign exchange if the value of the franc showed falling tendencies. As is quite clear from Figure 12.1 the National Bank purchased more gold than it sold throughout the years of the fixed rate regime to reach a peak of monetary gold holdings of 13.4 billion francs ($3.06 billion) in 1967. A previous 'peak' in 1965 also showed slightly

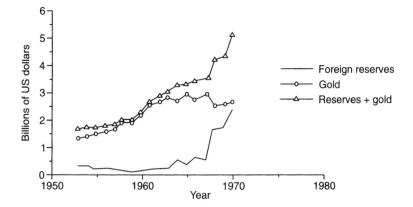

Figure 12.1   Swiss foreign reserves (billions of $ US)
Source: International Financial Statistics Yearbook, 1983, International Monetary Fund, Washington D.C, p. 483.

over 3 billion dollars in gold. It is interesting that the gold cover of the Swiss franc note actually reached 144.7 per cent in 1961 as compared to the legal cover of just 40 per cent.

The reasons, fundamentally, for the gold flowing into the Swiss National Bank at this time lay in the fact that in Switzerland, dealing in gold for any reason whatsoever has been perfectly legal ever since federal regulations on the import and export of gold were lifted in 1951. Until 1954, a turnover tax had been applied to gold transactions, but after this was discontinued, perfect freedom of gold movement has been assured. At the same time, the Swiss had maintained the most important (if not the largest) banknote market in the world. The heavy tourist traffic, the central location of the country, communication facilities with every location in the world, and the security of the government along with its neutrality all combined to enhance the prestige of this market. Thus, the exchange of banknotes into gold, and the reverse, became quite feasible, the banknote market being headquartered in Basle, and the gold market in Zürich.

With the return of the London gold market to full operation in the spring of 1954, sterling area gold was channeled directly to London. The reason for this has been that the London market is a 'two-way market' (meaning that arbitrage transactions may occur) resulting in very close spreads between buying and selling prices, hence the best 'deal' can be had from sales to that market. Indeed, many Continental markets closed after the opening of the London market, but not Zürich. In fact, the direction of flow of much of the gold sold in the London market was directed toward Zürich because gold purchasers in London had the advantage of selling at a higher buying price in the Zürich market.[17]

The combination of the banknote market and the gold market, as well as the fact that the Swiss banknote was directly exchangeable for gold, meant that as gold flowed to Zürich, the franc would inevitably appreciate in value unless the National Bank purchased gold from the market. This it did in steadily increasing amounts. The result was that, in the decade of the 1950s, the amount of gold in the National Bank rose from 6 billion francs in 1950 to 9.5 billion in 1959, a little more than a 50 per cent increase.[18]

In 1960, however, an interesting development within the world's monetary system took place. An erosion of confidence in the US dollar occurred with devastating results for the world's financial system. Aside from such 'externalities' as the war in Vietnam, there is little rational explanation for this phenomenon. But, for whatever reason, the US dollar standard began to deteriorate in value with the result that a general expectation of a rise in the price of gold followed. But the price of gold was a statutory price set at US$35.00 per ounce. Expectations of a rise in the price of gold, therefore, meant that there was a general wagering amongst market speculators that the US government could no longer hold that price by offering its own gold for sale at $35.00 per ounce. The effect of this was that speculators would sell US dollars and purchase gold in anticipation of selling gold at a higher price after US dollar depreciation.

The irrational nature of the speculation lay in the fact that speculators also purchased sterling, which would certainly devalue if the price of gold rose. Regardless of this obvious logic, the amount of the British gold reserves did increase sufficiently to pay off its 'Suez debts', as well as other outstanding debts, to the International Monetary Fund and still have some £11 million left to add to its total reserves – all of this within a single month, October. The United States, of course, reduced its gold reserve to a level of $18.5 billion as other countries, especially Germany, increased their gold holdings.

Similarly, the Swiss National Bank experienced a sharp increase (in the *rate* of increase) in its gold holdings (see Figure 12.1). These peaked at 13.4 billion francs in 1967. Thereafter, an enormous increase in foreign exchange holdings took place, as Euro-currencies began to flow into the country. These currencies had to be purchased by the National Bank because it became a matter of maintaining the value of the franc to within its IMF range, as the Swiss franc (as a 'hard' currency) was seen as the logical alternative to the dollar.

THE DEVELOPMENT OF THE 'NEW' SWISS BANK

Against this background of financial uncertainty, so characteristic of the declining years of the US dollar standard, the Swiss banks were able to approach their highest peak of efficiency. While it is almost a truism to state that banks, in general, can only achieve whatever their national economies make possible (they are, in the final analysis, only mediators of wealth, no more) we find that the Swiss banks during this period reached well beyond their Swiss national environment to become a major force driving the Swiss economy. It was their capacity to seize the initiatives which world circumstances had made available to them that seemed to set Swiss banking apart from the banks of other countries in those years of exchange rate uncertainties.

Probably the intitial step in this direction was taken by the Swiss government itself during the immediate post-war era. On 25 May 1946, in Washington, blocked Swiss dollar investments were finally released after some hard bargaining with the US government. From the spring of 1947 on, the National Bank was able to de-ration all its holdings of dollars and permit their use as payment for imports, with the result that the importers could then pay in full the Swiss franc counterpart for imports. In other words, trade, on the basis of the US dollar standard, became free. Blocked Swiss capital investments were freed as well so that payments of returns on those investments could also be made.

The price for these concessions, in retrospect, was both sad and harsh. Switzerland had to pay some 250 million francs in gold to the former wartime Allies as recompense for an alleged use of German gold as a 'circulating medium' stolen from occupied territories during the war, and was forced to release 400 million francs of blocked German assets to the Allied Control Council. Whether or not the allegations were true (they were, in fact, *not* true), the enforced release of German assets infringed the sovereignty of the country. All this was for the purpose of achieving freedom of trade and payments, a circumstances which ought to have been sought for its own merit and certainly not with a price attached.

Nevertheless, the Washington Agreement did unlock the potential for trade and payments which were so important to Swiss banks and for commercial exports and imports. For the banks, the simplification of payments was a major step toward the free market economy which the circumstances of war had temporarily removed. Domestically, the country had abandoned its wartime restrictions and price controls and rationing ceased; rationing ended in 1948 and price controls followed (except for rents), in 1950. This, combined with the general increase in world prices of commodities, the consequence of the Korean War, resulted in an increase in the Swiss cost of living–a world-wide phenomenon in which Switzerland shared. However, the Swiss were able to hold down their price increases at the same time that other countries were already experiencing inflation prior to 1950, and this was a contributing factor to the rise in exports during that period.

An interesting, and significant, development in the later forties was the introduction by the government of the Federal Old-Age and Surviving Dependents Insurance scheme in 1947. This Swiss form of social security had, as its initial impact, a reduction by as much as one-half in the rate of increase in the level of savings deposits that had been expected on the basis of the performance of the preceding year. The Swiss are noted for their penchant for savings and have generally created more capital in this way than they could use. The result has always been low interest rates, but the introduction of the insurance scheme temporarily (only temporarily) reduced the perceived need for savings on the part of the public with the consequence already noted.

But more significant for the banks proved to be the use of the proceeds of the surplus insurance collections, that is, those collections not required for immediate payment. To the surprise of many, this surplus amounted to 470 million francs by 1949. It meant that these funds had to be invested in the domestic capital market precisely at the time when investment requirements were already low. They therefore impinged directly upon the traditional prerogative of the banks, as mediators between savers and investors, to lower interest rates still further. It was not until the decade of the 1950s that the banks' fears regarding the potential competition from these new funds were proven to be groundless, because thereafter the investment possibilities inherent in the foreign sector became more and more obvious to them.[19]

It was not long after the war that the balance sheets of the banks began to exhibit the effects of change from war to peace. This was evidenced by the decrease in government securities in the balance sheets and the corresponding increase in private sector loans and advances.[20] The process of venturing into the foreign sector began with a syndicated loan (headed by the Swiss Bank Corporation) to the Belgian Telephone and Telegraph Administration in 1947. This was for 50 million francs at 4 per cent, an attractive interest rate at the time, and was offered to the public. It was highly successful and was soon followed by two other Belgian loans, each of the same amount, which were used for the purchase of Swiss railway equipment. Again these were equally successful, suggestive of the large degree of available savings which had already been accumulated by the Swiss public.

From this beginning, there appeared to be almost no end to the growth possibilities. Membership in international organisations, loans, aid, and so on, all assisted in the process of economic growth fostered, we might suggest, by the strategic position of Switzerland in its financial and commercial connections with foreign countries. The confidence which the nation enjoyed, particularly in banking, was remarkable. Political stability, neutrality, and confidence in the value of its currency all meant that Switzerland had become an island of stability in a world which was far from secure and far from stable. To be sure, the turmoil and strife accompanying the collapse of colonial empires, the formation of the European Economic Community and the European Free Trade Association, and even the war in Vietnam all held the promise of a future world order in process of realisation. But the turmoil existed nevertheless and the Swiss contribution remained precisely that–an island of stability within a sea of confusion. The result was that the banks themselves experienced an extraordinary period of growth which was well beyond the capacity of the economy of Switzerland alone to sustain.

In Figure 12.2, the total assets/liabilities of all category 1–5 banks the principal bank) are shown along with the Gross Domestic Product of Switzerland. Until about 1956, the growth rates of both are approximately the same; however, after that year and well into the 1960s, the spread between the two widens sharply until, by 1970, the total of assets/liabilities is almost double the GDP of Switzerland. It is the spread between these two which shows us clearly that the banks, particularly the commercial banks, were both acquiring deposits from outside the country and investing these deposits in industrial ventures in countries other than Switzerland. In other words, the economy of Switzerland

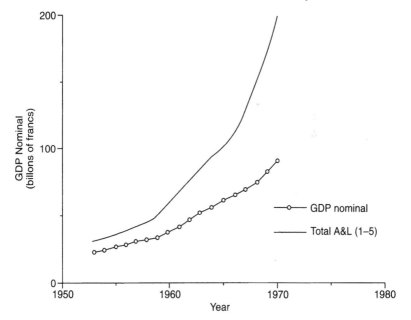

Figure 12.2   GDP and Total Assets/Liabilities, Categories 1–5 Banks
Source: Les banques suisses en 1984, Schweizerische National Bank, Zurich, Table 6.

alone could not possibly have supplied the deposits nor absorbed the investment. In performing these services for foreigners, the banks were making their own substantial contribution to the Gross Domestic Product of the country, increasing it as their activities expanded to become, ultimately, the major industry of the entire country.

In addition, the extent to which the Swiss banks participated in the investment activity of the Swiss domestic economy alone is considerable, especially when compared with other capital intensive countries. Simply put, it meant that Swiss banks, unlike those of the United States or Great Britain, participated directly in longer term capital requirements. This was the natural extension and evolution of the Saint Simonian tradition. It is most apparent when we compare the ratios of 'credit granted to the private sector by the commercial banks' to the Gross Domestic Product. We can do this on a comparable basis (as shown in Figure 12.3), thanks to the wonderful statistical reporting of the International Monetary Fund.

From 1953 to 1971, Swiss bank credit to the private sector practically equalled the level of the Gross Domestic Product. This is an extremely large amount, especially when comparisons are made with other countries such as France and Germany. During the same period,

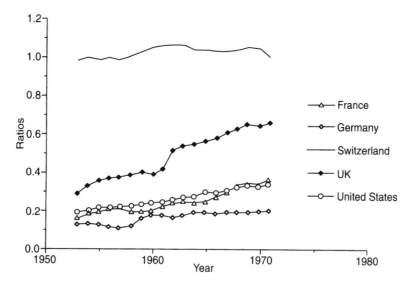

Figure 12.3   Ratio of private sector Credit to GDP
Source: International Financial Statistics Yearbook, 1983, International Monetary Fund.

the British banks increased their private credit/GDP ratio from 0.1 to almost 0.2. The British simply preferred to use their capital markets rather than their banks, especially for longer term investment. Germany, on the other hand, showed an increasing tendency to rely on its banks for capital such that the ratio rose from about 0.2 in 1953 to almost 0.7 by 1971.

The enormous growth of the Swiss banks relative to the GDP of Switzerland suggests also that the velocity of circulation of money must have been declining just as in the United States, as the Swiss too re-structured their financial assets. This is indeed the case as is apparent from the Figure 12.4.

Declining velocity, or a decline in the ratio of GDP to total money, has been a characteristic of Swiss banking since the turn of the century. This is the consequence of the growth of borrowed funds, as opposed to the banks' own resources (capital and reserves), as a proportion of the banks' total liabilities. It is these borrowed funds which have been used increasingly as savings deposits which have a lower velocity of circulation than demand deposits and cash.

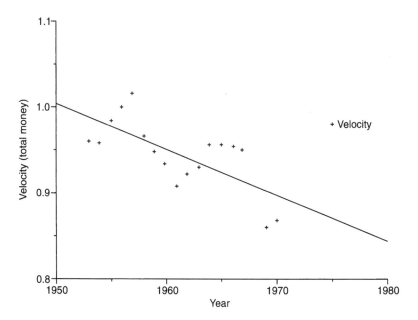

Figure 12.4 Income Velocity of Money, 1953–1970
Source: IFS Yearbook, 1983, IMF Washington DC

Much of the increase in borrowed funds is accounted for by foreign borrowing, that is, the influx of foreign funds. These increased to 39 per cent of the total liabilities in 1971 from just 13.6 per cent in 1946. We cannot ignore, however, the fact that deposits from domestic sources were also a significant portion of the growth in borrowed funds during this period.

Those of us familiar with the British banking system and its history must find this to be somewhat strange. After all, English banks have been taking deposits (or borrowing funds) for centuries, and certainly Italian banks have had a much longer history of the same banking process. One would be hard put to it, therefore, to explain the relatively late emergence of Swiss banks on the deposit-taking scene even though Johann Jakob Speiser had urged such banking practices in Basle as early as 1843. Nevertheless, the circumstances were such that until the turn of the century, Swiss banks were little more than 'investment houses' that placed the funds of shareholders with appropriate, and lucrative, investments.

The emergence of Swiss banks as deposit-taking institutions (both foreign and domestic deposits) has been a reflection of the world-wide trust Swiss banks have enjoyed. It is precisely this trust which underlies the phenomenal growth of the balance sheet totals of the banks as this new source of funds, deposits of the public, drove the banks to seek appropriate investment outlets for them. At the same time, the rising level of those funds borrowed from domestic sources accounts for the declining velocity of circulation of money (M2).

The enormous increase in liabilities during these years also meant that the Swiss banks had to recognise the existence of another problem typical of modern banks today. This was the *structural* balance of assets and liabilities. Thus it is not merely a matter of 'pushing' funds acquired through borrowing into investments, loans, and so on, but structuring these assets in such a way that maturing assets would fund the liabilities with sufficient liquidity when required by depositors. This is a problem which is considerably more significant with banks of the Saint-Simonian type which find that their investments are sometimes illiquid for longer periods of time. The rapid growth of the Swiss banks during this period made it absolutely essential to seek urgent solutions to this problem.

The Swiss Bank Corporation, probably the one major bank which had experienced more growth at this time than the others, found it necessary, in 1970, to enter the capital market for long-term bonded borrowings to run for a maximum term of twelve years. As the Chairman of the Bank had stated, in 1966, '. . . it has proved possible in these times of rapid and, indeed, sometimes turbulent development to maintain the structure of the balance sheet in equilibrium, a feat which is all the more difficult of accomplishment in that the volume of the various constituent items cannot be influenced at will'.[23]

Unquestionably the greatest achievement of Swiss bankers has been their ability to 'spin off' a large portion of these liabilities into foreign assets without, we must add, having any effect on the domestic money supply of Switzerland. The fact that geography and population limit the capacity of Switzerland to absorb large amounts of capital, combined with the fact that internal requirements for capital had already been satisfied by cantonal banks, meant that the major banks, the Grossbanken, which were the principal recipients of foreign capital, had to seek foreign assets in ever growing amounts. We can see this in Figure 12.5 which expresses as a ratio the foreign assets of the banks to the Gross Domestic Product. For comparison purposes, we include the equivalent ratios of both West Germany and Great Britain.

By the year 1971, foreign assets of Swiss Banks had almost equaled the Gross Domestic Product of the country itself – 91.87 billion francs as compared to a GDP of 103 billions. This is no small achievement for a banking system that still was required to maintain an equilibrium *within* the structure of its balance sheet. Foreign assets almost by definition are

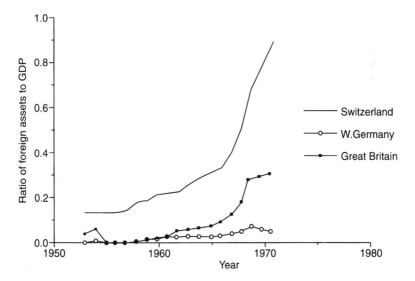

Figure 12.5 Proportion of foreign assets of banks to GDP
Source: International Financial Statistics, IMF

considerably more difficult to evaluate in terms of risk than domestic assets. Furthermore, it suggests that the Swiss banks themselves were making a net contribution to the balance of payments of the country in terms of interest earned from foreign investments. When compared to another major foreign investor, Great Britain, whose banks managed about £18 billion compared to a GDP of £57.34 billion in 1971, the Swiss achievement can only be recognised as outstanding.

CONCLUSION, SWISS BANKING DEVELOPMENT IN A WORLD OF MONETARY INSTABILITY

The changes outlined above did not come without considerable debate, discussion, risk-taking, and, finally, effort. The banks' immediate task after World War II was to divest themselves of the public sector's financing requirements in favour of the private sector. This they were able to do gradually, and we can recognise this in the decline in the securities portfolio and the concomitant increase in commercial loans and advances.[24] This change increased the earnings of the banks which were able to utilise their post-war abundance of funds for more lucrative assets than government securities. In the area of international trade and payments, the return to a market system, rather than the clearing-office method, greatly improved their efficiency.

Whence came this 'abundance of funds'? The post-war world was a world of sharp contrasts. It is no exaggeration to assert that Swiss banks were able to exploit this unusual circumstance, probably as no other contemporary banking system. The Cold War and the antagonism of the two great powers, the US and the Soviet Union, almost continuously generated tensions in the world which resulted further in expenditure on armaments amongst the other powers. Such expenditures weighed heavily upon the economies of the European nations, absorbing growing amounts of capital beyond the limits of some countries to provide. Foreign aid was required as a consequence, and this came from either the US or the Soviet Union depending upon the apparent allegiance of their governments. The outbreak of hostilities in Korea and in other centres in the Near and Far East added further to these tensions and uncertainties.

Along with the burden of establishing and maintaining armaments, there was a substantive change in economic thinking, at least partially due to the new philosophy which is generally associated with the Keynesian arguments of the 1930s. The practical result of this 'new economics' was a steady increase in the public sector at the expense of the private to such an extent that the public sector became dominant in the economy.

As such, it subjected the entire economic systems of the various countries to exogenous decision-making factors, giving great leverage effects to those decisions. Fiscal policy (that is, the amounts and types of taxation as well as government expenditures), have had a powerful impact to an extent unimaginable in the pre-war era. The nationalisation of industries, the welfare safety net, and mitigating or even eliminating the business cycle have all become the accepted area of the governments' responsibilities.

Additionally, the emphasis of economic direction has shifted toward economic growth. Through growth, the burden of welfare is steadily diminished. The economic load of social security becomes lighter as pensions of the elderly are paid from a growing base of economic activity. Taxes are more readily collected. Public sector expenditures, such as for the military, are likewise more readily available from a growing economy than from a static one. Most important, rising living standards of the populace assure governments of reelection.

This change in economic philosophy was accompanied by enormous strides made in the collection and interpretation of statistics. Those in responsible positions felt that they had the tools at their fingertips to 'fine tune' the economy and maintain a steady upward growth trend, thereby counteracting any tendency within the economy to turn downward. As events proved, such an objective was much more difficult to achieve in practice than in theory.

The ultimate result of this change in economic philosophy was the creation of steady pressures toward a monetary inflation. Government expenditure unrelated to taxation revenue, the economic objective of full employment as opposed to production processes under the most efficient conditions, and a shift away from classical monetary theory to the extent that the money supply and monetary policy became secondary in importance to fiscal policy, all contributed to the structure of economies with biases toward inflation. This was (and still is) a world quite different from the pre-war past. It is a world in which each generation becomes wealthier (in real terms) than the one preceding. It is a world in which growth can eliminate all our economic problems, and most important, it is a world in which the government can take responsibility for jobs, welfare, and social security.

Finally, it is a world in which financial considerations remain in a subsidiary position to matters of full employment and economic growth. Under the gold standard régime, the situation was quite the reverse because the balance of payments and the means of financing deficits were of primary importance. The 'real' economy, under those conditions, became secondary. But in a world in which the real national income is of primary importance, as well as the means by which aggregate demand might be encouraged (or discouraged), the command of economic affairs shifted from the banker to the politician. With elections looming in the short term, the political party is eager to please the electorate with full employment; hence, the stimulation of aggregate demand, in order to achieve this goal, must mean that the money supply will grow with deficit financing.[25] In the end, the result is inflation which, though it may be relatively long in coming, is nonetheless inevitable.

Another characteristic of the post-war world had its beginnings with the collapse of empires. European nations, those who were forced to face the loss of their colonial empires, found that by institutionalised cooperation in the form, first, of the European Coal and Steel Community, and, second, the European Economic Community with its own sovereign rights, they could enhance their own well-being through cooperation. Through a Common Market with the free flow of goods and services and factors of production, the advantages of the nineteenth century Cobden Treaties could be attained. Similarly, the European Free Trade Area (EFTA) was an attempt to accomplish the same objective, though it was considered to be just a preliminary stage in the process, whereas the EEC, which in the end proved to be the more successful, had a time table for its eventual achievement of a united Europe.

What does this new world have to do with the development of Swiss banking? A great deal. Balance of payments problems attendant upon the process of economic growth and the stimulation of aggregate demand inevitably proved to be too severe for the fixed exchange rate system of the International Monetary Fund. The Fund was in no position to sustain the chronic imbalances of Great Britain, for example, nor the continued balance of trade surpluses of Western Germany. Devaluations and revaluations in accordance with the realities of trade were inevitable, but in the process severe losses (or great gains) in wealth could be experienced. From all of this stemmed the massive inflow of capital into Switzerland seeking security in the stable Swiss franc, a currency which was still tied to gold.

At the same time, the Swiss banks were already reaching a level of world wide respect, certainly greater than that of the domestic banks of those countries which were subject to inflationary pressures. Not only was the foreign exchange value of a currency in jeopardy through balance of payments difficulties but also the purchasing power of the domestic currencies was subject to severe erosion. It was, to summarise in a sentence, the confluence of wage/price inflation, stemming from the policies of governments, and the exchange rate difficulties, which arose from the balance of payments problems and the ensuing international monetary markets, which was characteristic of the post-war era.

The western world had never witnessed such extraordinary circumstances as these – certainly not under the gold standard. From this turmoil, Switzerland grew to become a world-class banking nation, not necessarily because the Swiss themselves are a conservative lot, but because they became an island of monetary stability in a sea of financial *instability*.

Ultimately, it was the development of the Euro-currency, probably the most unique single achievement of our modern western banking system, which proved to be the more significant source of Swiss bank growth and development. As currencies became free from restrictions, the banks were able to transfer the claims on the wealth of one country (its domestic currency) into another currency maintaining the integrity of the first currency. It then became a Euro-currency. This is indeed remarkable, well beyond the imaginings of past generations of bankers. Both in the development of Euro-currency markets and investment of Euro-currency loans, Swiss banks have been virtual 'pioneers'.

But not everything was moving in Switzerland's favour. The post-war world was also characterised by a nationalisation movement in which basic industries, state economic planning (especially in Eastern Europe), and entire firms came under state management and control. This meant that considerable effort had to be exerted by the Federal Government in conjunction with the Swiss Bankers Association to repatriate even small portions of investments made under the former clearing agreements.

In retrospect, however, these proved to be trifling annoyances. The development of the Euro-currencies proved to be far more significant as far as the banks were concerned. With these new sources of international liquidity, Swiss banks were able to tap not only the great amounts of foreign savings but to spearhead the movement into consolidation and combinations and to establish themselves as powerful players in the financial capitals of the world. One is truly hard put to it to recognise the original Swiss grossbanken in the new financial institutions which supply all possible services to business enterprises and investors world-wide. Indeed, it is precisely this which justifies the title of this final chapter '. . . the Dawn of a New Era'.

CONCLUSION

It is incorrect to argue that the Swiss banks profited from the tragedy of World War II nor did the Swiss people as a nation or as individuals. No one profits from such a tragedy – some only lose less than others. Neutral countries were spared the physical damage to their nation and the casualties so characteristic of modern warfare. As far as Swiss banks were concerned, they lost most of their foreign investments especially in Germany and Eastern Europe.

To recover from these losses was no small achievement. Other banking systems, particularly the British, French, and German, lost heavily as well. However, these others were able to recover more quickly because their asset structure was more strongly based on their respective domestic economies. As the domestic economies of Europe recovered from the war so did their banks. This was not true for the Swiss banks which relied so heavily on foreign assets.

For Swiss banks there was no substitute for the process of re-building foreign assets in the form of loans and investments. At the same time, they were able to take advantage of the new post-war developments in trade and payments by being in the forefront of both Euro-currency growth and the new risk-management measures of bank derivatives. It has been these latter which have been characteristic of Swiss banks as truly international.

We regret that the recent attacks on the reputation of these banks, based upon their conduct in wartime, have been so widely publicised and have resulted in negative reports in the world's press. What is missing in these reports is the entire story in the sense that only that portion of historical circumstance is used by news reporters to justify their pre-conceived notion of the truth. We refer, of course, to the freezing of the Swiss bank dollar assets, along with the bank assets of the belligerent powers in June of 1940 by the Americans. This forced the Swiss into direct gold transfers and required much more gold for necessary imports than otherwise would have been the case. To add further to the insult, the Swiss had to pay 250 million Swiss francs in gold, in accordance with the Washington agreement, just to free their dollar assets.

Under any circumstances it surely is better not to attempt to attribute guilt during that unfortunate period of history when all have contributed in some measure to the guilt of humanity.

Notes

1. Burckhardt, Carl J., *Meine Danziger Mission*. Prof. Burckhardt was the last High Commissioner of the League of Nations to Danzig.
2. The name 'Mefo' is an acronym deriving from Metall-Forschungs, a state sponsored research company. Companies engaged in armament production were paid in Mefo bills which were then used to pay for their production requirements. The Reichsbank guaranteed these bills in full when tendered, but the fact was that a secondary market developed because these bills, short term, yielded a handsome 4 per cent. They were seen by business enterprise as an excellent investment for unused short term funds. In effect, investors, including banks, with unused capital paid for armaments by purchasing these bills! Any Mefo bills that were not absorbed by the market were quickly taken up by the Reichsbank, and these amounted to about one-half of the total of 12 billion marks worth of Mefo bills issued during a four year period. For the invention of this instrument, Schacht must receive full credit. Schacht, H., *My First Seventy-Six Years, an Autobiography* Allan Wingate (London: 1955, pp. 316–18).
3. As reported in the *Seattle Post-Intelligencer*, 21 September 1996, p. A4.
4. Transcript of Hearings Before the United States Senate Committee on Banking, Housing and Urban Affairs, Washington, DC, Tuesday, April 23, 1996, pp 90–1.
5. Quoted from the *Financial Post*, October 5 1996, p. 6.
6. The Netherlands is also attempting to claim gold looted by the Nazis if still held in Swiss bank vaults. While they had already received some 64 tonnes under the 1946 agreement, there is, apparently, another 68 tonnes still outstanding. The *Financial Post*, October 12 1996, p. 13.
7. *Schweizerische Bankiervereinigung*, Press information, 20 September 1996.
8. Ibid. 9 February, 1996.
9. Ibid., 8 August 1996.
10. *Schweizerische Bankiervereinigung*, Press information, 'Bankiervereinigung zum Schweizerisch-Polnischen Wirtschaftsabkommen von 1949', 22 October 1996. We should point out that the information included in our text is based upon our own translation from the German and is subject to possible misinterpretation, though we hope it is accurate. Swiss German is not an easy language, especially when couched in 'defensive terminology'. What is important, though, is that the 'secret treaty', as reported by the press, was only a commercial exchange of letters leading to an agreement. That is our interpretation of the term *Wirtschaftabkommen*.

11. In 1962, a law was passed by the Legislative Assembly requiring all bank deposits to be registered as to those individuals who were 'persecuted for religious or racial reasons'. Such wording included, obviously, those deposits which were made on behalf of Jewish refugees; hence Swiss lawyers, accountants, and trustees, who were most likely to have acted as intermediaries, were not to be overlooked. Nevertheless, it was a difficult law to enforce. This is just an example of the complexity of the problem. Testimony of Julius Baer before the US Senate Committee on Banking, Housing and Urban Affairs. Washington, DC pp. 78–9.

12. The *Globe and Mail*, Wednesday, November 13 1996.

13. For the record, the list includes Prof. Klaus Jacobi, Prof. Curt Gasteyger, Dr Peider Mengiardi, Hans Bär, (the most respected banker in the country), and Prof. Rene Rhinow. Press information, *Schweizerische Bankiervereinigung*, 19 November 1996.

14. *Schweizerische Bankiervereinigung*, Press information, 13 December 1996. We must again point out that the translation from German is our own and may be subject to some slight misinterpretation. We hope not.

15. Statement by the Federal Council on the occasion of its application to become a full member of the OEEC on 20 August 1948. Reported by Bauer, Hans, *Swiss Bank Corporation, 1872–1892*, Swiss Bank Corporation, Bosle, 1972, p. 317.

16. See Blackman, W., *Swiss Banking in an International Context*, (Basingstoke: Macmillan 1989) pp. 175 ff. In addition to the monetary base of the Swiss banks, there is the legal requirement that Swiss currency (the franc) must be backed by either gold or foreign exchange. The distinction is made here between the currency (paper) and bank credit which requires a monetary base.

17 It is estimated that two-thirds to three-quarters of London gold found its way to Zürich where the concentration of buyers was so great that the Zürich price was always higher than the London selling price.

18 Vol. 81, *Geschæftsbericht, 1988 Schweizerische Nationalbank*, Table 2, Hauptposten der Bilanz seit 1951, p. 74.

19 For our North American, and also British, readers, we should observe here that the Swiss did not fall into the trap of investing their surplus insurance funds in government bonds, thereby funding national debt. Indeed, there were no Swiss Federal bonds at the time. Perhaps unwittingly or by design the Swiss have been able to avoid the modern North American and European problem of financing a growing population of elderly with an ever-narrowing sector of working population at a time when the national income refuses to grow to the same degree that it has in the past.

20 Once again we use the balance sheet of the Swiss Bank Corporation as typical of the larger Swiss banks.

21 Categories 1–5 include the major banks of Switzerland, viz 1. Grossbankern, 2. Kantonal bankern, 3 Regional bankern and Sparkassen 4 Darlehens and Raiffeisenkossen and 5 Übrige bankern.

22 Velocity of circulation used here is for M2 (money and 'quasi-money' in the IFS terminology). Quasi-money includes savings deposits. Interestingly,

the velocity of circulation of cash alone actually rises during this period and velocity of demand deposits is static. Clearly the Swiss public was becoming more aware that savings deposits were almost as good as cash and were minimising their use of cash for transactions purposes, hence the increasing velocity of circulation for the cash that is left over after savings deposits have been made.

23 Annual Report of the Swiss Bank Corporation, 1966.

24 We use the Swiss Bank Corporation and its balance sheet as typical of the major Swiss banks. In this case, investment in government securities fell in value from 595 million francs in 1946 to 363.5 million in 1950 – a decline of 39 per cent. At the same time loans and advances rose from 625.2 million to 809.3 million, an increase of 29 per cent.

25 The subordination of money and finance in an economy to the objective of full employment through stimulating aggregate demand and real economic growth has a long history. In the pre- depression era of the 1920s the Fisher equation of exchange and the Cambridge 'k', the equivalent English version of the equation of exchange, meant that money or its substitutes was *the same as* (that is, an identity) economic activity. This was accepted doctrine in the English speaking world. Beginning with the publication of Keynes' *Tract on Monetary Reform*, followed, of course, by the Great Depression, the role of money and finance shifts to a subordinate one – in effect, disappearing from the forefront. No longer is the Quantity Theory of Money the central focal point. According to Prof. Friedman, the Quantity Theory did not disappear altogether, however, but took refuge in the University of Chicago, to re-emerge at a later point in time.

Concluding Thoughts

Despite the fact that thoughtful readers are quite entitled to arrive at their own conclusions regarding Swiss banking, the temptation to set forth a few significant after-thoughts is simply too strong to resist.

We cannot avoid noting that the Swiss Banking Law, which set forth the operating principles of the banks, was the culmination of centuries of development – trial and error, mistakes, corrections, etc. through the centuries since the banks of Switzerland were hardly more than money changers. The result was the Banking Law which, after some decades of debate on the subject, carefully distinguished between the banks' responsibilities and those of the government. While banks should be free to make their own decisions (yet not *too* free) and, at the same time exert their own internal controls over their own affairs, the government (in the form of the Banking Commission) must regulate (but not *over*-regulate). It is the judicious exercise of responsibilities as between the banks and the government which characterises the Swiss banking system and has contributed to its extraordinary success.

Swiss banks have the highest liquidity requirements of any banking system in the world. Indeed, their capital/assets ratio well exceeds the 8 per cent minimum set by the Basle Committee on Banking Supervision. Additionally their liquid reserves (including 'hidden reserves') are more than ample for any conceivable need for liquidity. This is largely why they are both safe and stable and is also why a Swiss bank account is widely respected throughout the world.

All of this is unique to Switzerland. One could not argue that other countries might emulate the Swiss; quite the contrary, each country must find its own individual banking system suitable to the peculiar requirements of each country. India's government-owned banks may serve that country well; or the practical experiences of both Brazil and Mexico will likely prove that those countries must also evolve their own particular techniques of banking as well.

What is so impressive, though, and can hardly be overlooked is that the Swiss banks, by their very existence, act as a driving force toward the development of more efficient banking throughout the world. Capital is lost to domestic banks as savers in other countries prefer the Swiss bank account. It is as simple as that. This force of competition requires a general improvement in banking efficiency in other countries. Thus, while the Basle Accord is useful enough, the gentle pressure exerted by Swiss bank competition reinforces the necessity for liquidity as an insurance for depositors against bank failures in their own respective countries.

All of this is particularly important in developing countries which have not yet developed the 'banking habit'. The banking intermediation function of allocating scarce capital to its most efficient use is essential for such countries to achieve any reasonable degree of economic growth. Since banking habits require an amount of security of savings, sound banking principles must be followed; otherwise, local populations will refuse to trust their own banks.

Meantime, the great Swiss banks have, literally, ceased to be Swiss. They are now international. It is an interesting question as to how much, if any, of indigenous Swiss banking practices have actually infiltrated into the international banking sphere. Should such be case, competition in the field of international banking might well result in all of the large international banks, Japanese, British, American, German, etc. also becoming 'Swiss'. That is an interesting question which only time can answer.

Bibliography

It would be an exercise in futility to attempt to include all the many references which Dr. Bauer had used in preparation for this book. Most, if not all, are already out of print and the Swiss publishers have long ceased to exist. In the list which follows we include only those which have been included in footnote references. In some cases, publishers have been omitted for the reason that in Switzerland, publishers are often created for the purpose of publishing a single work, then promptly disappear. In others, the publishers are not known.

Annual Reports of the Swiss Bank Corporation, 1925 and 26

BOREL, FREDERIC, *Les Foires de Geneve au Quinzieme Siecle*, H. Georg, Libraire-Editeur, 10, Corraterie, Geneve, 1892.
BRAUDEL, F. 'Prices in Europe from 1450 to 1750', *The Cambridge Economic History of Europe*, Cambridge University Press, 1967.
BRAUDEL and SPOONER, Ch. VII *Cambridge Economic History*, Vol iv, Cambridge University Press, Cambridge, 1967.
BAUER, H., *Vom Wechsler zum Bankier*, Friedrich Reinhardt Verlag, Basel, 1989.
BAUER, HANS, *Swiss Bank Corporation, 1972–1972*, Basle, 1972.
BAGEHOT, WALTER, *Lombard Street*, John Murray, London, 1919.
BERGIER, JEAN-FRANCOISE, *Wirtschafts Geschichte der Schweiz*, Benziger Verlag AG, Zurich, 1990.
BURCKHARDT, CARL J., Meine Danziger Mission, quoted in Bauer, *op. cit.*
BLACKMAN, W., *Swiss Banking in an International Context*, Macmillan Press, Ltd. Basingstoke, 1989.
BERNASCONI, JEAN-LUC, 'Derivatives – Another Look at the Basics', Swiss Bank Corporation, Special, 1994.
BOSSARD, WIRTH, and BLATTNER, 'The Swiss Banking Sector: Development and Outlook', Swiss Bankers Association, 1991.
CLAPHAM, J. H., *Economic Development of France and Germany, 1815–1914*, Cambridge University Press, 1961.
COURTNEY, Rt. Hon. LEONARD H., 'Banking', *Encyclopaedia Brittanica*, Ninth Edition, Vol. III.
CROWTHER, GEOFFREY, *An Outline of Money*, Thomas Nelson & Sons, London, 1949.
CUNNINGHAM, W., *The Growth of English Industry and Commerce in Modern Times*, Cambridge University Press, 1892.
Deutsche Bundesbank Monthly Report, April 1995.
'Depression in the Swiss Industry, 1868–69' Report by H.M. Secretaries of Embassies and Legations, (Parl. Papers, 1868–69).
Die Schweiz als Internationaler Bank-und Finanzplatz, Orell Füssli Verlag, Zurich, 1970.

258

DE ROOVER, RAYMOND, *The Rise and Decline of the Medici Bank*, 1397–1494, Harvard University Press, Cambridge, 1963.

DE ROOVER, RAYMOND, *Money, Banking, and Credit in Medieval Bruges*, The Medieval Academy of America, Cambridge, 1948.

Economist, 21 January, 1995, 'The Battle of Trafalgar'.

Economic and Financial Prospects 'Understanding Derivatives' Swiss Bank Corporation, Special, 1994.

Eleventh Annual Report of the Chamber of Commerce to the Basle Association of Commerce and Industry on the year 1886.

FEHRENBACH, T. R., *The Swiss Banks*, McGraw-Hill, New York, 1966.

FRIEDMAN, M, and SCHWARTZ, A., *A Monetary History of the United States, 1867–1960*, NBER, Princeton University Press, 1963.

Geschœftsbericht, 1988 Schweizerische Nationalbank, Vol. 81, Table 2, Hauptposten der Bilanz seit 1951, p. 74.

GEHR, MARTIN, Der Verhaltnis Zwischen Banken und Industrie in Deutschland seit Mitte des 19 Jahrhunderts bis zur Banken krise von 1931, Tubingen, 1959, (a doctoral dissertation quoted in Documents of European Economic History, Vo. 2, p. 123.)

GIDE, C. and RIST, C., *A History of Economic Doctrines*, Harrap and Co., London, 1948

Gilbart on Banking, Vol. 1, Bohn's Economic Library, George Bell and Sons, York Street, Covent Garden, London, 1881.

GILBART, J. W., *The History, Principles, and Practice of Banking*, A. S. Michie, ed., Bohn's Economic Library, George Bell & Sons, London, 1882, Vol. 2.

GUERDAN, RENE, *La Vie Quotidienne a Geneve Au Temps de Calvin*, Librairie Hachette, Paris, 1973.

HAUSER, HENRI, *Germany's Commercial Grip on the World, Her Business Methods Explained*, Manfred Emmanuel, New York, 1918

IKLE, MAX, *Switzerland, an International Banking and Finance Centre*, Dowden Hutchison, and Ross, Stroudsburg, Pa., 1972.

International Financial Statistics, 1983, International Monetary Fund, Washington D.C.

International Banking and Financial Market Developments, Bank for International Settlements, Basle, November 1996.

Jubilee Report of the Swiss Bankers Association, Basle, 1962.

KOENIGSBERGER, H. G. and MOSSE, G. L., *Europe in the Sixteenth Century*, Holt, Rinehart and Winston, New York, 1968.

KELLENBERGER, E., *Kapitalexport und Zahlungsbilanz*, Vol. I.

LANDMANN, J., 'Geldmarkt und Bankpolitik,' published in *Zeitschrift fur Schweizerische Statistik und Volkswirtschaft, 1914*.

LUSSER, Dr. MARKUS, Address before the Finnish Bankers Association, Helsinki, 30 May, 1994.

MCCULLOCH, J. R. 'Introductory Discourse' *The Wealth of Nations* by Adam Smith, Edinburgh: Adam and Charles Black, 1889.

MARSHALL, A. *Industry and Trade*, Macmillan and Co. Ltd., St. Martin's Street London, 1923.

MAST, HANS J., *The Swiss Banking System*, Credit Suisse Special Publications, Zürich, vol. 27.

MICHAELIS and SCHRAEPLER, Ursachen und Folgen, Vol. X.

MILL, J. S. *Principles of Political Economy*, Longmans Green and Co., London, 1902.

MILWARD, ALAN S. and SAUL, S. B. *The Development of the Economies of Continental Europe 1850–1914*, Allen and Unwin, London, 1977.

POLIAKOV, LEON, *Jewish Bankers and the Holy See, From the Thirteenth to the Seventeenth Century*, Routledge and Kegan Paul, London.

POLLARD, SIDNEY, and HOLMES, COLLIN, *Documents of Economic History*, Vol 2, Edward Arnold, London, 1972.

RITZMANN, FRANZ, *Die Schweizer Banken*, Verlag Paul Haupt, Bern and Stuttgart, 1973.

REINHOLD, PETER P., *The Economic, Financial, and Political State of Germany since the War*, Yale Univ. Press, New Haven, 1928.

RIESSER, J., *The German Great Banks and their Concentration*, U.S. Monetary Commission, Document 593, Washington, 1911.

Report of the McKenna Committee, 1927.

Reports on Tariff Wars between Certain European States, British Parliamentary Papers, 1904, XCV.

SMITH, ADAM, *The Wealth of Nations*, McCulloch's Edition, Adam and Charles Black, Edinburgh, 1889.

SMALL, ALBION W, *The Cameralists*, Burt Franklin, New York, 1909.

H. LUTHY, *La Banque Protestante en France*, S. E. V. P. E. N., Paris, 1959.

SIME, JAMES, 'Switzerland' *Encyclopaedia Britannica*, Ninth Edition, Vol xxii.

Sixteenth Annual Report of the Basle Chamber of Commerce.

Sixteenth Annual Report of the Chamber of Commerce to the Basle Association of Commerce and Industry, 1891.

SCHULZE-GAEVERNITZ, GERHARD von, Die Deutsche Kreditbank, Tubingen, 1915.

SCHUMPETER, JOSEPH, *Capitalism, Socialism, and Democracy*, 2nd Edition, Harper & Bros. New York, 1947.

SCHACHT, H., *My First Seventy-Six Years, An Autobiography*, (Translated by Diana Pyke), Allan Wingate, London, 1955.

Schweizerische Bankiervereinigung, Presse Information, September 1996.

9 February, 1996.

8 August, 1996.

'Bankiervereinigung zum Schweizerisch-Pölnischen Wirtschaftsabkommen von 1949', 22 October, 1996.

19 November, 1996.

13 December, 1996.

29 September, 1995.

7 September, 1993.

Transcript of Hearings Before the United States Senate Committee on Banking, Housing and Urban Affairs, Washington, D. C. Tuesday, April 23, 1996.

'U.K. Banks' External Liabilities and Claims in Foreign Currencies,' *Bank of England Quarterly Bulletin*, June, 1964.

WEISZ, LEO 'Der organisierte Kredit in Zurich von der Reformation bis zum Jahre 1835', *Geld und Kreditsystem der Schweiz*, Schultheiss and Co. AG, Zurich, 1944.

WELLS, D. A., 'Recent Economic Changes and their Effect on the Production and Distribution of Wealth and the Well Being of Society' (New York, 1893). Pollard and Holmes, Documents of European Economic History, Vol. 2. Edward Arnold, London, 1972.

WILSON, C. H. 'Trade, Society, and the State', *Cambridge Economic History of Europe*, Vol IV, Cambridge University Press, 1967.

The following is a short list of some references, most of which are out of print, that could not be included as direct footnotes but which nevertheless were extremely useful in the preparation of the text:

BAUER, HANS, *Bankgeheimnis, nicht nur in der Schweiz*, Verlag Universum Press Wyler & Cie, Genf-Zurich, October, 1972.

BOREL, FREDERIC, *Foires de Geneve*, Ch. 6, 'Coins, Weights and Measures.' (see above).

BRADY, T. A. J. *Turning Swiss, Cities and Empire*, 1450–1550, Cambridge Univ. Press, 1985.

BÜCHNER, RICHARD, 'Geld und Kredittheorie im Wandel des Wirtschaftslebens', included in *Geld und Kreditsystem der Schweiz*.

HYDE, H. MONTGOMERY, *John Law*, W. H. Allen, London, 1969.

IKLE, MAX, *Die Schweiz als Internationaler Bank-und Finanzplatz*, Orell Füssli Verlag, Zurich, 1970.

KÖRNER, *Solidarite Financiere Suisses Au Seizieme Siecle*, Edition Payot Bibliotheque Historique Vaudoise, 1980.

LÜTHY, H., *La Banque Protestante en France, (1730–1794).*, S. E. V. P. E. N., Paris, 1959.

STAMPFLI, ARTHUR, 'Die Banken in der Schweizerischen Kreditorganisation,' essay included in *Geld und Kreditsystem der Schweiz*.

Veröffentlichungen der Schweizerischen Kartellkommission und des Preisuberwachers, 3#, 1989, Bern.

WEBER, ERNST, 'Das Kreditgeschäft der Schweizerischen Nationalbank', included in *Geld un Kreditsystem der Schweiz*.

WEISZ, 'Der Organisierte Kredit in Zurich von der Reformation bis zum Jahre 1835' essay included in *Geld und Kreditsystem der Schweiz*, Schulthess and Co., Zurich, 1944.

Index